Conferences and Conventions

Conferences and Conventions
A global industry

Tony Rogers

ELSEVIER
BUTTERWORTH
HEINEMANN

AMSTERDAM BOSTON HEIDELBERG LONDON NEW YORK OXFORD
PARIS SAN DIEGO SAN FRANCISCO SINGAPORE SYDNEY TOKYO

Elsevier Butterworth-Heinemann
Linacre House, Jordan Hill, Oxford OX2 8DP
200 Wheeler Road, Burlington, MA 01803

First published 2003
Reprinted 2004

British Library Cataloguing in Publication Data
A catalogue record for this book is available from the British Library

Library of Congress Cataloguing in Publication Data
A catalogue record for this book is available from the Library of Congress

ISBN 0 7506 5747 2

For information on all Elsevier Butterworth-Heinemann
publications visit our web site at www.bh.com

Composition by Genesis Typesetting, Rochester, Kent
Printed and bound in Great Britain by Biddles Ltd, King's Lynn, Norfolk

Contents

Forewords   ix

Preface   xi

List of case studies   xiii

1   A global industry   **1**
Introduction   1
The origins of the conference industry   2
The foundations of a proper industry   4
The industry's recent globalization   7
World rankings of leading cities and countries   8
Certain industry shortcomings   13
Industry parameters and definitions   19
Business tourism and leisure tourism   20
The benefits of conference and business tourism   23
Summary   25
Review and discussion questions   25
Notes and references   26
Further reading   26

2   The structure of the conference industry   **27**
Introduction   27
Buyers   28
Suppliers   46
Agencies   50
Other important organizations   59
Summary   61
Review and discussion questions   62
Notes and references   63
Further reading   63

3 The economics of conferences and conventions	**64**
Introduction	64
Conferences within the wider tourism context	65
Factors affecting conference sector demand	66
The inadequacy of the information base	68
The size of the global conference industry	70
The value of the industry	70
Research findings	76
Summary	93
Review and discussion questions	95
Notes and references	95
4 Conference industry marketing activity	**96**
Introduction	96
Marketing principles	97
Relationship marketing and customer relationship management	104
A definition of destination	106
The branding of cities and other destinations	106
Destination marketing organizations	108
Conference venue marketing	133
The branding of hotel venues	135
Overseas marketing	137
Summary	138
Review and discussion questions	139
Notes and references	139
Further reading	140
5 Conference management – an organizer's perspective	**141**
Introduction	141
A general introduction to conference organizing	142
Pre-conference planning and research	143
Budgeting and financial management	149
Sourcing and selecting a venue	153
Negotiating with venues	158
Programme planning	162
Event marketing	164
Conference management and production	165
Event evaluation	167
Summary	169
Review and discussion questions	169
Notes and references	170
Further reading	170
6 Conference management – a venue perspective	**172**
Introduction	172
Client-focused product innovations	173
Professional inspection visits and showrounds	176
Yield management and 'REVPAR'	177

Negotiating with clients   181
Venue case studies   183
Discussion questions   192
Notes and references   192
Further reading   192

7 A people industry   **193**
Introduction   193
The importance of people skills   194
Education and training opportunities   198
Development of occupational standards for the
meetings industry   206
Careers in the conference industry   208
Salary levels   210
Career profiles of leading industry figures   211
Summary   225
Review and discussion questions   226
Notes and references   226

8 Leading industry organizations   **227**
Introduction   227
The activities of international organizations and
associations   228
The roles of selected national trade associations   239
An assessment of the conference industry's
fragmentation   245
Summary   246
Review and discussion questions   246

9 The future of the conference industry   **247**
Introduction   247
Market trends   248
Issues and developments   255
In conclusion   266
Summary   267
Review and discussion questions   267
Notes and references   268

Case studies   **269**

Appendix A   List of conference industry trade magazines   314

Index   317

Forewords

Mady Keup

Conferences are about communication, whether between executives of blue-chip companies, world experts in medical science, members of a political party or United Nations aid workers.

The list of users is diverse and international, as are their goals: to spread a message, to discuss new developments, to learn from stories of scientific breakthrough or to energize employees and other major stakeholders.

An industry has developed to facilitate the satisfaction of the objectives of face-to-face communication: the conference industry. Suppliers to the industry are as diverse as their clients: conference centres, hotels, specialist intermediaries, convention bureaux, caterers, production companies, and many others – all cooperate to create the right atmosphere and infrastructure, conducive to communication.

The industry is both global and localized: the need to communicate is universal and conference products and services are being developed around the world. At the same time, the strategic importance, and tourist appeal, of destinations play a significant role in the selection of where a conference is to be held. Competition is fierce, with a constant stream of new entrants on all levels, in both product offering and service delivery. Substitutes, such as teleconferencing or virtual conferences, may or may not pose a threat to the established industry over the years to come, as may the Internet, with its 24-hour information flow.

This book, therefore, makes for essential reading for anyone interested to learn more about the processes, business models and key success factors that characterize the conference industry. A must for present, or potential, practitioners!

Mady Keup
Chair of the British Association of Conference Destinations
Head of London Convention Bureau

Peter Mainprice

In its various forms, the conference and events industry must be one of the oldest in existence. Perhaps originating early on in human evolution when our language was rudimentary and skills relatively basic, meetings occurred and have continued throughout history.

Today our human communications are complex and truly global, and the means of communication are ever expanding. These advances mean that conferences can be a forum of a few people or an international event involving tens of thousands in different locations.

And thus conferences have evolved to incorporate the most modern technologies and the use of facilities built to impress, or just ensure people are comfortable. Conferences and events allow people to impart facts, exchange opinions and change behaviours, but perhaps most importantly, motivate people to learn, improve performance and enjoy themselves.

The principles of conferencing are indeed simple, but the implementation is complex and requires vision, efficiency, experience, energy and confidence. Anyone can organize a conference, but there is a direct and transparent link between its quality and the skills of the organizer.

Events large or small do not happen on their own, and professional organizers through to volunteers are involved in creating the environments and opportunities for people to get together at a local level or on a global scale.

This book offers an insight into this evolving industry, which is both complex and exciting. It will be an excellent reference for those starting out in the industry, and for those involved in leading or teaching others to create great events, and to meet the challenges of this most stimulating of professions.

Peter Mainprice
Chairman of the Association of British Professional Conference Organisers
Managing Director, Index Communications Meeting Services

Preface

This is my second book about the fascinating conference industry in which I have been privileged to work for the past 13 years. In that period there have been huge changes and developments in the way the industry is marketed, in the organization and presentation of meetings and conferences, in the competition for a share of the lucrative economic 'cake' that conferences and conventions represent, and in a multitude of other ways. Yet the essence remains the same: it is about bringing people together to communicate by sharing information and ideas, to motivate and inspire, to launch new products and disseminate the latest research, and to negotiate in order to reach a consensus on the different challenges facing our world.

I have attempted to describe the many facets of this global industry and to provide both an insight into how it is organized and a broader picture of an industry in its totality. It can be dipped into for discrete pieces of information on specific aspects of the industry, or read in its entirety by those wanting a better understanding of the parameters and characteristics of this true 21st-century industry. I hope very much that it will be of interest and practical use to students and lecturers, to those working in the industry as well as to those who may be looking to make a future career in the industry, to politicians (local and national), to journalists and consultants, and indeed to anyone seeking an overview of this dynamic, endearing, varied but still under-recognized sector of national and global economies.

The book would not have been possible without the unstinting help, advice and provision of data and material that I have received from literally hundreds of colleagues around the world. One of the delights of the conference industry, for me, is this very openness and willingness to share that I have experienced at every turn. To everyone who has helped in any way, I owe an enormous debt of gratitude. I hope they will understand if I do not mention them individually. To do so would certainly take up several pages, but I am very afraid of missing someone out and unwittingly giving offence. Please be assured that my appreciation is heartfelt – I just hope that they each feel that the book justifies the efforts and contributions they have made.

Each chapter follows a similar pattern with an introduction, main theme, summary, review and discussion questions, and references. There is also a series of case studies after the main text giving more in-depth illustrations and elaboration of points made in particular chapters. The numbering of the case studies relates back to the chapter in which the point occurs, e.g. Case study 4.2 refers to text in Chapter 4. However, there are also several short case studies embedded in particular chapters.

In the text I have, for stylistic simplicity, used 'he' rather than '(s)he' where appropriate, but such uses should be interpreted as applying equally to both genders. Indeed, I should perhaps have used 'she' throughout, as women are represented very strongly at all levels of the industry, probably outnumbering men in many sectors.

Finally, I have used mainly UK spellings and terminology. I give below several common words/phrases for which different words/phrases are used in North America and in certain other countries:

UK terms	North American equivalents
Accommodation	Housing
Exhibition	Exposition
Professional conference/congress organizer (PCO)	Destination management company (DMC)
Delegates	Attendees

Tony Rogers
October 2002

Case studies

1.1 Manchester
1.2 Pattaya Exhibition and Convention Hall, Pattaya, Thailand
1.3 Dubai
1.4 Creta Maris Hotel and Conference Centre, Hersonissos, Crete, Greece
2.1 Sydney's bids to host two major international congresses
2.2 International Federation of Library Associations and Institutions
3.1 Cape Town International Convention Centre (CTICC), South Africa
4.1 The Aberdeen and Grampian Convention Bureau
4.2 Tourism Vancouver
4.3 Vienna Convention Bureau
5.1 A PCO philosophy
5.2 Conference planning budget
6.1 The Majestic Hotel, Harrogate
6.2 The Westin Turnberry Resort, Ayrshire
6.3 The International Convention Centre, Birmingham
6.4 Cranfield Management Development Centre

CHAPTER 1

A global industry

Introduction

The conference industry is a young, dynamic industry, which is growing and maturing at a rapid rate. From origins in Europe and North America, it is now a truly international industry, witnessing huge investments across all continents. Its youthfulness, however, does mean that it lacks some of the necessary characteristics of more established industries, such as well-defined terminology, adequate market intelligence, appropriate education and training structures, and clear entry routes. Conferences are part of the business tourism (or business events) sector, a major though often undervalued sector of the wider tourism industry.

This chapter looks at:

- the origins of the conference industry
- the foundations of a proper industry
- the industry's recent globalization
- world rankings of leading cities and countries
- certain industry shortcomings
- industry parameters and definitions
- business tourism and leisure tourism
- the benefits of conference and business tourism.

The origins of the conference industry

American Presidents hosting the latest Middle East Summit at Camp David in Maryland, the Royal College of Nursing holding its annual conference in Bournemouth, members of the International Congress and Convention Association gathering for their assembly and congress in Copenhagen, shareholders of Microsoft or HSBC attending the company's annual general meeting, the sales force of GlaxoSmithKline coming together for a regular briefing or training event, or their high achievers jetting off for an incentive-cum-meeting trip to an exotic overseas destination.

The different events described above have one thing in common: they are all to do with bringing people together, face-to-face, to exchange ideas and information, to discuss and in some cases negotiate, to build friendships and closer business relationships, to encourage better performance by individuals and organizations. They are different facets of the same dynamic, international, economically vibrant conference industry. The terms used ('summit', 'meeting', 'conference', 'assembly', 'convention', 'congress', 'AGM', 'briefing', 'training', 'incentive') may vary, and the events themselves may have different formats and emphases, but the essential ingredients and objectives are the same.

Conferences are at the forefront of modern communications, whether this is for internal communications (sales meetings, training seminars, board retreats, major annual conferences, for example) or as a vehicle for communicating with key audiences (such as press briefings, product launches, annual general meetings, some technical conferences). 'Conferences' is a generic term to describe a diverse mix of communications events.

The phrase 'conference industry' is of very recent origins, and is certainly not one that would have been heard until the second half of the 20th century. Yet people's need to congregate and confer is one of the things that defines our humanity and, for a multitude of different reasons, meetings and gatherings of people have taken place since the early days of civilization. Shone (1998) traces the evolution of meetings since Roman times in Britain and Ireland, and the development of meeting rooms and meeting places to accommodate these, driven largely by the needs of trade and commerce.

One of the highest profile events in the past couple of hundred years, perhaps almost a launch event for our contemporary conference industry, was the Congress of Vienna held from September 1814 to June 1815. The Congress was called to re-establish the territorial divisions of Europe at the end of the Napoleonic Wars and representatives included all of the major world powers of the day (with the exception of Turkey). It is tempting to imagine what the 'delegate spend' must have been like, with delegates such as Alexander I, Emperor of Russia, Prince Karl August von Hardenberg from Prussia, and Viscount Castlereagh and the Duke of Wellington as the principal British representatives. Each representative would have been accompanied by a substantial delegation of support staff and partners, requiring accommodation, social programmes, lavish corporate entertainment, ground handling, not to mention state-of-the-art conference facilities. The Vienna Convention Bureau no doubt celebrated long and hard its success in attracting such a high-profile, high-spend event to the city!

As the 19th century progressed, universities increasingly provided facilities for the dissemination of information within academic circles, while the boom in spa towns and, in the UK, Victorian resorts with assembly rooms, began to make available larger public spaces for entertainment and meetings. At the same time, the development of the railway network was accompanied by the construction of railway hotels alongside major stations. Many of these hotels had substantial function rooms available for hire.

Shone contends that the dawn of the 20th century was accompanied by a change in the demand for meetings:

> Though assemblies and congresses continued to be driven by trade and industry, there was a slow and gradual increase in activity which, rather than promoting products, or reporting a company's annual progress, looked to developing staff and sales. The precursors of the sales training meeting, the 'congress of commercials' (or commercial travellers) of the 1920s and 1930s, began to develop into something more modern and recognizable.

The situation was somewhat different in North America during the latter half of the 19th century, particularly across the eastern seaboard of the USA where various trade and professional associations, as well as religious groups, were being formed and, as they became more established, beginning to hold conventions for their membership. Gartrell (1994) records that, in due course, a number of committees were also created to 'lure the growing convention business from these expanding and thriving associations'. As more and more cities became aware of the value of convention business, Gartrell suggests that it was 'inevitable that the solicitation of these conventions would be assigned to a full-time salesperson; and, while this might have happened in any one of many major cities, history records that it first happened in Detroit, Michigan, when a group of businessmen decided to place a full-time salesperson on the road to invite conventions to their city. Thus, in 1896, the first convention bureau was formed, and an industry emerged.' Detroit was shortly followed by other US cities, which established their own convention bureaux: Cleveland (1904), Atlantic City (1908), Denver and St Louis (1909), Louisville and Los Angeles (1910). Now many cities around the world have their own convention bureau, or convention and visitor bureau.

The foundations of a proper industry

While the origins of today's conference industry lie in the political and religious congresses of earlier centuries, followed by business meetings and, in the USA, trade and professional association conventions, the development and recognition of a proper 'industry' is a much more recent phenomenon, in Europe especially, effectively dating from the middle to latter part of the 20th century.

The foundation of trade associations is often a useful, objective way of marking the real formation of an industry. Some of the principal conference industry associations were founded as follows:

International Association for Exhibition Management (IAEM)	1928
Professional Convention Management Association (PCMA)	1957
Association Internationale des Palais de Congrès (AIPC)	1958
International Congress and Convention Association (ICCA)	1963
European Federation of Conference Towns (EFCT)	1964
International Association of Professional Congress Organizers (IAPCO)	1968
British Association of Conference Destinations (BACD)	1969
Meeting Professionals International (MPI)	1972
Meetings Industry Association of Australia (MIAA)	1975
Association of British Professional Conference Organisers (ABPCO)	1981
Asian Association of Convention and Visitor Bureaus (AACVB)	1983
Meetings Industry Association (MIA) (UK)	1990

The International Association of Convention and Visitor Bureaus, on the other hand, with a predominantly North American membership, was founded as long ago as 1914.

Since the 1960s there has been a steadily increasing investment in the whole infrastructure that supports conferences, meetings and related events, an investment which accelerated into a rapid growth during the 1990s. The 1990s were almost certainly the decade that recorded the highest sustained investment to date in global conference infrastructure. Tables 1.1 and 1.2 give details of new conference and convention facilities built in just two countries, Australia and the UK, epitomizing the huge scale of investment that has taken place over the past decade or so. This list does not include other substantial investments in buildings which, though not purpose-built for the conventions industry, are capable of staging very large conferences, such as (in the UK) the Sheffield Arena (12 000 seats, £45 million), Birmingham's National Indoor Arena (13 000 seats, £51 million), Manchester's £42 million Bridgewater Hall and the 19 000-seat Nynex Arena, and the Newcastle Arena (10 000 seats, £10.5 million) in Newcastle upon Tyne.

Case study 1.1 traces the developments and investments made by the City of Manchester in its convention 'product' over recent years.

But it is not just in Europe, Australasia and North America that major investments are being made. In the past five to ten years, large-scale infrastructure projects have been undertaken throughout much of Asia and the Pacific rim, in the former East European countries, such as Hungary and the Czech Republic, in the Middle East and in a number of African countries, particularly South Africa. Case Studies 1.2 and 1.3 give detailed examples of two such investments, one at venue level (Pattaya Exhibition and

Name of centre	Year of Opening	Cost (AU$m)
Adelaide Convention & Exhibition Centre	1987	Not available
Sydney Convention & Exhibition Centre	1988	230
Canberra National Convention Centre	1989	Not available
Melbourne Exhibition & Convention Centre	1990 (1996 for Exhibition Centre)	254 (combined cost)
Brisbane Convention & Exhibition Centre	1994	200
Cairns Convention Centre	1995 (Convention Centre extension opened in 1999)	Not available
Convention Centre South – Sydney	1999	60
Federation Concert Hall and Convention Centre – Hobart	2000	16
Extension to Adelaide Convention & Exhibition Centre	2001	85
Alice Springs Convention Centre	2003	14.2
Perth Convention & Exhibition Centre	2004	310

Source: Pannell Kerr Forster Consultants Australia (PKFCA) Research.

Table 1.1
Investments in major Australian conference centres since the mid-1980s

Name of centre	Year of opening	Cost (£m)
International Convention Centre (Birmingham)	1991	180
Plymouth Pavilions	1992	25
Cardiff International Arena	1993	25
North Wales Conference Centre	1994	6
Edinburgh International Conference Centre	1995	38
Belfast Waterfront Hall (Conference Centre And Concert Hall)	1997	32
Clyde Auditorium at the Scottish Exhibition and Conference Centre	1997	38
Millennium Conference Centre (London)	1997	35
Manchester International Conference Centre	2001	24

Table 1.2
Investments in major UK conference centres since 1990

Convention Hall in Thailand) and one at a national level (Dubai).

There appear to be a number of reasons for these investments, many of which are paid for out of central government and other public sector funds:

- Such countries and destinations are probably already active in the leisure tourism sector and have developed much of the infrastructure for this sector, which is the same infrastructure (airports and other communications facilities, three-star/four-star/five-star hotels, attractions, trained staff, for example) as that required to attract international conference business. And, although additional investment in purpose-built conference and exhibition facilities may not be an insignificant cost, it is likely to be a relatively small additional amount compared with the total infrastructure investments already made.
- Such destinations quite rightly see conference business as complementary to leisure tourism business, in the same way that the longer-established destinations do.
- Conference and business tourism, being at the high-quality, high-yield end of the tourism spectrum, brings major economic benefits for developing as well as for developed countries. Such benefits include year-round jobs and foreign exchange earnings. There is also the potential for future inward investment from conference delegates, who have liked and been impressed by what they have seen of a country while attending a conference there, and return to set up a business operation, or persuade their own employers to do so.
- There is undoubted prestige in being selected to host a major international conference and some less developed countries would see this as a way of gaining credibility and acceptance

on the international political stage. There is perhaps an element of conferences and conference centres being developed as status symbols, signs of having 'arrived' as destinations to be taken seriously.

Such huge infrastructure investments are driven by a number of demand factors, both economic and social (analysed in further detail in Chapter 3). The challenge for those planning major new purpose-built convention centres (usually local authorities or municipalities, and public sector organizations) is to anticipate future demand accurately. Lead time from the initial idea for a convention centre until its opening can be as much as ten years. The process involves, *inter alia*, identification of a suitable site, design and planning stages, assembly of the funding package, construction of a venue and its related infrastructure, and recruitment and training of staff. In such a period, substantial changes in the wider marketplace may have occurred.

There is less of a risk for hotel and smaller venue developments, where the period between initial concept and completion is much shorter (typically 3–5 years), but the same principles apply. Many venues conceived, for example, in the boom times of the late 1980s found that they were opening in a very different market in the early 1990s, with the economy in full recession, and many of the venues struggled or foundered as a result. A similar economic cycle was experienced in the late 1990s and early years of the new millennium.

The industry's recent globalization

Conference and business tourism is a very important sector of the tourism industry, an industry that, in all its guises, is claimed to be the world's largest industry. Conference tourism is now a truly global industry, as evidenced by the examples of international investments described earlier in this chapter. But there is much other evidence to substantiate such a claim. Nowhere is its truth better demonstrated than in the evolution of one of the industry's major trade shows, the European Incentive and Business Travel and Meetings Exhibition (EIBTM), which is held in Geneva in May each year (but is moving to Barcelona in 2004). In 1988, 54 countries were represented as exhibitors at EIBTM, a number that had almost doubled by 2002 to 100 countries. In the same period the number of visitors increased from 2850 in 1988 to 5560 in 2002, with 88 different countries supplying visitors to the show in 2002.

And yet, while competition is increasing from countries seeking to act as suppliers to the conference industry, the markets from which to win business still remain relatively few in number. A total of 83 per cent of the visitors to EIBTM 2002 were drawn from just eight countries (see Table 1.3).

Market	%	Market	%
Benelux	8.7	Spain	3.3
France	10.6	Scandinavia	3.3
Germany	17.4	Switzerland	17.3
Italy	6.2	UK	16.1

Source: Reed Travel Exhibitions.

Table 1.3
Markets supplying visitors to
EIBTM 2002

There are a number of reasons for this:

- The national economies of many of the emerging nations are not yet sufficiently strong for their corporate sector organizations to be planning events overseas (e.g. sales meetings, product launches, incentive events).
- The headquarters of many international associations and intergovernmental organizations are located in Western Europe and North America. Such headquarters are also where those organizing events on behalf of these bodies are based.
- Market intelligence is much better developed in respect of the 'buyers' (conference organizers) in the most experienced conventioneering countries. Quite sophisticated databases exist detailing the buying requirements and preferences of conference organizers in the more established North American and European markets. Such data do not yet exist, either in quantity or quality, for many of the newer markets.

World rankings of leading cities and countries

The global nature of the conference industry is also very well illustrated by figures produced annually by the International Congress & Convention Association (ICCA), from its headquarters in Amsterdam, and by the Union of International Associations (UIA), which is based in Brussels. Such figures record the staging of international conferences and conventions by country and city. They enable trends to be monitored and give an indication of which countries and cities are gaining market share and which may be losing it.

International Congress & Convention Association rankings

ICCA maintains an association database that holds meeting profiles with information on the location of international meetings. All association meetings in the ICCA database must meet the following criteria:

- be organized on a regular basis;
- rotate between at least four different countries;
- attract a minimum of 50 participants.

The database allows ICCA to provide rankings (by country and city) showing market share in respect of such meetings. ICCA's figures for 1999–2001, published in May 2002, and given in Table 1.4, show market share for the top 25 countries by number of events in that three-year period. It underlines the global nature of conferences, including as it does many countries that would not have appeared at all, even just a few years ago, such as the Republic of Korea and the Czech Republic.

Although international conventions are tracked by country as shown in Table 1.4, the events are actually won by individual destinations (normally cities) through a bidding process, and

	Country	1999	2000	2001
1	USA	265	262	185
2	UK	179	209	139
3=	Germany	176	187	138
3=	Japan	104	111	138
5	Australia	114	162	129
6=	Italy	141	136	128
6=	Spain	169	154	128
8	France	157	161	113
9	Finland	107	89	101
10	Denmark	75	59	83
11	Austria	80	79	78
12	Netherlands	113	132	77
13	Canada	95	101	76
14	Republic of Korea	52	28	73
15	Brazil	76	89	63
16	Portugal	45	46	59
17	Switzerland	62	68	51
18	Norway	67	74	49
19	Sweden	79	85	48
20=	Greece	52	37	45
20=	Poland	28	40	45
22	South Africa	51	49	42
23=	Belgium	61	59	40
23=	Czech Republic	45	30	40
25	Singapore	48	45	39
	Total	2441	2492	2107

Source: ICCA data (website: www.iccaworld.com).

Table 1.4
ICCA rankings (number of association meetings per *country* 1999 – 2001)

ICCA's record of where events were held on a city basis in 2001 (see Table 1.5) provides a challenging test to anyone's knowledge of world geography. As well as confirming the strength of international competition for convention business, it also suggests that Europe's pre-eminence is being challenged by destinations in Asia (e.g. Seoul, Singapore, Taipei), Australia (e.g. Sydney, Melbourne) and South America (e.g. Rio de Janeiro).

It should be noted that ICCA rankings are based purely on the *number* of meetings that meet the ICCA criteria, not their economic *value*. In other words, a destination would achieve a higher ranking than another destination because of a higher number of events held, even though such events might be considerably smaller in delegate numbers than a destination staging fewer events but with greater delegate numbers (and hence greater economic value).

	City	1999	2000	2001
1	Copenhagen	55	40	70
2	Vienna	63	53	57
3	Seoul	43	17	51
4	Helsinki	48	42	48
5	Barcelona	44	43	45
6	London	36	59	42
7	Paris	41	60	42
8	Sydney	45	52	41
9=	Rio de Janeiro	37	50	38
9=	Singapore	48	44	38
11	Madrid	50	55	36
12=	Berlin	48	44	34
12=	Lisbon	24	28	34
14	Prague	42	26	32
15	Edinburgh	36	42	30
16=	Melbourne	28	35	29
16=	Rome	30	23	29
18=	Budapest	48	40	28
18=	Dublin	23	20	28
18=	Taipei	25	18	28
21	Munich	25	22	27
22	Amsterdam	44	47	26
23	Kuala Lumpur	19	15	25
24	Glasgow	15	22	23
25	Beijing	21	28	22
	Total	938	925	903

ICCA statistics produced by ICCA data (website: www.iccaworld.com).

Table 1.5
ICCA rankings – number of association meetings per *city* 1999 – 2001

Union of International Associations statistics

Since 1949, the UIA has undertaken annual statistical studies on international meetings taking place worldwide. The statistics are based on information collected by the UIA Congress Department and selected according to very strict criteria. Meetings taken into consideration include those organized and/or sponsored by the international organizations, i.e. non-governmental organizations (NGOs) and intergovernmental organizations (IGOs), which appear in the UIA's *Yearbook of International Organizations* and *International Congress Calendar*, and whose details are subject to systematic collection on an annual basis by the UIA. Broadly, these meetings comprise the 'sittings' of their principal organs (notably IGOs) and their congresses, conventions, symposia, and regional sessions grouping several countries. Other meetings of 'significant international character', especially those organized by national organizations and national branches of international associations, are included provided that they meet the following criteria:

- minimum number of participants: 300;
- minimum number of foreigners: 40 per cent;
- minimum number of nationalities: five;
- minimum duration: three days.

These more stringent criteria for inclusion account, in large measure, for the differences between the UIA and ICCA rankings.

The UIA figures for 2001 (published in August 2002) include 9259 international meetings organized worldwide in 188 countries. The total number of meetings represents a decrease of 1.8 per cent on the 2000 figures, with just Africa (+3.7 per cent) and Europe (+0.7 per cent) recording increases. The decreases experienced in other continental regions were as follows: America: −6.9 per cent, Asia: −4.0 per cent, and Australasia/ Pacific: −7.9 per cent.

Some of the key findings of the 2001 figures, by continental region, highlighted by the UIA, were as follows.

Africa • • •

The rise in the number of meetings represents a small recovery from the significant falls of several years. In absolute terms, however, the number of meetings (+7 per cent) is not much changed from a decade ago and is below the global growth in meetings (+13 per cent) for the same period. Meeting numbers for individual countries are mostly too small to detect longer-term trends, except to note that South Africa continues to maintain its very strong position within the region. Morocco maintained good growth (+62 per cent).

America • • •

The fall in international meetings on the American continent in 2001 unexpectedly reversed the robust growth (+27 per cent) of the previous decade. Over the past decade, both Cuba (+57 per cent) and Argentina (+39 per cent) had made noteworthy advances. However, the USA, as the unchallenged world leader in international meetings (average annual growth of approximately 40 per cent), was decimated in 2001 with a reduction of –8 per cent compared with 2000, especially due to 'September 11th'. Canada also experienced a downturn (–14 per cent) over 2000 figures.

Asia • • •

The fall in international meetings in 2001 continued the downward trend of the previous four years, though this needs to be placed against a general growth of 10 per cent in the previous decade (slightly below the global growth figure of +13 per cent). South Korea experienced exceptional growth (+300 per cent over the decade) and continued to feature strongly, while Vietnam and Lebanon also signalled potential rapid growth in 2001. Regional leaders Japan, China, Singapore, Malaysia and Thailand held fairly stable positions.

Australasia/Pacific • • •

The fall in the number of international meetings in 2001 was unremarkable in this, the smallest of the regions, which overall experienced a 105 per cent real growth over the previous decade. Meetings in Australia fell by 15 per cent, back to 1999 levels, but New Zealand recorded a 67 per cent increase compared with 2000.

Europe • • •

There was not much change in 2001 compared with the previous year. Scandinavian countries (especially Sweden, Finland and Denmark) performed well, and the UK overtook France as the lead country. There was evidence of former Soviet Union countries in Eastern Europe re-emerging as important meetings destinations.

The UIA produces rankings by both country and city. Table 1.6 shows the leading countries covered by the UIA research.

Other countries hosting a significant number of international meetings in 2001 were: Brazil (94), Russia (90), India (85), Thailand (81), Argentina (79), Czech Republic (78), Mexico (75), Turkey (75), Ireland (64), Malaysia (55) and New Zealand (55).

	Country	Number of meetings	Percentage of all meetings
1	USA	1195	12.91%
2	UK	615	6.64%
3	France	600	6.48%
4	Germany	544	5.88%
5	Italy	414	4.47%
6	Spain	340	3.67%
7	Belgium	317	3.42%
8	Australia	308	3.33%
9	Netherlands	293	3.16%
10	Switzerland	240	2.59%
11	Austria	231	2.49%
12	Japan	215	2.32%
13	Canada	208	2.25%
14	Sweden	194	2.10%
15	Finland	184	1.99%
16	China and Hong Kong	159	1.72%
17	Denmark	152	1.64%
18	South Korea	134	1.45%
19	Singapore	120	1.30%
20	Portugal	116	1.25%
21=	Greece	110	1.19%
21=	Norway	110	1.19%
23	Poland	105	1.13%
24	Hungary	99	1.07%
25	South Africa	95	1.03%

Source: Union of International Associations.

Table 1.6
UIA rankings: top international meeting countries in 2001

Table 1.7 shows the UIA rankings of leading cities. It should be remembered that it is the cities that are the actual 'destinations' for the meeting, conference or convention. Other cities hosting a significant number of international events, but not in the top 26, in 2001 were (in order): Munich (57), Montreal (55), Istanbul (52), Dublin (51), Edinburgh (50), Chicago (49), Tokyo (46), San Diego (43), San Francisco (42), Glasgow (42), and Kuala Lumpur (40).

Further information can be found at the website www.uia.org/statistics.

Certain industry shortcomings

Limited market intelligence

It has been seen that, in comparison with many other industries, the conference industry is still a very young industry, barely 50

	City	Number of meetings	Percentage of all meetings
1	Paris	229	2.47%
2	London	191	2.06%
3	Brussels	188	2.03%
4	Vienna	140	1.51%
5	Singapore	120	1.30%
6	Geneva	119	1.29%
7	Berlin	114	1.23%
8	Seoul	107	1.16%
9	Copenhagen	105	1.13%
10	Sydney	95	1.03%
11	Amsterdam	91	0.98%
12=	Barcelona	90	0.97%
12=	Stockholm	90	0.97%
14	Washington	89	0.96%
15	Rome	81	0.87%
16=	Hong Kong	77	0.83%
16=	Budapest	77	0.83%
18	Helsinki	76	0.82%
19	New York	74	0.80%
20=	Strasbourg	73	0.79%
20=	Madrid	73	0.79%
22	Lisbon	67	0.72%
23	Melbourne	64	0.69%
24	Prague	62	0.67%
25=	Bangkok	59	0.64%
25=	Buenos Aires	59	0.64%

Source: Union of International Associations.

Table 1.7
UIA rankings: top international meeting cities in 2001

years of age in Europe and North America, and even younger in most of the rest of the world. Although it is maturing at a very rapid rate, it is indisputable that one of the legacies of its relative immaturity is a lack of reliable statistics and regular research to provide a base of intelligence and information on trends and on the size and value of the industry (the ICCA and UIA statistics quoted in this chapter are something of an oasis in what has generally been a rather barren statistical landscape). This, in turn, has meant that governments have not taken the industry seriously as a major benefactor to national economies because it has been impossible to demonstrate clearly the economic impact that conferences can have (except in some of the so-called less developed countries who have very quickly realized its potential and invested accordingly).

An important initiative to enhance statistics and research on the international conference industry was launched in 1997. Known as 'DOME' (an acronym for Data on Meetings and Events), the project is managed by a Board of Governors comprising leading figures from the industry and from academia, and is supported financially by a range of organizations (convention centres, convention bureaux, airlines, etc.). DOME is an international not-for-profit research foundation, whose mission is to 'improve the quality and accessibility of global research and data on the world's convention and meetings industry'. In some respects DOME has not made the progress hoped for in its first five years and it is still to establish itself as a leading resource for the industry. However, one of the major DOME research programmes is moving ahead: this measures the economic impacts of conventions by asking delegates to provide information on types of accommodation used and the duration of their stay, as well as details of air seats used by airline, flight segments and class of service (Chapter 3 gives further details of this programme). Further information on DOME is available through the website (www.domeresearch.com) or by emailing the DOME Secretariat at Johnson & Wales University (Rhode Island, USA): dmorales@jwu.edu.

Other important research projects are being developed in a number of countries (see examples in Chapter 3) so that overall market intelligence is increasing. However, there is undoubtedly still a long way to go before industry practitioners will feel that they have the information resources that meet their needs and accurately reflect the scope and importance of the industry.

Non-standardized terminology

One of the reasons for the limited statistics on the size and value of the industry is the lack of an accepted and properly defined terminology. At a macro level, arguments still rage over whether the term 'business tourism' is an accurate or appropriate one to describe the sector encompassing conferences, exhibitions and incentive travel. The link with 'tourism' is thought to be confusing and overlaid with a number of negative perceptions ('candy floss' jobs of a seasonal and poorly paid nature, for example, and dominant associations with holidays and leisure tourism). Business tourism is the phrase now widely in use in Europe as the accepted generic term. In Australia, the industry has adopted the term 'business events' to describe its essential focus.

The acronym MICE (for meetings, incentives, conferences, and exhibitions or events) is also still in widespread use around the world, despite its somewhat unfortunate connotations! In Canada this is adjusted to MC&IT: meetings, conventions and incentive travel.

At the micro level, words such as 'conference', 'congress', 'convention' and 'meeting' even, are often used synonymously or indiscriminately. Other words are also used with similar but more specialized connotations, such as 'symposium', 'colloquium', 'assembly', 'conclave' and 'summit', although it is probably only the last of these for which it might be easy to reach a consensus on its precise meaning (namely, a conference of high level officials, such as heads of government).

A first attempt was made by a number of industry professionals in 1990 to produce a *Meetings Industry Glossary*. A finished version of the *Glossary* was published in 1993 under the auspices of the Convention Liaison Council (now the Convention Industry Council – see page 230) and the Joint Industry Council (now the Joint Meetings Industry Council – see page 236) as the *International Meetings Industry Glossary*. It is revealing to see how the definitions changed from the first draft to the final version. Both are given below, with the draft version followed by the published definition (in italics).

Conference · · ·

Conferences can be used as an appropriate tool by any organizational group, private or public body, corporation, trade association, scientific or cultural society wishing to confer, exchange views and, consequently, to convey a message, open a debate or give publicity to some area of opinion on a specific issue. Most conferences are for 'study' purposes, generally involving some sort of special research input or conveyance of findings and require an active contribution from the participants. Compared with a congress, a conference is on a smaller scale and this gives a somewhat higher social connotation and makes it easier to exchange information. An example of the latter can be seen in a meeting of heads of state, ministers or official representatives of various states to examine, discuss and resolve, preferably by mutual agreement, political, economic or juridical problems of common interest. By and large, conferences are intended to facilitate communication and establish position reports or papers as a result of exchange of views. No tradition, continuity or periodicity is required to convene a conference. Although generally limited in time, conferences are usually of short duration with specific objectives.

An event used by any organization to meet and exchange views, convey a message, open a debate or give publicity to some area of opinion on a specific issue. No tradition, continuity or periodicity is required to convene a conference. Although not generally limited in time, conferences are usually of short duration with specific objectives. Conferences are generally on a smaller scale than congresses.

Congress • • •

The regular coming together of several hundreds, even thousands, of individuals on a representational basis belonging to one professional, cultural, religious or other sphere, who are generally united in associative groups. A congress is often convened to discuss a particular subject. Contributions to the presentation and discussion of the subject matter come only from members or the promoting associative group. A congress will often last several days and have several simultaneous sessions. The length of time between congresses is usually established in advance of the implementation stage, and can be either pluri-annual or annual. Most international or world congresses are of the former type while national congresses are more frequently held annually.

The regular coming together of large groups of individuals, generally to discuss a particular subject. A congress will often last several days and have several simultaneous sessions. The length of time between congresses is usually established in advance of the implementation stage, and can be either pluri-annual or annual. Most international or world congresses are of the former type while national congresses are more frequently held annually.

Using this definition, it may be felt that the Congress of Vienna, to which reference was made at the beginning of this chapter, should more accurately have been called the 'Convention' of Vienna.

Convention • • •

A general and formal meeting of a legislative body, social or economic group in order to provide information on a particular situation and in order to deliberate and, consequently, establish consent on policies among the participants. Usually of limited duration with set objectives, but no determined frequency. (The draft version was unchanged.)

• • • • •

Meeting ● ● ●

A general term indicating the coming together of a number of people in one place, to confer or carry out a particular activity. Can be on an ad hoc basis or according to a set pattern. (The draft version was unchanged.)

The descriptions listed above help to shed some light on the nature of different kinds of 'communications' events, but it is perhaps not surprising that they have not as yet been adopted as succinct, easy-to-remember definitions for the modern conference industry.

However, a new on-line initiative is striving to make further progress in standardizing and providing a common source for industry definitions. Known as the APEX (Accepted Practices Exchange) Initiative Terminology Project, it is spearheaded by the Convention Industry Council and is designed to 'bring together all stakeholders in the development and implementation of industry-wide accepted practices, which create and enhance efficiencies throughout the meeting, convention and exhibition industry'. APEX is located on the University of Las Vegas website, and browsers are invited to comment on definitions and/or add new terms for scrutiny by an expert panel. To access the APEX website use: www.conventionindustry.org/apex/Panels/Terminology.htm (and click on the link) or go directly to www.unlv.edu/Tourism/apex.html (ensuring a capital 'T' for Tourism) or http://tca.unlv.edu/apex.

It could be argued that the variety of available vocabulary is more a reflection of the rich diversity of the English language than a symptom of an industry with myriad events, each with its own distinct characteristics. It may not really matter whether an event is called a 'conference' or a 'convention', and certainly there are as many misuses of these terms are there are correct interpretations, if indeed such a thing as a correct interpretation really exists.

What is important, however, is the need to ensure that statistics are being collected and interpreted in a standardized way on a worldwide level, as befits a truly global industry. This will enable the real size and value of the conference industry to be established and monitored. This is critical to the national and international recognition and support, which the industry now deserves and demands.

Underdeveloped educational framework

One of the other reasons for the lack of a standardized terminology is that, for many of those now working in the industry, it is a second or even third career. They have come into conference work from related disciplines, such as hotel and catering, travel, sales and marketing, public administration, but also from what might appear superficially to be unrelated spheres of employment. Whereas many, if not most, other professions have a formal induction and training process for new entrants, which provides opportunities for them to be educated in the use of the accepted, clearly defined terminology, such opportunities and structures do not yet exist within the conference industry (although this is beginning to change with the advent of university and college courses providing modules on the conference industry).

Professional qualifications specific to the industry have existed for some years in North America. Such qualifications are now emerging elsewhere (see Chapter 7) and it is likely that, within the next five years, an appropriate range of educational courses and qualifications will have been established at both national and international levels. Such a development will provide overdue support and recognition for what is a highly sophisticated industry but, none the less, one in which many conference organizers have received no formal training nor obtained recognized qualifications to prepare them for their event management responsibilities. It is also frequently the case that conference organizing is only a small part of a person's job, undertaken for just a limited period of time. These are again factors that help to explain the problems sometimes experienced with semantics and the lack of clear, well-understood terminology.

Industry parameters and definitions

Even if precise definitions are not yet in regular use, it is important, at the beginning of a book on the conference industry, to set out certain parameters for the measurement of conference events and facilities.

In the UK, the sponsors of the annual *British Conference Market Trends Survey* (to be renamed the *British Conference Venues Survey* from 2003), namely the British Tourist Authority, British Association of Conference Destinations, CAT Publications, International Congress and Convention Association (UK & Ireland Chapter), Meetings Industry Association, Northern Ireland Tourist Board and VisitScotland, agreed to use the following criteria in respect of the *Survey*. A conference: 'an out-of-office meeting of at least six hours' duration involving a minimum of eight people'. For 2003, this definition was amended to read 'an out-of-office meeting of at least four hours' duration involving a minimum of eight people'.

In Australia, the definition used for the 1996–1997 'Meetings Make Their Mark' research was 'a meeting of 15 or more people using dedicated meeting space' at a venue away from their normal place of work.

Other research programmes use somewhat different definitions, while major conference hotel chains often base their own conference statistics on meetings with two or more people.

One definition of a conference venue that has been used is 'a conference venue must be able to seat 20 or more participants theatre-style'. However, this is so hopelessly inadequate that it could even describe a large living room or den in a private house! In October 2002, leading industry bodies in the UK agreed to use the following definition of a conference venue: 'a conference venue must be an externally-let facility (i.e. not a company's own meeting rooms), have a minimum of three meeting/conference rooms with a minimum seating capacity of 50 theatre-style in its largest room'.

The conference industry forms one sector within 'business tourism', itself a subsector of the overall tourism industry, which comprises both leisure tourism and business tourism. Apart from conferences, the other main components of business tourism are: exhibitions and trade fairs, incentive travel, corporate events/ hospitality and individual business travel (also referred to as 'corporate travel').

Table 1.8 provides a matrix of the main segments of business tourism and highlights some of their key characteristics.

One useful definition of a business tourist is 'a traveller whose main purpose for travelling is to attend an activity or event associated with his/her business or interests'.

Conferences, exhibitions and trade fairs, incentive travel and corporate events (sometimes referred to as corporate hospitality) are the four business tourism sectors that are the prime focus of marketing activities by venues and destinations because decisions about where the events take place are open to influence. The organizers of the event may have great flexibility in deciding where it is to be held, and are able to use their own judgement or discretion. For this reason, these four business tourism sectors are sometimes described as 'discretionary'.

Individual business travel or corporate travel relates to those whose work regularly involves travel within their own country or overseas, such as a lorry driver or sales representative, as well as to people who may have to travel away from their normal place of employment from time to time (e.g. a management consultant or an engineer responsible for installing a new piece of equipment in a client's factory). In all such business travel, which represents a major portion of business tourism, the opportunities to influence where the individual travels to are minimal, and this sector is consequently referred to as 'non-discretionary'.

Business tourism and leisure tourism

Reference has already been made to the broad division of tourism into the two sectors of business tourism and leisure tourism,

Segment	Corporate organization	National association	International association/intergovernment	Public sector/government
Meetings	An out-of-office meeting of at least 6 hours' duration involving a minimum of 8 people. Includes sales meetings, training, board meetings and retreats, AGMs	Board meetings, regional meetings, training events, information events	Limited number of board-level meetings, typically lasting 1–2 days maximum. Also international meetings hosted by national associations	Mainly organizing non-residential meetings of up to 1 day's duration. Also training courses, which may last for several days, and information events
Conferences	Typically of 1 or 2 days' duration with a formal programme that has been promoted in advance. Delegates are often compelled to attend	Usually an annual conference/congress/convention for members lasting 2–3 days	An annual (or less frequent) congress or convention rotating around different countries or continents, with selection based on bids received from individual cities. Typically of 3–5 days' duration	Mostly 1-day conferences (occasionally 2 days) attracting delegates from the local area or region
Incentive travel	A business tourism trip to motivate and reward employees and dealers, usually containing a conference element	Not applicable	Not applicable	Not applicable
Exhibitions	Product launches, attendance as an exhibitor at trade and consumer shows organized by specialist exhibition organizers or trade associations. Also attendance as a corporate visitor ('buyer') at trade shows	May include the organization of an exhibition to run alongside its own conference; also participation in other industry trade shows as an exhibitor. Trade associations are also primary exhibition organizers	May include the organization of an exhibition to run alongside its own conference; occasional participation in other industry trade shows as an exhibitor	Information/regional trade events
Corporate events (previously known as corporate hospitality)	Hosted entertainment at major sporting events, concerts and other high-profile functions, and/or participation in sporting or outdoor pursuits-type activities	Not applicable	Not normally applicable	Not applicable

Table 1.8
'MICE' matrix (illustrating the segments which make up the business tourism sector)

although these two sectors share much common ground. As Davidson (1994) points out:

> business tourism, in particular, can involve a substantial leisure element. Incentive travel, for example, may consist entirely of leisure, sport and entertainment. But, even for conference delegates, visitors to trade fairs and individual business travellers, excursions to local restaurants and places of entertainment, or sightseeing tours, can be a way of relaxing at the end of the working day. Socializing in this way can be an important part of the business tourism experience for groups, as it gives delegates or colleagues the opportunity to unwind together and get to know each other on a less formal basis.

This is why bidding destinations sell the concept of 'destination' and place great emphasis on everything from leisure, cultural and entertainment assets to shopping, sports and dining options.

Davidson also makes clear that:

> the distinction between the two categories of tourism is further blurred by the presence of 'accompanying persons' alongside many business tourism events. Incentive travel often includes the husbands or wives of those selected for such trips. But also, it is not uncommon for those travelling to exotic destinations for conferences or trade fairs and exhibitions to take their spouses along and make a short holiday out of the trip. In such cases, the couple may prolong their stay in order to have the time to tour around the destination after the business part of the trip is over.

The phrase 'leisure extenders' is emerging in the UK to describe the latter activity.

Business tourism and leisure tourism rely on the same, or a very similar, infrastructure to take place successfully. Both sectors need accommodation (hotels, guest houses), transport and communications (airports, railway stations, good road networks, coach and taxi services, modern telecommunications links), entertainment (shopping, bars and restaurants, night clubs/ casinos, visitor attractions), as well as information and advisory services, emergency medical services and an attractive, welcoming, safe and secure environment.

The Creta Maris Hotel in Hersonissos, Crete, is a good example of a tourism product catering equally well for both the business and leisure tourism sectors by focusing on several niche markets: conferences and conventions, incentive trips, and leisure tourism for higher spending holidaymakers. Case study 1.4 gives a more in-depth analysis of the Creta Maris product and business strategy.

But conference and business tourism has additional infrastructure needs, such as appropriate venues, specialist contractors (e.g. audiovisual suppliers, exhibition contractors, interpreters) and, perhaps most importantly, staff who are trained to be aware of and to respond to the particular needs of conference organizers and delegates. It is in the provision of this latter service that venues and destinations most frequently fall down, a theme that is further developed in later chapters of this book.

The benefits of conference and business tourism

Although business tourism and leisure tourism rely on a similar infrastructure, the former brings with it a number of significant extra benefits, which makes it particularly attractive to destinations.

Greater profitability

Conference and business tourism caters for the high-quality, high-cost and, therefore, high-yield end of the market. In 2001, for example, conference visitors to the UK from overseas spent an average of £146 per day compared with an average of just £56 per day for all categories of visitors (source: *International Passenger Survey 2002*). The greater spending power of business tourists means increased economic benefits for the host destination and a greater return on its investment in infrastructure and marketing.

All-year-round activity

Conference and business tourism takes place throughout the year. Spring and autumn are the peak seasons of the year for conferences (with most of the larger, high-profile association and political party conferences taking place at these times in the UK), but many smaller conferences and meetings are also held during the winter months. In the northern hemisphere, January, July and August are the months of least activity, which, for many resort-type destinations, is an added benefit because it means that there is no clash between the demands of leisure and business tourism, but rather they are complementary.

The all-year-round nature of conference and business tourism also leads to the creation and sustenance of permanent jobs, as opposed to the seasonal, temporary jobs, which are a frequent characteristic of the leisure tourism sector. This, in turn, ensures that 'careers' rather than simply 'jobs' can be offered to new entrants, although clearly defined structures and opportunities for career progression are not yet fully established.

Future inward investment

Those organizing a conference or incentive travel trip will always be very keen to make sure that it is as successful as possible. One of the ways in which this can be achieved is by giving delegates and participants a pleasant, positive experience of the destination in which the event is being held. This usually means showing delegates the most attractive, scenic parts of the destination in the hope that, by creating a memorable experience for them, many will return.

Where this has been undertaken successfully, some delegates/attendees return as leisure visitors, often bringing their partners and families for a holiday or short break. Some, it is hoped, will have been so impressed that they may decide to relocate their business to the destination or look to set up a subsidiary operation there. As Davidson (1994) says:

> a business visitor who leaves with a good impression of the conference, trade fair or incentive destination becomes an unpaid ambassador for that place . . . these are often influential people, whose opinions of the destination will be instrumental in determining its image in the minds of others who have not visited it.

'Green' tourism

Conference and business tourism has fewer negative impacts on the environment than mass leisure tourism. It is concerned with smaller numbers, but a much higher spend. It is characterized by the use of coach transfers and public transport (or Shanks' pony) within a destination, minimizing traffic congestion and environmental pollution.

Conference delegates are together as a group, so that it is possible to inform and educate them about the local community in which their conference is being held in order to maximize the enjoyment of their stay, but also to minimize any disruption and possible inconvenience to the local resident population. It is very much harder to manage, in the same way, the impact of individual leisure travellers on a destination.

However, it would be naïve to claim that business tourism does not have its negative impacts, especially on the physical environment. These are well summarized by Swarbrooke and Horner (2001): 'If we want to make business travel and tourism more sustainable, we have to recognize that there are characteristics of business tourism, which make it particularly problematic in relation to the concept of sustainable tourism. First, most business tourists take more trips in a year than the average leisure tourist, thus making more demands on transport infrastructure and destination services. Business tourists tend to be very demanding and want high-quality facilities, even in towns and cities in developing countries. While both of these are difficult to reconcile with the concept of sustainable tourism, the positive side of business tourism is the fact that business travellers tend to be higher spending than leisure tourists.

Summary

- The USA was the first country to recognize the potential economic benefits of conference business for a city or local destination. Detroit was the first US city to establish a convention and visitor bureau in 1896, followed by a number of other US cities in the early years of the 20th century. Europe did not follow suit until the latter half of the 20th century, and it was at this time also that conference tourism came to be recognized as an industry in its own right.
- The final two decades of the 20th century and the early years of the 21st century have witnessed spectacular investment in the infrastructure that supports both leisure and conference/business tourism. Such investments are taking place not only in the more established conference destinations of Western Europe and North America, but in every continent and region.
- The conference industry is now a truly global industry, with almost 200 countries vying for a share of the lucrative international conferences and meetings market. A greater market share is now being won by countries in Eastern Europe and in the Asia/Pacific region in particular.
- The conference industry is still young, though maturing at a rapid rate. Symptomatic of the industry's youthfulness, yet contributing to its lack of proper recognition in commercial and political circles, is the lack of a comprehensive statistical base to measure its true size and value. Its relative immaturity is also shown in its use and misuse of terminology.
- Conference/business tourism and leisure tourism are closely intertwined, relying on similar infrastructure and support services. However, conference tourism also has a number of unique characteristics and advantages, which can bring additional benefits to those destinations successful in attracting conference business.

Review and discussion questions

1 Analyse the destination and/or venue case studies in this chapter (Manchester, Dubai, Pattaya Conference and Exhibition Hall, Creta Maris Hotel) and identify the principal features which each have in common and which are contributing to their success as conference destinations or venues. Then compare these with a destination or venue that

has been less successful and put forward reasons why it has
fared less well in the international conference marketplace.

2 Summarize the main changes in international convention
market share experienced by one continent over recent
years, giving examples of national and city destinations, and
drawing comparisons with another continent. Suggest
strategies for increasing its market share.

3 Compare and contrast the conference industry with another
young industry (e.g. computing and information technology,
the fitness and health food industry). Draw conclusions on
which has progressed further, and give reasons why.

4 Choose a resort destination active in both the leisure and
conference/business tourism sectors. Identify the best niche
markets for both sectors (see also Chapters 2 and 3), and
produce the 'ideal calendar' of business for a year that
maximizes use of its facilities and generates the highest level
of economic benefit.

Notes and references

Davidson, Rob. *Business Travel*. Addison Wesley Longman Limited (1994).

Gartrell, Richard B. *Destination Marketing for Convention and Visitor Bureaus*. Published under the auspices of the International Association of Convention and Visitor Bureaus by Kendall/Hunt Publishing Company (second edition, 1994).

ICCA data are used by permission of the International Congress and Convention Association, Entrada 121, 1096 EB Amsterdam, The Netherlands.

International Passenger Survey – Overseas Visitors to the UK 2001. Office for National Statistics and BTA Statistical Research (2002).

Meetings Industry Glossary. Published under the auspices of The Convention Liaison Council and Joint Industry Council (1993).

Shone, Anton. *The Business of Conferences*. Butterworth-Heinemann (1998).

Swarbrooke, John and Horner, Susan. *Business Travel and Tourism*. Butterworth-Heinemann (2001).

UIA statistics are used by permission of the Union of International Associations, Congress Department, Rue Washington 40, B-1050 Brussels, Belgium.

Further reading

Davidson, Rob and Cope, Beulah. *Business Travel*. Pearson Education (2002).

Dictionary of Meeting Industry Terminology. Available from the International Association of Professional Congress Organizers (IAPCO)(see Chapter 8).

The structure of the conference industry

Introduction

The conference industry is highly complex, comprising a multiplicity of buyer and supplier organizations and businesses. For many conference organizers ('the buyers'), the organization of conferences and similar events is only a part of their job, and often one for which they have received little formal training and may only have a temporary responsibility. Suppliers include conference venues and destinations, accommodation providers and transport companies, agencies and specialist contractors. Both buyers and suppliers are welded together, and supported by national bodies and associations, trade press and educational institutions, each contributing to the overall structure of this fast-developing global industry.

This chapter looks at the roles and characteristics of:

- the buyers (corporate, association, public sector, entrepreneurs);
- the suppliers (venues, destinations, other suppliers);
- agencies and intermediaries;
- other important organizations (trade associations, trade media, national tourism organizations, consultants and educational institutions).

Buyers

In common with other industries, the conference industry comprises 'buyers' and 'suppliers'. The buyers in this case are conference organizers and meeting planners, who buy, or more accurately, hire conference venues and related services in order to stage their events.

Most people working within the conference industry refer to two broad types of buyer: 'corporate' and 'association'. However, in some cases, 'public-sector' buyers are treated as a separate entity, rather than being included within the 'association' category. There is also a category of risk-taking, entrepreneurial conference organizer, who puts together a conference and hopes to be able to attract sufficient delegates for the event to be profitable. All of the above may also employ the services of various kinds of 'agency' to assist them in the staging of their events.

The corporate buyer

Definitions ● ● ●

The term 'corporate' is used to describe conference organizers (often called 'meeting planners', especially in North America), who work for corporate organizations. Corporate organizations are companies established primarily to generate a profit and thus provide a financial return for their owners, whether these are the proprietors of a family-run business or the shareholders of a large publicly quoted company. They can be manufacturing or service companies.

Corporate organizations are to be found in most, if not all, industry sectors. The sectors that are particularly prominent in generating corporate conference business include:

- oil, gas and petrochemicals;
- medical and pharmaceuticals;
- computing/IT and telecommunications;
- motor manufacturing and other manufacturing;
- financial and professional services;
- food, drink and tobacco;
- travel and transport.

Identifying the corporate buyer ● ● ●

Relatively few companies have a dedicated conference or event-management department. Indeed, during times of economic recession, this is often an area where many companies have opted to make savings by closing down their event-management departments and putting the work out to agencies on a contract

Job title/Responsibility	% of interviewees
Administration (including secretaries and PAs)	25
Sales and marketing	23
PR/Communications	18
Training/Human resources	11
Conferences/Events	18
Other	5

Source: UK Conference Market Survey 2002.

Table 2.1
Principal job titles/responsibilities of staff engaged in conference organizing

basis. In some cases, they contract the employees from their former event-management departments to continue to organize their events, but such employees now work on a freelance basis and so are not a direct overhead to the company.

The larger corporate organizations are, of course, multidivision entities located on a number of different sites, often in a number of different countries. Staff involved in organizing meetings and conferences appear in a whole range of guises and job titles. Research carried out for the *UK Conference Market Survey 2002* found that fewer than one in five of the 600 conference organizers interviewed (300 corporate, 300 association) had job titles or responsibilities directly associated with 'conferences or events'. Table 2.1 gives further details of this research.

In broad terms, most corporate events will fall within the ambit of the following departments: sales and marketing; training and personnel/human resources; and central administration, including the company secretarial activities.

Staff involvement in organizing events often varies considerably. At one extreme, their task may simply be to obtain information on potential venues for an event, while at the other, they will be given complete responsibility for planning and running the event. It is estimated that, in the UK at least, around 80 per cent of corporate organizers have received little formal training in conference and meeting planning. Such activities account for just a part of their overall responsibilities and their responsibility for conference organizing may only be of a short-term nature. (In the USA, the role of a meeting planner is more established, with better-defined training and career structures.)

Identifying the corporate buyer is, therefore, a major and continuous challenge for those organizations wishing to market their facilities and services to him. The transience of many corporate conference organizers also makes it difficult to provide an effective education and training framework for them, and thus develop their expertise and increase their professionalism. It is only when such support systems are in place that proper recognition can be given to the role of the corporate conference organizer as a crucial component of any company's communications strategy.

Corporate buying patterns

Decisions about the conference or meeting (choice of venue, budget, size of event, visiting speakers, programme content, and so forth) will be taken by the corporate conference organizer, line manager or the managing director, or by a group of such people in consultation. The decision-making process is relatively straightforward and more-or-less immediate.

Corporate events can be of many different types and sizes. The most common of these events are shown in Table 2.2.

Table 2.2
The main types of corporate meeting/event

Annual general meeting (AGM)	Product launch
Board meeting/retreat	Sales conference
Corporate hospitality/entertainment	Training course/seminar
Exhibition/exposition	Technical conference
Incentive travel	Team-building event
Roadshow	Symposium

It is worth drawing the distinction between internal and external events. In the former case, the participants are employees of the company (typically sales conferences, general management conferences, rallies for the staff, etc.). External events are a vital part of Customer Relationship Management (CRM) strategies (see Chapter 4) with companies trying to build a long-term relationship with their key clients. One way of doing this is to invite such clients to be part of the company's development process through attending events. Such events can include new product launches, educational meetings explaining complex new products or upgrades (especially in the field of IT). Participation in these events enables account managers to get close to such clients over coffee breaks or in the bar. One of the benefits for companies in running these events is that they get real-time feedback and can measure the return on investment (ROI) in a way that is impossible with traditional internal sales conferences.

The majority of corporate conferences and meetings are held in hotels. Some take place in purpose-built conference centres and management training centres. Incentive events and corporate hospitality will often make use of unusual venues. Civic venues and town halls tend to attract relatively few corporate events because of a perception that they may be staid and 'basic', which is often far from the reality. Some corporate meetings are held in university and academic venues, especially where such venues have invested in dedicated conference facilities with high-quality, *en suite* accommodation/housing (as, indeed, an increasing number are doing).

Corporate events often have a fairly short 'lead time', especially compared with association conferences, with just a matter of weeks or a few months available to plan and stage them. In 2001, there was an average lead time of five months for corporate meetings in the UK (*UK Conference Market Survey 2002*). The majority of such events involve relatively low delegate numbers (e.g. from 10 to 200). Delegates are told to participate by the company; they are often not given a choice.

Corporate conferences and events take place throughout the year, peaking in spring and autumn. In the northern hemisphere, July and August are the months of least activity because of holidays, although the corporate hospitality sector is buoyant at this time with its links to major sporting events, such as Wimbledon, test match cricket, Grand Prix motor racing and international golf tournaments.

The budget for corporate conferences, expressed in terms of expenditure per delegate, is generally much higher than that for many 'association' conferences, as it is the company that pays for delegate attendance, not the delegates themselves. The costs can be incorporated into a company's marketing or staff-training budgets, for example, and the selection of an attractive quality venue coupled with a professionally produced conference will reinforce the importance of the event in delegates' minds and contribute to the successful achievement of its objectives, whether these be motivational, information sharing, team building or other.

However, research undertaken by Ian Flint & Associates (and published in *Business Travel World* magazine – July 2002) among major national and multinational companies in France, Germany, Italy, Spain and the UK found that, while such companies were claiming an estimated annual expenditure on meetings of between US$2 million and US$10 million, 67.5 per cent of them said that they did not know how much they spent overall on meeting planning. There is a clear case for changing and introducing more effective management systems to, and indeed professionalizing, the whole meeting-venue procurement process. The same research found that the three countries spending most on meetings were (in order) the UK, Germany and France, while the highest spending sectors were pharmaceutical, IT and motor manufacturing.

Web-based tools are now arriving, which will provide much more effective management of venue-purchasing activities across major corporations, while at the same time enabling these companies to make significant savings by obtaining bulk purchase discounts, particularly from hotel groups. One such tool is Meeting Management Solutions (MMS) developed by the PlanSoft Corporation in Ohio, USA (www.plansoft.com).

Corporate conferences are now more intensive, business-related events than was the case during the 1980s, when they were often seen as something of a 'jolly'. Return on investment is one of the buzz phrases across the industry, emphasizing the need to measure the effectiveness of all investments and activities, including those investments made in a company's workforce. Despite this, research suggests that around one-third of corporate conference organizers do not evaluate their events after they have taken place, a finding that calls into question their professionalism and the investment that the company is making in them as people who place a high value on the virtues of two-way communications.

Typical delegates

A survey of 300 corporate organizations on behalf of the *UK Conference Market Survey 2002* found the following.

- The average age of a delegate attending a corporate event during 2001 was 38.
- 67 per cent of corporate delegates were male, attending on average three events per year.
- At least 70 per cent of organizers categorized their delegates as senior or middle management, or sales and marketing professionals. A total of 43 per cent were also organizing events for accountants or accountancy-related positions, but only 31 per cent for general administration. Eleven per cent were organizing events for medical professionals.
- 88 per cent of those corporate conference organizers interviewed believed that their delegates were satisfied with their venue choice most of the time. An additional 11 per cent believed that they were satisfied all of the time.
- The most frequent cause for complaint by delegates was food, which far outweighed complaints about presentations or meeting content.

A profile of typical delegates attending conferences in Germany is given in Chapter 3.

In summary, therefore, the corporate sector of the conference industry is characterized by events with fewer than 200 delegates, fairly short lead times, and high spend with costs being borne by the company. Conferences are one of the prime ways in which corporate organizations communicate with their employees and their customers, although the generic term 'conferences' may describe a variety of sizes and types of events. Conferences are a high-profile communications vehicle conveying important messages about the company. It is vital, therefore, that conferences are successful in meeting the objectives set for them. This often means that the budget for the event will be a generous one, making it an attractive piece of business for venues and other suppliers.

The association buyer

Definitions • • •

The term 'association' organizer or buyer covers those representing a wide range of organizations, including:

- professional or trade associations/institutions (whose members join because of their employment);
- voluntary associations and societies (whose members join primarily to further an interest or hobby);
- charities;
- religious organizations;
- political parties;
- trades unions.

The acronym 'SMERF' groups (social, military, educational, religious and fraternal) is sometimes used in North America to describe those types of organizations that are not work-related.

Very few, if any, of these organizations are established mainly to generate a financial return. They are 'not-for-profit' organizations, which exist to provide a service to their members and to the community at large. There is, however, an equal need for association conferences, as with corporate conferences, to be run extremely professionally, not least because they are often in the public eye, through press and media exposure, in a way that corporate conferences are not. And, while the associations themselves may be 'not-for-profit', association conferences must cover their costs and, in some cases, be planned with the aim of generating a profit, which can then be reinvested in the administrative and promotional costs of future conferences.

There are also specialist association management companies, which make a living by providing a professional 'secretariat' for associations, which do not have the resources or management expertise to run their association themselves. They can pay a management fee to such companies to administer the association on their behalf, including the organization of their meetings and conferences. The Society of Incentive and Travel Executives (SITE – see Chapter 8) is now run by an association management company. Such association management companies will typically have a meeting planning department, which, in essence, operates like a professional conference organizer (see below) on behalf of the organizations they represent.

Delegate characteristics ● ● ●

Delegates attending association conferences usually share a number of the following common characteristics.

- They normally choose to attend the conference or other event run by the 'association', rather than being asked to attend by their employer.
- They are often required to pay their own expenses to attend (except perhaps for trade association delegates), which means that the conference organizer must keep the costs as low as possible if it is important to maximize delegate attendance. In certain cases, particularly where the delegate is attending as a representative of a group of colleagues or fellow workers, as with trade union conferences, the delegate will receive a daily allowance to cover his costs while attending the conference.
- A range of accommodation will usually be required, from guesthouses to five-star hotels. At least one major association insists that a destination must have a caravan park before it can be considered to stage its conference!
- The number of delegates attending the main annual conference will typically be much higher than for corporate events. Indeed, association conferences can attract hundreds and sometimes thousands of delegates, and frequently receive much media attention.
- The *UK Conference Market Survey 2002* found that the average age of an association delegate was 38 (42 in 2001), with 62 per cent of delegates being male and attending an average of two events per year.

These general characteristics may apply across the association sector, but they should not be allowed to hide some important differences between different types of associations. For example, delegates attending an annual surgeons' conference would expect to stay in accommodation of at least three-star hotel standard (a 1000-delegate conference with many delegates bringing spouses would require a destination with a substantial number of high-quality hotels), whereas a charity or religious conference is likely to require more modest accommodation at the budget end of the spectrum.

Buying patterns ● ● ●

The association decision-making process is different from that in the corporate sector. Even though many of the larger associations have dedicated conference organizers and, in some cases, event organizing units/departments, the decision on where the annual conference is to be held will normally be taken by a committee elected by the membership. The conference organizer will do much of the research and related groundwork, producing a shortlist of the most likely destinations and venues from which the committee will choose, and even making recommendations.

Destinations will put forward detailed 'bid' proposals outlining how they could help the association to stage a successful event (and, indeed, will also do this for corporate buyers). Such a bid document is likely to contain a formal invitation, often signed by the mayor or other civic dignitary, a full description of the destination highlighting its attractions, access and communications details (e.g. road and rail links, the number of scheduled flights from the local airport), information on the support services available in the destination (transport operators, exhibition/exposition contractors, interpreters, audiovisual companies, and so on), a list of the services provided by the convention and visitor bureau or conference office, details of hotel and other accommodation and, of course, full details of the venue being proposed to stage the conference. The convention and visitor bureau/conference office, acting on behalf of the destination, may be invited to make a formal presentation to the selection committee of the association, in competition with other destinations similarly short-listed.

Bid proposals may also be put forward by host committees (i.e. local chapters of an association) (an example of this in relation to international association conferences is shown in Case study 2.2 – the same principle applies to national association events). Such host committees have an important influence on site selection. It should also be noted that internal 'politics' can also have a major influence within such organizations, e.g. the President or Chairman's wife wants to meet in Florida!

Before a final decision is made, the selection committee may undertake an inspection visit to the destination to assess at first hand its strengths and weaknesses. The whole decision-making process can, therefore, be very protracted, sometimes taking many months to complete.

Lead times for association events are much longer than for corporate events. It is not uncommon for associations organizing a 1000-delegate conference to have booked venues for several years ahead. In part, this is because there is a much more limited choice of venue, in part because there is significantly more work involved in staging a 1000-delegate conference than one for 100 delegates. Some of the larger, purpose-built conference/convention centres have provisional reservations for more than ten years ahead from association conference organizers.

National associations tend to follow one of several patterns or rotations in the staging of their main annual conference. The examples given below relate to the UK but similar rotations are likely to apply to most other countries with a significant 'national association' conference market:

- Some associations adopt an alternate north–south rotation, holding the conference in the north of England/Scotland one year, and then in the south of England the next, returning to the north in year three.
- Some associations operate a three- or four-year rotation, moving to different regions of the country in order to be seen to be fair to their members who are probably drawn from most parts of the country.
- Other associations appear to be quite immobile, opting to use the same destination year after year.
- Finally, certain associations look for somewhere different each year, following no clear geographical pattern.

For those destinations and venues seeking to win their business, it is clearly important to have an understanding of which pattern a particular association has adopted.

Many association conferences have both delegates and their partners attending, a characteristic much less frequently found with corporate events, unless they include an incentive element. The partners do not normally attend the business sessions of the conference but they will be fully involved in the social events, which form part of the conference programme. Partner programmes are designed to entertain partners while the conference is in progress. Quite often destinations will work with the conference organizer to help in the planning of partner (or spouse) programmes, as well as in coordinating tours and activities both pre- and post-conference. Such activities, together with the attendance of partners, can add significantly to the economic benefits that the conference brings to the destination, encouraging a number of countries to examine and adopt best practice in maximizing these 'leisure extenders'.

Association conferences, because of their larger size, are often held in purpose-built conference or convention centres. Hotels are also popular (particularly so in the USA, where major resort hotels can cater for large conventions, all under one roof), while some associations will use town hall and civic venues, and others book university and college venues. Where hotels are used, this will often be over a weekend because the hotel is offering cheaper rates than for weekday bookings. The peak seasons for association conferences are autumn and spring, but some conferences take place over the summer months and a limited number during the winter.

Table 2.3 summarizes the similarities and differences between corporate and association conferences.

Corporate conferences	Association conferences
Corporate buyers are employed by 'for profit' organizations	Association buyers are employed by 'not-for-profit' organizations
Corporate organizations are to be found in both the manufacturing and service sectors	Associations are to be found in the manufacturing, service and voluntary sectors
The event decision-making process is straightforward, and more or less immediate	The event decision-making process is prolonged, often involving a committee
Events have a relatively short lead time (usually measured in weeks or months)	Major conferences have a relatively long lead time (often measured in years)
Corporate buyers may organize a wide range of events	Association buyers organize a more limited range of events
Delegate numbers are typically less than 200 (and frequently well under 100)	Delegate numbers are often several hundred and, for the larger associations, can be several thousands
Mainly held in hotels, purpose-built conference/convention centres and unusual venues	Mostly use purpose-built conference/convention centres, conference hotels, civic and academic venues
A higher budget per delegate, with the company paying	A lower budget per delegate, with the individual delegate sometimes paying. There are variations both by type of association and by country
Events are organized year-round	Major events primarily in the spring and autumn, with some in the summer
Events typically last 1–2 days	Major conference typically lasts 3–4 days
Accommodation normally in hotels (three-star and upwards)	Wide range of accommodation may be required, dependent on the type of association, and whether participants are paying out of their own pockets or whether their employers are paying
Delegates' partners rarely attend	Delegates' partners quite frequently attend

Table 2.3
Similarities and differences between corporate and association conferences

Table 2.4 summarizes the key findings from the *UK Conference Market Survey 2002* from interviews conducted with 300 corporate conference organizers and 300 association conference organizers. The findings relate to events organized in 2001, with findings for 2000 shown in brackets.

Table 2.5 summarizes comparative data on the corporate and association meetings sectors in the USA. The information was taken from the Meeting Professionals International (MPI) website (www.mpiweb.org/members/membership/facts.asp) in July 2002, and is based on several surveys: 'Meetings & Conventions'

	Corporate sector	Association sector
Average number of events organized	9.2 (9.7)	12.8 (13.2)
Total number of events organized by sample	2760 (2910)	3840 (3960)
% decline on previous year	−5%	−3%
% who cancelled events following 'September 11th'	26%	12%
% who postponed events following 'September 11th'	25%	11%
% expecting to organize more events in 2002	6%	34%
Average number of delegates	111 (128)	186 (118) (regular meetings, not major annual meeting for which the figure is 397)
Most popular types of events	Management meeting Presentation Sales conference Training	Annual meeting Education Member communication Technical updates
Average duration of event, in days	1.3 (1.6)	1.8 (2.1)
% residential	40% (38%)	34% (35%)
Most popular days of week for holding events	1. Thursday 2. Wednesday 3. Tuesday	1. Wednesday 2. Tuesday 3. Thursday
Average lead times (months)	5 (4.7)	13.9 (13.6)
Average spend per organization (£ sterling) on events	£109 700 (£133 000)	£112 800 (£84 500)
Top three destinations used	1. Central England − 52% 2. London − 49% 3. South East England − 34%	1. London − 54% 2. Birmingham − 30% 3. Manchester − 23%
% of conferences held outside UK in 2001	6%	6%
Most popular venue type	1. Out of town hotel − 70% 2. City centre hotel − 65% 3. Residential conference centre − 27%	1. City centre hotel − 58% 2. Purpose-built convention centre − 34% 3. University/academic venue − 25%

Table 2.4 Key findings from the *UK Conference Market Survey 2002* from interview conducted with corporate and association conference organizers

	Corporate sector	Association sector
Top five factors influencing venue selection	1. Location – 64% 2. Price/value for money – 49% 3. Access – 33% 4. Quality of conference facilities – 27% 5. Quality of service – 27%	1. Location – 80% 2. Price/value for money – 59% 3. Access – 52% 4. Capacity of conference facilities – 42% 5. Quality of service – 38%
Top five sources of help with venue selection	1. Own knowledge – 96% 2. Internet – 43% 3. Venue-finding agency – 42% 4. Word of mouth – 34% 5. Brochures – 20%	1. Own knowledge – 65% 2. Word of mouth – 47% 3. Venue finding agency – 26% 4. Directories/guides – 25% 5. Internet –19%
% who visit trade shows/ exhibitions	21% (28%)	48% (44%)
Factors causing dissatisfaction at venues	1. Value for money 2. Lack of a dedicated person	1. Customer service 2. Value for money
% always or nearly always asked for feedback from venues	33% (30%) (22% in 1999)	44% (37%) (25% in 1999)
Top three audiovisual items used	1. Flip chart – 87% 2. PC/data projection – 86% 3. Video and monitor – 77%	1. Sound system – 65% 2. OHP – 61% 3. PC/data projection – 59%
Forms of communication most used in addition to face-to-face meetings	1. Email – 99% (83%) 2. Website – 96% (73%) 3. Teleconferencing – 72% (60%)	1. Email – 63% (46%) 2. Website – 54% (39%) 3. Teleconferencing – 37% (17%)
Using the Internet to market their events	16% (19%)	60% (59%)
Communicate with delegates/ attendees via email	96% (72%)	66% (47%)
Seek venue information via Internet	35% (25%)	41% (37%)
Booking venues via Internet	11% (5%)	12% (15%)
Take registrations via website	7% (7%)	42% (23%)
Delegate joining instructions sent via website	7% (6%)	49% (27%)

() = 2000 figures

Table 2.4 Continued

	Corporate	Association
Expenditure	Corporate meetings expenditure totalled $US 10.2 billion in 1999	Association meetings expenditure in 1999 totalled $US 13.7 billion
Expenditure breakdown	58% on hotels, food and associated costs; 19% on air transportation; 8% on speakers, audiovisual and entertainment; 6% on ground transportation	33% on food and beverage; 30% on hotels; 12% on speakers, audiovisual equipment and entertainment; 5% on ground transportation
Delegate/ attendee numbers	Total number of corporate meeting attendees in 1999 was 51 million	The total number of association meeting attendees in 1999 was 15.6 million
Planner ages	52% of corporate planners are female, 48% male, with an average age of 47	62% of association planners are female, 38% male, with an average age of 45
Other characteristics	The top meeting cities for corporate meetings in 1999 were: Chicago, Las Vegas, Orlando, San Francisco	More than 70% of association planners named cost as the most important factor in the selection of meeting facilities
	82% of corporate planners selected the meeting venue, 75% chose the destination, 72% planned entertainment and social functions, 63% set the budget, and 62% planned the agenda/programme	In 1999, associations held 61 800 educational meetings, 40 300 board meetings, 33 900 technical meetings and 29 200 regional/local meetings. They also held 11 700 conventions

Table 2.5
Characteristics of the corporate and association meetings sectors in the USA

2000 Meetings Market Report', 'The Meeting Professional', and the MPI Foundation's 'Making Meetings Work – An Analysis of Corporate Meetings'.

International 'association' conferences

The above characteristics of national associations apply equally to those associations that are primarily international in nature, as well as to international governmental organizations and to academic bodies planning international scientific conferences. Destinations bidding to stage major international conferences have to be extremely professional in their approach and be prepared to begin working for such an event many years before it is due to take place. It is not unusual to find lead times of five years or more, necessitating a great deal of research by those destinations seeking to host the conference, particularly in their cost calculations. It could be all too easy to offer certain hotel rates and venue hire charges to the association, which, because of the effects of inflation and other possible changes in the macroeconomic climate, bear little relation to what should be being charged when the event actually takes place.

Case study 2.1 illustrates the lead time involved in Sydney's attempts to secure and stage two major international medical conventions, both held in 2002.

Case study 2.1

Sydney's bids to host two major international congresses

XIVth World Congress of Cardiology – 5–9 May 2002

The possibility of Sydney bidding to host the 2002 Congress was first confirmed in 1990, following preparatory work undertaken during the late 1980s. A formal bid was presented at the 1994 Congress held in Berlin, and was based on extensive collaboration between Sydney Convention and Visitors Bureau, the New South Wales State Government, a group of leading Australian cardiologists (which became the nucleus of the Organizing Committee), and the congress organizer ICMS Pty Ltd. Sydney faced stiff competition from Singapore, Japan and Thailand, but was successful in its bid. The Congress is held every four years and the 1998 Congress in Rio de Janeiro was used to promote the 2002 event in Sydney to potential delegates and exhibitors. A total of 8000 cardiologists attended the 2002 Congress.

XXIXth International Congress of Ophthalmology – 21–25 April 2002

Research into this Congress also began in the late 1980s and Sydney was invited to present its bid at the 1994 Congress held in Toronto. Competing destinations in 1994 were Hong Kong and Manila. Sydney was again successful and was then invited to attend the 1998 Congress held in Amsterdam to confirm sponsors for the 2002 event. A total of 5000 ophthalmologists attended the Congress in 2002, held at the Sydney Convention and Exhibition Centre.

Both events took some 14 years to bring to fruition. They were expected to generate an economic impact of AU$106 million for Sydney, creating 66 jobs.

International associations and international governmental organizations also operate rotational patterns or cycles in the staging of their events, often on a continental basis: for example, an international conference held in Europe one year may well not return to a European country for at least another five years. The Union of International Associations (UIA) and the International Congress and Convention Association (ICCA) both devote considerable resources to tracking where international conferences and congresses are held (see Chapter 1). In recent years there have been some moves by international associations to hold a greater proportion of their conferences in developing countries as a way of building up their memberships in such countries.

Bids to host an international conference will often be channelled through the national member representatives of that organization. For example, a small group of Canadian or French members of an international association will form a committee to plan and present a bid to the selection committee. They are likely to get support and assistance from the destination that they are putting forward to stage the conference, while the national tourism organization or national convention bureau may also play a part in helping to fund the bid and contributing to it in other material ways.

Other characteristics of international association conferences include:

- the frequency may be annual, biennial, or even every five years;
- the destination is chosen by the international organization (the Board, the General Assembly, or a special committee);
- the local host committee that has won the bid will choose the venue and other suppliers, often drawing on the services of a Professional Conference Organizer (PCO);
- the programme of the event is made up by a special programme committee, which can be part of the local organizing committee or a separate international body.

Case study 2.2 gives details of the annual conference of the International Federation of Library Associations and Institutions, including the criteria used to assess locations wishing to host the conference and the proposal document that has to be prepared by potential hosts.

The public sector buyer

The public sector (sometimes referred to as 'government') has much in common with the association sector (and, indeed, for research purposes is often subsumed within it), covering organizations such as local authorities/municipalities, central government departments and agencies, educational bodies, and the health service. These organizations are all 'not-for-profit' organizations and are accountable for the ways in which they spend public funds. Although delegates from public-sector organizations are not normally expected to pay their own expenses to participate in a conference, it is likely that the events will be run on fairly tight budgets, often using the less expensive venues, such as civic facilities, universities and colleges, and hotels up to three-star standard.

There is, even so, a discernible trend for such public-sector organizations to book higher standard facilities. Delegates' expectations are rising constantly and, whereas sharing a room or staying in bedrooms that are not *en suite* might have been the norm some years ago, this is now much less acceptable. Such trends help to account for the major investments, which university venues, in particular, are making to upgrade their accommodation stock, to enable them to compete in this highly competitive marketplace.

In the context of public-sector and government organizations, it is worth noting the phrase *'per diem'* (literally 'per day'). In the USA, *'per diem'* is a daily allowance, which public sector employees can spend on food, accommodation and other expenses when attending a meeting or conference. The phrase may also be encountered outside the USA, if hotels are dealing with US armed services or embassy personnel stationed overseas. In the USA, some large hotel chains have a Director of Sales specializing in this area, assisting the group's hotels and also their government clients, when quoting for conferences at which delegates are on this *'per diem'* allowance.

The entrepreneurial buyer

The fourth type of buyer is one who does not have a recognized descriptor but who is essentially acting as a conference entrepreneur. In other words, someone who identifies 'hot topics' in the business or academic world, and then plans and produces a conference at which the topics can be presented, discussed and debated by high-profile speakers and experts. The entrepreneur aims to sell places at the conference to anyone interested in paying to attend. Clearly, as with any entrepreneurial activity, there is a financial risk to be borne, as the entrepreneur will incur various costs (e.g. venue deposit, promotional costs, possibly cancellation charges to the venue and to speakers, if the event does not go ahead) with no guarantee that he can run the conference successfully and make a profit. However, it is also possible to make significant profits on such conferences, with delegate fees for a one-day conference often being as much as £300–£500.

Entrepreneurial conferences are typically organized by publishing houses, trade associations, academic bodies and independent conference producers/organizers. It can be seen from the brief description above that one of the prerequisites for success in this area includes having a finger on the pulse of specific industrial and business sectors to understand what are the contemporary issues and challenges that might provide the material for a conference. It is also important to have access to quality databases of potential invitees to whom the conference can be promoted.

Corporate		Non-corporate		Sector description
Sector code	Numbers	Sector code	Numbers	
01	170	21	26	Mining, energy (gas, electricity), water companies, petroleum, chemicals
02	333	22	455	Pharmaceuticals, medical, cosmetics, toiletries
03	155	23	26	Engineering
04	469	24	10	Computer manufacturing and services, information technology, telecommunications
05	367	25	49	Manufacturing/processing
06	152	26	37	Building and construction, civil engineering, surveying, architecture, estate agency, housing associations
07	562	27	39	Communications and media (radio, TV, newspapers, PR/marketing consultancy, advertising, publishing)
08	244	28	13	Commerce: retail and wholesale distribution, import/export
09	808	29	79	Financial and professional services: banking, insurance, building societies, finance/credit companies, solicitors/legal, accountants, management consultants, training consultants
10	166	30	21	Service companies (e.g. couriers/ logistics, security, cleaning)
11	1948	31	223	Leisure and entertainment, hotels and catering, transport, travel (including professional conference/ event/exhibition organizers, venue finding agencies)
12	23	32	101	Agriculture, forestry, environment, animals
13	53	33	194	Education
14	13	34	724	Central and local government departments and agencies (not covered above), public bodies, charities, religious groups
15	2998	35	293	Others
	8461		**2290**	**Total** (A further 934 records were awaiting coding)

Source: British Association of Conference Destinations.

Table 2.6
BACD conference buyer database sector coding

Tables 2.6 and 2.7 show a classification system developed by the British Association of Conference Destinations (BACD) for its Conference Buyer Database. The system differentiates between corporate and association buyers (and also has a section for Agencies – see later in this chapter) by industry sector (based loosely on the Standard Industrial Classification). It also gives numbers of records held for each buyer category (as at July 2002). A search on Sector Type 04, for example, would pull out all of the corporate organization contacts in the Computing and Tele-communications Sectors, while the inclusion of Sector Type 24

Buyer code	Numbers held in database	Buyer code description
		Corporate
10	651	Others
11	707	Conference/event/incentive organizer
12	32	Exhibition (exposition) organizer
13	1691	Secretary/PA, administration manager/assistant
14	862	Training and personnel manager/assistant, training consultant
15	1913	Sales and marketing manager/executive, PR/manager/executive
16	1015	Company secretary, managing director, chief executive
	6871	**Total corporate**
		Agency
20	243	Other (e.g. incentive travel house, business travel agency)
21	1650	Professional conference/event organizer, conference production company
22	154	Venue-finding agency (only)
23	41	Exhibition (exposition) organizer (independent)
	2088	**Total agency**
		Association
30	115	Others
31	1234	Professional or trade association/institution/society
32	425	Voluntary association/society, charity, religious group, political party
33	59	Trade union
34	497	Local or central government, educational body, health authority, other public agency
	2330	**Total association**
	11 289	**Grand total** (A further 396 records were awaiting coding)

Source: British Association of Conference Destinations.

Table 2.7
BACD conference buyer database buyer coding

would bring in all of the association contacts for the same industry sectors.

Suppliers

The suppliers are those who make available for external hire the venues, destinations and many other specialist services without which today's conferences could not take place.

Suppliers to the conference industry have grown in quantity and diversity in tandem with the overall growth of the industry over the past 50 years. Relatively few of these suppliers are dedicated exclusively to the conference industry, however.

This summary will divide the supply side of the conference industry into three main categories:

- venues;
- destinations;
- others.

While the examples given relate mainly to the British Isles, most countries with a well-developed conference product will have a similar base of suppliers, although the numbers and proportions will vary from country to country.

Venues

Within the British Isles alone there are around 5000 venues being promoted as suitable for conferences, meetings and related events. It is impossible to give a precise number because new venues are regularly becoming available for external hire. There has been discussion about the establishment of a grading or classification system for conference venues, but nothing of this kind is yet in place. In theory, therefore, almost any type of building could be promoted as a conference venue.

A clearer idea of which are the leading conference venues would no doubt emerge if it were possible to ascertain what proportion of their turnover is accounted for by conference business. There are probably fewer than 1000 venues in the British Isles in which conference business contributes more than 40–50 per cent of their annual turnover.

What is certain, however, is that hotels make up around two-thirds of all conference venues, being particularly important to the corporate market sector. The main types of hotel active in the conference market are:

- city-centre hotels;
- hotels adjacent to the national and international communications infrastructure (airports, motorways and highways especially);
- country house hotels.

In addition to the conferences that they stage as venues in their own right, hotels located close to large conference centres also benefit as providers of delegate accommodation/housing when a major conference comes to town. Additionally, the larger association conferences often choose one hotel as their 'headquarters' hotel, and there can be significant public relations benefits with the hotel being featured in national, and sometimes international, television and media coverage.

The larger hotel chains have, in recent years, invested very heavily in the design and equipping of their conference facilities, recognizing that the standard multipurpose function room was no longer adequate for the needs of the contemporary conference organizer. Many have also branded their conference product (see Chapter 4) to assist in the promotion of these facilities and services, seeking to assure the buyer that he will receive the same level of service whichever hotel in the chain is used. Staff trained and dedicated to meeting the needs of conference organizers and delegates are to be found in all the major conference hotels (see Chapter 6).

Alongside hotels, other principal types of venue include the following.

Purpose-built centres

These can be residential or non-residential, and are specifically designed to host meetings and conferences, whether they are the larger events for hundreds or even thousands of delegates (venues such as the International Convention Centre in Birmingham (England), the Orlando (Orange County) Convention Center in Florida, Hong Kong Convention and Exhibition Centre, Durban International Convention Centre in South Africa, Melbourne Convention and Exhibition Centre (Australia), or smaller, day and residential, events (venues such as Henley Management College, Oxfordshire, England, and Belmont Square Conference Centre in Rondebosch, Cape Town, South Africa).

It should be noted that, in the USA, the term 'convention center' is used to describe a building with exhibition (referred to as 'exhibit') halls and convention/meeting rooms but no residential (sleeping) facilities. The term 'conference center' is used to describe a building with meeting rooms, bedrooms but no exhibition (or exhibit) space.

College, university and other academic venues

There are around 150 academic venues in the UK, many only available for residential conferences during student vacation periods (but still staging some non-residential events during term time). Germany has over 300 universities, such as Kiel and Karlsruhe, available for use as meeting and convention venues.

An increasing number of academic venues have been investing in the construction of conference facilities that are available throughout the year, providing accommodation equivalent to a good three-star hotel standard. In the UK, the University of Warwick, UMIST in Manchester, and the University of Strathclyde are three very good examples of such investments. The East Midlands Conference Centre, located on the campus of the University of Nottingham, can seat up to 550 delegates in its main auditorium, complemented with exhibition/exposition or banqueting space and a range of syndicate rooms, and might equally be classed as a purpose-built conference centre.

Civic venues

These are council chambers and committee rooms, town halls and other civic facilities, which are available for external hire. Brisbane City Hall, Portsmouth Guildhall, and Bremen's Stadthalle are just three examples of such facilities.

Unusual venues

This is a somewhat ill-defined term to describe a very wide range of venues (sometimes described as 'unique' venues) that do not fit into the more common categories listed above. The attraction of unusual venues is that they can give an event a special appeal and can make it memorable for years afterwards. Some have very high-quality meeting and conference facilities, others may be quite limited in this respect but the setting in which the event is being held compensates for such shortcomings in the eyes of the conference organizer (and, it is hoped, of the delegates). Unusual options include sporting venues (e.g. football and rugby club facilities, racecourses, cricket grounds), cultural and entertainment venues (museums, theatres, television studios, stately homes), tourist attractions (theme parks, historical sites, castles, heritage centres), transport venues (ferries, steam trains, canal barges), even a lighthouse or two! In the British Isles around a quarter of the 5000 venues being promoted to the conference market can be classified as unusual venues.

Destinations

Conference organizers attach greater importance to 'location' than to any other single criterion when selecting their sites. Location may be expressed in terms of 'town', 'city' and 'region of the country'. The widely accepted term to describe each of these is 'destination'. A destination may, of course, be an entire country (as a national destination), but within a country it is a discrete area with identifiable boundaries (usually!). Each conference destination must contain a range of venues, facilities, attractions, support services and appropriate infrastructure to help it to attract conference business.

Within the British Isles, the British Association of Conference Destinations represents almost all of the leading destinations active in serving the conference industry. Its 80 member destinations may be classified as follows:

- cities – 29;
- towns – 18;
- counties/regions – 30;
- islands – 3.

A list of current BACD members is accessible on the BACD website (www.bacd.org.uk). A consolidation of member destinations since the mid-1990s has led to mergers and a growth in organizations representing larger geographical areas, i.e. counties/regions.

Destination marketing organizations (DMOs), often trading as 'convention and visitor bureaux (CVBs)' or 'conference desks' (see Chapter 4), bring the destination to the market-place, offering a 'one-stop shop' enquiry point to the conference and event organizer. Their role is to promote the destination, highlighting all its strengths and facilities, generating and converting enquiries into confirmed business. They are also involved in product development: identifying weaknesses in venues and facilities, and in general infrastructure and working to rectify such shortcomings. However, the role of CVBs is changing and evolving because of a range of factors and pressures, a point examined further in Chapters 4 and 9.

Other suppliers

The conference industry has to draw upon the services of many different supplier organizations in order to offer a complete service to its buyers. Those suppliers who fulfil a 'buying' role on behalf of corporate or association clients are described in the next section (Agencies). Examples of other key suppliers include the following, individually or in combination:

- audiovisual contractors (supply and operation of specialist audiovisual equipment);
- telecommunications companies (video/tele/satellite conferencing);
- transport operators (airlines, coach and rail companies, car hire, taxi firms, ferry companies);
- interpreters and translators (for international conferences);
- after-dinner speakers, entertainers, corporate events companies (e.g. companies running 'murder mystery' events, sporting and outdoor activities);

- speciality caterers (banquets, receptions, buffets);
- floral contractors (flower displays for conference platforms, registration areas, exhibition/exposition stands);
- exhibition/exposition contractors;
- companies that develop specialist computer software (e.g. venue-finding and event-management programmes).

Agencies and intermediaries

'Agencies' is a generic term used to describe a range of different organizations that are both suppliers and buyers. They undertake a buying role on behalf of their clients, who may be companies or associations. They act as intermediaries or 'middle-men', and can be contracted to assist in the planning and running of a conference or similar event.

In the agency field in the UK, there are a number of agencies that are just 'one-man bands', some of whom lack professionalism, and the poor quality of service they provide has tainted the industry and given the term 'agency' a derogatory meaning.

Agencies come in a number of forms, and the nomenclature can be somewhat confusing, but below are listed the principal kinds of intermediaries operating within the conference and events industry.

Professional conference organizer

The professional conference organizer, sometimes professional congress organizer, is often referred to simply as a PCO (but may also be described as an event management company). In the USA, the term PCO is not widely used and reference is more likely to be to a destination management company (DMC) fulfilling this role (see description of a DMC below, although in the USA a DMC may have a more restricted role, focusing on ground handling for incentives and meetings). Multi-management firm is another term used in the USA with a similar connotation, i.e. a company offering complete turnkey organizational support for a meeting, including administration and meeting management services.

Employed to assist in the organization of a conference, the PCO's role can include researching and recommending a suitable venue, helping to plan the conference programme including the social programme, marketing the conference and handling delegate registrations, booking accommodation/housing for delegates, planning an exhibition (exposition) to run concurrently with the conference, producing a budget and handling all of the conference finances. The PCO will normally be paid a management fee by the client organization, calculated on the basis of a registration fee per delegate (with a guaranteed minimum number of delegates) or on the estimated staff costs

- Venue selection, booking and liaison
- Reservation and management of delegate accommodation
- Event marketing, including the design of conference programmes and promotional materials, PR and media coordination, presentations to committees and boards
- Programme planning, speaker selection and briefing
- Provision of an administrative secretariat, handling delegate registrations, recruitment and briefing of conference staff, coordinating delegates' travel arrangements
- Organization of exhibitions/expositions, including sales and marketing functions
- Advising on and coordinating audiovisual services and the production of the event, including the provision of multilingual interpretation and translation services
- Planning the catering for an event, liaising with chefs, conference and banqueting staff, and independent catering companies
- Arranging social events, tour programmes and technical visits
- Arranging security cover and advising on health and safety issues
- Recording, transcribing and producing the proceedings of meetings for publication, arranging poster sessions, processing of abstracts
- Preparation of budgets, managing event income and expenditure, generating revenue through sponsorship, exhibitions/expositions and satellite meetings, handling VAT and insurance issues
- Preparation of contracts with venues and other suppliers

Source: Association of British Professional Conference Organisers.

Table 2.8
Typical portfolio of services offered by a professional conference organizer (PCO)

required to manage the event (number of staff needed × number of days × amount per day). PCOs may also charge a commission to the conference venue (usually 8–10 per cent of the value of the conference to the venue itself), and also on accommodation bookings and on other services provided.

Table 2.8 shows a typical portfolio of services offered by a PCO. Further insights into the work of a PCO are given in Chapters 5–7.

Venue finding agency

As their name implies, such agencies offer a more limited service, restricted to researching and recommending a suitable venue for an event. They normally put forward a shortlist of three potential venues to their client (or in some cases just one venue initially) and expect to receive a commission (paid to them by the venue chosen for the conference) of 8–10 per cent of the value of the booking to the venue. Venue finding agencies may also get involved in booking accommodation for delegates, and again would expect to charge commission to the hotels and other accommodation providers. The agency's services to the client are usually provided free of charge.

However, in the UK at least, many of the most successful venue-finding agencies have moved into the field of event management in order to develop a longer-term relationship with their clients. They have introduced client–management team structures within the company, comprising an account manager, a venue finder and an event planner, who often manage a handful of major accounts. This approach is attractive to major corporations and pharmaceutical companies, who are constantly looking to obtain benefits from the economies of scale that the large agencies claim to deliver.

Conference production company

Such companies specialize in the actual staging of the conference: designing and building conference sets, providing lighting, sound systems, presentation technology (e.g. video/dvd, data projection, rear projection, overhead projection, satellite conferencing, webcasts) and special effects. Their expertise lies in audiovisual and communications technology, but they are required to match this to the needs of different clients. They also need creative and theatrical skills, recognizing that conferences have to be professionally stage-managed and should be a memorable, striking experience for the delegates.

Shone (pages 91–103) describes in greater depth the technical equipment used by conference production companies and conference venues, but the technology is developing at such a rapid rate that it is highly likely that new equipment and presentation systems that will be in use in three or four years' time will not have even been heard of at the time this text is being written (Summer 2002).

Incentive travel house

All-expenses-paid travel, often to overseas destinations, is still regarded as one of the best incentives a company can use to motivate and reward its employees, distributors and retailers. 'Incentive travel', as this has come to be known, was developed in the USA in the first half of the 20th century, and is now an important industry sector in its own right. The official definition, according to the Society of Incentive and Travel Executives, is as follows:

> Incentive Travel is a global management tool that uses an exceptional travel experience to motivate and/or recognize participants for increased levels of performance in support of the organizational goals. (SITE, 1998)

It is notoriously and frustratingly difficult to get accurate global figures on the worth of incentive travel, but we do know that the value of spend by US companies on 'merchandise and travel' was US$26 billion in 1999 (a rise from US$23 billion in

1997), with the wider US meetings, convention and incentive industry being worth US\$41.8 billion in the same year. Research commissioned by the British Tourist Authority *et al.* put the value of incentive travel to the UK (both inbound and domestic markets) at £180 million in 1995 (source: Incentive Travel). In 1999, the UK outbound incentive travel industry was worth £1.025 billion (including air travel costs), a figure that had reduced to £956 million by 2000 (source: SITE UK & Ireland Chapter). However, generally research into the volume and value of incentive travel globally, or even by country, is extremely limited.

The specialized nature of the incentive sector has led to the growth of incentive travel houses, as these 'agencies' are generally known. Companies operating in the automotive, financial services, pharmaceutical and information technology sectors are among the leading users of outbound (overseas) incentive travel from the UK.

Incentive travel programmes should be tailored to the needs of each client company. An 'off-the-shelf' incentive programme is really a contradiction in terms. Incentive travel has been described as an 'extraordinary reward for extraordinary perform-ance' (Paul Flackett, SITE member and Managing Director, IMEX Ltd). Incentive travel programmes are, therefore, designed to create an allure or dream, which will make people want to produce that extra effort, achieve that exceptional performance and strive to be the winners within a corporate organization. From the company's perspective, it is also about strengthening the loyalty of its best employees to the company, making them want to belong to the organization and giving them reasons to perform even better in the future.

Attention is now being paid to developing incentive travel as a tool for motivating achievers across the board. David Hackett, Chairman of UK incentive travel specialists TMO, elaborated this point as follows (*Conference & Exhibition Factfinder* magazine, June 1997):

> League tables are frequently created in order to offer rewards and create motivation at all levels. This can include lower targets to encourage first-time qualifiers or graduated awards for top achievers to ensure they still strive to maximize their performance, even when they have qualified to participate in the travel programme. Individual benefits can include superior room allocation, upgraded flights and hosting allowances (for example, providing top achievers with budgets to host cocktail parties in their suites).

Incentive travel programmes may have an educational element for the participants, such as visits to factories and businesses in the same industry sector as that of the award winners. Other ingredients of an incentive programme can be team-building activities, and a conference-type session with an award presentation ceremony and announcements of corporate plans, designed to encourage the incentive winners to reach future performance targets. Other trends in incentive travel programmes noted by Carolyn Dow, 2001 President of SITE, in a presentation to the UK Business Tourism Partnership Research Group (June 2001) were:

- smaller groups;
- shorter lead times;
- shorter qualification periods;
- more 'exotic' locations;
- active not passive programmes, for example participating in an activity rather than merely watching it;
- many incentives now include a meeting.

This final point is a way of delegates avoiding the need to be taxed on the benefit of the incentive trip. However, it also makes good business sense to build a more formal work-related element into the incentive programme.

The most popular incentive destinations for groups travelling from the UK, according to *Meetings & Incentive Travel* magazine's 'Trends and Spend Survey 2001' (published June 2002) were Spain, France and Germany as short-haul destinations and the USA, South Africa and the United Arab Emirates as long-haul destinations. The Survey found that trips lasted on average just over four days. It estimated the value of the UK outbound incentive travel market at £1.085 billion.

Incentive travel is probably more susceptible to the ups and downs of the national and global economies than most other sectors of business tourism. In some cases, however, an economic downturn in a particular industry or country can actually encourage incentive travel schemes. The beauty of incentive schemes is that they are totally self-funding, with the travel award being paid for by the success of the incentive travel programme. If no one meets his sales targets, no one wins. It is, therefore, one of the best promotional tools.

Perhaps even more important than economic factors in the health of this business sector is the national/international political situation. The Gulf War in 1990, for example, virtually wiped out the American incentive travel market, even to Europe. Similarly, the impact of 'September 11th' on the American travel industry was huge and it will take some time to recover.

Incentive travel houses charge a fee to their clients for the work they undertake on their behalf.

Destination management company

Destination management companies are specialist ground-handlers operating in the incentive travel market (who may also provide services to conference organizers, especially where a conference is being organized overseas). The definition of a DMC in the *Handbook of the Society of Incentive and Travel Executives* (SITE) is as follows: 'A DMC is a local service organization that provides consulting services, creative events and exemplary management of logistics based on an in-depth knowledge of the destination and the needs of the incentive and motivation markets.'

Such services are provided on a professional, fee-charging and commission-charging basis (although some provision of information may be offered free of charge to established clients). By comparison, ground-handlers have a more limited role, defined as: 'A ground handler provides transportation in a locale, i.e. coaches, rental cars, etc.'

DMCs, therefore, have detailed knowledge and expertise of a specific destination, be this a city, an island or other discrete region, and sometimes even a whole country. They also have access to unusual venues, such as private houses and stately homes, that are not normally open to the general public. They have considerable buying power, which makes them very useful to incentive travel houses situated in countries other than the one in which the incentive travel award is to be taken.

Incentive travel houses and DMCs, therefore, work very closely together. However, the relationship between an incentive travel house and a DMC can sometimes be fraught, often centring upon the definition of 'creativity', or the requirement to meet extremely tight deadlines and even tighter budgets. Incentive travel houses demand more and more creativity, wanting things that have never been tried before for their clients, but the budget or time available to achieve this may be insufficient, putting the DMC under great pressure to meet and satisfy such objectives. From a DMC perspective, it is very difficult to assemble a creative event programme unless they are given a thorough brief of what is to be achieved, a realistic budget to make such creativity possible and a destination that can do full justice to creative ideas (e.g. a DMC can only put forward a unique venue if there are unique venues within the destination). A DMC would probably contend that what is more important than 'creativity' is delivering a memorable programme, which has achieved its aim.

When a company knows that it wants to hold an incentive event (or conference) in a particular destination, it can employ the services of a DMC to locate a venue, to handle delegate accommodation/housing, to assist with transport arrangements, and to put together itineraries and social programmes (e.g. special interest visits, theme parties, unusual activities), even to provide 'pillow gifts' for award winners. DMCs are expected to develop tailor-made programmes within budget for their clients. They need to be creative and innovative, and provide an experience that will give the participants an insight into a country or region that will be beyond the reach of the normal visitor or holidaymaker.

Most DMCs earn their income from commission, but the level of commission varies enormously, depending on how much of the programme the DMC is handling. The growing trend for hotels to offer to clients some of the special programme organization that has traditionally been the preserve of DMCs has inevitably eroded DMC revenue streams.

It can be seen that there is significant overlap between the work of a PCO and that of a DMC, and nowadays a DMC often has to have some PCO expertise.

The following websites give details of DMCs around the world: www.conworld.net/quick-finder and www.travelcontacts.com.

Corporate events company

Corporate events (also known as 'corporate hospitality') are one of the discrete sectors of the business tourism industry, which, while being separate from the conference sector, is often closely aligned to it. Corporate hospitality and corporate entertainment frequently involve the exploitation of major sporting and cultural events to strengthen the links between an organization, usually a corporate organization, and its clients or potential clients (e.g. inviting clients to spend a day watching tennis at Wimbledon, or being wined and dined at Grand Prix races at Monza or Indianapolis). Alternatively, activities may be arranged specifically for a client company, and typically involve drinks receptions, dinners and banquets, and dances and discos. Wherever possible, such activities will include a formal presentation or short speech to ensure that the company 'gets its message across'.

Specialist corporate hospitality/entertainment companies are usually hired to organize such events and programmes for their clients. Others may act in an entrepreneurial fashion (rather similar to conference entrepreneurs described earlier in this chapter), putting together corporate hospitality packages around major sporting or cultural events for sale to interested parties.

Corporate hospitality/events companies are also involved in corporate team building exercises and activities, aimed at clients and/or employees. Such activities include golf days, clay pigeon shooting, off-road driving, go-karting, 'paint ball' and many, many more. In recent years there has been a noticeable trend towards the active, participatory kinds of corporate events, rather than the more traditional, passive, spectator type of hospitality.

Business travel agency

This is a form of travel agency, but one which seeks particularly to cater for the needs of business customers rather than the general public and which will not normally have a presence on the local high street. The main thrust of their work is usually business travel: making air, rail, coach and ferry as well as hotel reservations to meet the needs of people travelling nationally and internationally for business purposes. However, many of the larger business travel agencies also get involved in sourcing venues for conferences and similar business events, and may contribute in other ways to the planning and organization of such events.

Some of the larger business travel agencies have staff physically located in the offices of their major corporate clients. Such arrangements are referred to as 'agency implants'.

Exhibition/exposition organizer

Exhibitions (expositions) are, of course, a major business tourism sector in their own right, but any clear divide between exhibitions and conferences that may have existed in the past has now been greatly eroded, especially as far as business-to-business exhibitions are concerned (less so for consumer exhibitions catering for the general public). Many exhibitions have a conference programme running alongside as a way of adding value to the exhibition and making it even more worthwhile for business people to visit. Similarly, many of the larger conferences and conventions have an exhibition running in parallel: for the exhibitors, the conference delegates are seen as important customers or potential customers, and for the conference organizer the exhibition is an important source of revenue, which will help to offset the costs of the conference.

While some conference organizers undertake the organization of their exhibition themselves, others prefer to employ the services of a specialist exhibition organizing company. In the UK, there are 200 exhibition organizing companies represented by the Association of Exhibition Organisers (AEO).

When contracting a specialist exhibition organizer, conference planners will either pay them a management fee for their work or negotiate a payment based on the size of the exhibition itself (e.g. the net exhibition area in square metres, where 'net' means the floor coverage taken up by stands alone, thus excluding aisle space and other space in the exhibition area). A further alternative is for the exhibition to be contracted out for a set period to an exhibition organizer in return for a fee paid to the owner of the exhibition (i.e. the conference organizer).

Agreements or contracts may well include incentives or bonuses linked to the sale of space or cost savings achieved by the exhibition organizer, although this latter approach could encourage the cutting of corners and result in an exhibition of unacceptable quality.

The larger exhibition organizing companies can bring added value to an event through their own network of contacts or simply via bulk purchasing power, which would not be accessible to a conference organizer working independently. Exhibition organizers may already have links with airlines, hotel groups, stand and electrical contractors, carpet and furniture suppliers, as well as knowledge of the exhibition venue and specialist technical expertise. The services of such trade contacts can be made available to their conference organizer client at preferential rates, while first-hand knowledge and experience can be another invaluable asset.

There is a very broad spectrum of relationships possible between conference and exhibition organizer, from just buying into certain specialist expertise to handling specific aspects of the exhibition (e.g. visitor badging and registrations, stand erection), right through to contracting out the organization of an exhibition in its entirety. The reasons for such variations on the part of the conference organizer include: in-house staff resources (numbers of staff available and their experience and expertise), the need for a guaranteed financial return from the exhibition (minimize risk by opting for a known income, even if this is less than it might have been possible to achieve), the overall profile of the event and the need to ensure its success, the benefits of having a well-known exhibition organizer working alongside, thus giving confidence to potential exhibitors that the exhibition will be well organized and successful.

Some useful websites for additional information on the exhibition sector include:

- www.iaem.org (International Association for Exhibition Management);
- www.aeo.org.uk (services of the Association of Exhibition Organisers);
- www.exhibitionswork.co.uk (information for marketeers about the benefits of exhibiting);
- www.exhibitionvenues.com (promotional and informational network for the UK's main exhibition venues provided by the Exhibition Venues Association);
- www.beca.org.uk (website of the British Exhibition Contractors Association).

Other agencies

There are other companies who will undertake at least part of a conference-organizing role for their clients, although this would not usually be the main focus of their work. Such companies include: public relations and advertising consultancies (who will organize conferences and seminars, press launches, product launches, for example); management consultancies (organizing 'retreats', meetings, training events); and training companies (running training, motivational and team-building events).

Other important organizations

As an industry emerges and matures, it requires other bodies and structures to help it to function professionally, to establish standards and codes of practice, to represent the industry to other industrial/business sectors as well as to government departments and public agencies. Within the conference industry, such bodies include, *inter alia*:

- trade associations;
- trade media;
- national tourism organizations;
- consultants;
- educational institutions.

Trade associations

Trade associations are formed to serve the interests of their members. Their activities usually include lobbying and representation, establishing codes of practice, marketing and promotion, education and training, and research and information.

Within the conference industry, some trade associations are international in the composition of their membership; others are strictly national. Among the leading international associations are:

- Association Internationale des Palais de Congrès (AIPC);
- Asian Association of Convention and Visitor Bureaus (AACVB);
- European Federation of Conference Towns (EFCT);
- Incentive Travel & Meetings Association (ITMA);
- International Association of Convention & Visitor Bureaus (IACVB);
- International Association of Professional Congress Organisers (IAPCO);
- International Congress & Convention Association (ICCA);
- Meeting Professionals International (MPI);
- Professional Convention Management Association (PCMA);
- Society of Incentive and Travel Executives (SITE).

Further details of the services and activities of these associations, as well as those of leading national associations, are given in Chapter 8.

Trade media

The conference industry trade media are primarily magazines published on a monthly, bi-monthly or quarterly basis. They contain articles on new developments, topical issues, how to stage successful events, destination reports, personnel changes, summaries of new books and reports, a correspondence section, and so on. They fulfil a very important role in keeping the industry abreast of the constant changes and developments taking place. Through their circulation to buyers, they also provide an important advertising and PR medium for suppliers wishing to promote their facilities/services to potential clients. Most of the magazines are international in content, emphasizing once again the global nature of the conference industry.

A list of the principal trade magazines is given in Appendix A.

National tourism organizations

Most countries in the world now have some form of national tourism organization, publicly funded, established for promotional activities to the international tourism industry. Such bodies are primarily concerned with marketing, but some may also fulfil a lobbying and representational role. Within the conference sector of the tourism industry, a number of countries have established a national convention bureau specifically to market to this sector. There is no standard format for such national convention bureaux. Indeed, it would be difficult to find two that operate in the same way with similar levels of funding and resources, and providing the same kind of services.

Examples of the roles of national tourism organizations are given in Chapter 4.

Consultants

Consultants play an important role in undertaking projects on a fee-paying basis for clients who are normally operating on the supply side of the conference industry. Typically, consultancy covers:

- the potential market for a proposed new conference centre;
- the specification for a new conference centre or for a major refurbishment to an existing venue;
- advice on marketing strategies for a destination or venue;
- a feasibility study to establish and run a new convention and visitor bureau.

Consultancy can, however, cover any aspect of the industry. Consultancy is carried out either by specialist staff within the larger management consultancies (e.g. KPMG, Deloitte & Touche, PriceWaterhouseCoopers and Pannell Kerr Forster) or by one of the smaller consultancies catering specifically for the tourism industry.

Educational institutions

The education and training of the conference industry's future workforce is vitally important in ensuring the continued growth and development of the industry. College and university institutions are now giving attention to conference and business tourism in their course programmes and syllabuses. A number of trade associations have developed educational programmes and certificated courses available to both members and, sometimes, non-members. Other training programmes within the wider tourism industry, such as 'Welcome Host' and 'Investors in People', also contribute significantly to the improvement of skills and expertise for those already working in the industry.

Further details of education and training opportunities are given in Chapter 7.

Summary

- The buying side of the conference industry includes corporate organizations, associations and government/public sector agencies, and conference entrepreneurs.
- Corporate organizations plan a wide variety of conferences, meetings and other events. Staff involved in the organization of these activities have many different job titles, but relatively few are employed as full-time event organizers. For the most part, corporate events attract less than 200 delegates and have comparatively short lead times. They have a higher average per capita expenditure than association conferences, with costs being borne by the companies themselves.
- The term 'association' is used to describe a sector of the industry, which encompasses professional and trade bodies, voluntary organizations, charities, political parties and other non-corporate entities. Association conferences are different in many respects from those held in the corporate sector, especially in their average size, duration, types of venues used and accommodation/housing required. International association and intergovernmental conventions form a major segment of the 'association' market in their own right.
- Government/public sector organizations have many similar buying characteristics to associations, although delegate expectations are rising and some comparisons with the

corporate sector may be drawn, particularly in respect of the types of venues used.

- Conference entrepreneurs develop conferences in response to an identified demand as a purely commercial activity.
- The supply side of the conference industry comprises venues, destinations and myriad other companies offering specialist services, from audiovisual equipment supply to contract catering, from interpreting to coach hire.
- The industry also features an important group of inter-mediary agencies, which provide services ranging from conference management to venue finding, and from incentive travel planning to exhibition organizing.
- This complex industry is reliant on a range of other institutions to enable it to operate professionally and develop in a structured way. Such institutions include trade associations, trade media, national tourism organizations, consultants and educational bodies.

Review and discussion questions

1 Assess the benefits and disadvantages, for a corporate organization, of maintaining its own, in-house event department. Include an analysis of the pros and cons, for the company, of employing a business travel agency as an 'implant'.

2 Compile two incentive travel programmes to reward:
- a company's top sales executives;
- the same company's most productive 'blue collar' employees.

Explain any differences in the programmes offered.

3 Identify and give reasons for the most appropriate types of conference/events business for the following venues:
- a four-star city-centre hotel with 250 bedrooms and conference facilities seating up to 400 delegates (choose a city that has an important manufacturing or service industry base);
- a multipurpose heritage building in a resort location with a seating capacity of 1500;
- a residential conference centre with six conference rooms (the largest seating 80) and accommodation of three-star standard, situated in a rural location.

4 As an employee of a major trade association that holds an annual convention for approximately 1200 delegates, with an exhibition running alongside the convention, you have been asked to contract out the planning of the convention and exhibition. Describe the kinds of agencies you would consider and give reasons for your choices.

Notes and references

Flint, Ian. Buying power. *Business Travel World* magazine (EMAP Communications)(July 2002).

Shone, Anton. *The Business of Conferences*. Butterworth-Heinemann (1998).

Society of Incentive and Travel Executives Handbook (1998).

The UK Conference Market Survey 2002. Research carried out by The Right Solution on behalf of the Meetings Industry Association (June 2002).

Trends and Spend Survey 2001. *Meetings & Incentive Travel* (CAT Publications)(June 2002).

Further reading

Incentive Travel Usage and its Impact on UK/Ireland. A report prepared by Travel Business Consulting Limited, Gordon Simmons Research Group Limited for the British Tourist Authority/English Tourist Board, Northern Ireland Tourist Board, Scottish Tourist Board, Wales Tourist Board, Bord Failte Eireann (October 1996).

UK Exhibition Facts. Published annually by the (UK) Exhibition Industry Research Group.

CHAPTER 3

The economics of conferences and conventions

Introduction

Conferences are a vital economic benefactor for both local and national economies. Investment in conference facilities and infrastructure can bring substantial returns through the expenditure of organizers and delegates, with both direct and indirect benefits for the destinations in which conferences are held. While statistics and intelligence about the industry are not yet as well developed as those working in the industry would wish to see, sufficient information and research findings do exist to enable estimates of its value and potential to be made with confidence.

This chapter looks at:

- conferences and conventions within the wider tourism context;
- factors affecting conference sector demand;
- the inadequacy of the information base;
- the size of the industry;
- the value of the industry, and measurement of economic impact;
- research findings, using the results of a range of national surveys.

Conferences within the wider tourism context

It has already been seen that conference tourism is a subsector of business tourism, itself a sector within the overall tourism industry, comprising both business and leisure tourism. All projections by economists confirm that the tourism industry was set to become the world's largest industry by the millennium or in this first decade thereafter. A press release entitled 'Millennium Tourism Boom in 2000', issued by the World Tourism Organization (WTO) in January 2001, shows that world tourism grew by an estimated 7.4 per cent in 2000, with the fastest developing region being East Asia and the Pacific, which recorded a 14.5 per cent increase over the previous year. In 2001, owing to factors such as 'September 11th' and economic slowdown in many countries, there was negative growth (a decrease of 0.6 per cent) but projections for 2002 were for a return to growth. In 2001, the top six tourism destinations were (in ranking order): 1, France; 2, Spain; 3, USA; 4, Italy; 5, China; 6, UK (www.world-tourism.org/newsroom/releases).

Figures published by the British Tourist Authority put the total value of tourism to the UK in 2001 at approximately £74 billion, supporting around 2.1 million jobs, some 8 per cent of total UK employment. This compares with a value of £40 billion in 1996, when the industry supported 1.7 million jobs, an employment growth approaching 25 per cent in just a five-year period. (www.visitbritain.com).

Within the UK, estimates suggest that business tourism (business/corporate travel and conferences/exhibitions/incentives), worth between £15 and £20 billion a year, accounts for between a third and a quarter of the total value of tourism. Some £7.3 billion of business tourism revenues were contributed by the conference and meetings sector in 2001, according to the *British Conference Market Trends Survey*. If it were possible to produce aggregated figures for the conference industry on a global scale, the totals would certainly reach hundreds of billions of pounds.

There are a number of research projects now underway that are beginning to build a more accurate and comprehensive picture of the size and value of the conference industry. This chapter will draw on these and on other sources, using material from Australia, Germany, Ireland, New Zealand, South Africa, the UK and the USA, to illustrate and emphasize that the conference industry is a major benefactor to both local and national economies, as a job creator and sustainer, as an income generator, and as a vehicle for attracting inward investment.

Factors affecting conference sector demand

The health of national and international economies

In line with most other industries, demand for conferences is driven to a large extent by the buoyancy of the national, and increasingly global, economy. There is strong evidence to show that, during the recession of the early 1990s, during the crash of many Asian economies in the late 1990s, and again during the global recession in the early years of the 21st century, business activity levels declined with conferences being cancelled or, more typically, being run on much lower budgets. At such times, companies trade down, reducing delegate numbers, cutting out the residential aspect of conferences, spending less on catering and using lower quality venues (e.g. three-star hotels rather than four-star).

Similarly, fluctuations in the value of a country's currency can have both positive and negative effects on its conference industry: a weakening of the currency may assist it to win more international events as costs for incoming delegates and organizers will be lower and the country may be perceived as good value for money. However, it will be more difficult, and certainly more expensive, for delegates to travel abroad from that country to attend conferences and meetings because of the relative weakness of their national currency. The opposite situation applies when a currency is strong compared with other currencies.

However, one of the positive characteristics of the conference industry is its resilience, even in times of economic downturn. While there may be a trading down, many events still go ahead: public companies are required to hold an Annual General Meeting for their shareholders, senior managers need to engage in management retreats to explore ways of reviving their business, new products are launched, staff have to be trained and motivated, sales forces need to be brought together for briefings, and many other types of 'conference' take place, albeit with reduced budgets.

The impact of crises, conflict and emergency situations

'September 11th' (or '9/11') is a phrase now firmly embedded in our international vocabulary, describing an appalling act of terrorism in New York, which had an immediate, catastrophic impact on travel around the world. It led to the cancellation or postponement of conferences and meetings scheduled to take place in the weeks and months following.

In the USA itself, conference delegates and business travellers refused to attend events held more than a short distance from their homes. A combination of 'September 11th' and economic recession led to 37 per cent of US associations experiencing a decline in attendance at their events in 2001. This compares with a figure of just 9 per cent that had forecast a reduction in attendance a year earlier ('Meetings Market Survey 2002' published by *Convene* magazine, March 2002).

Research carried out in the UK among conference organizers, as shown in Chapter 2 (Table 2.4), found that around a quarter of corporate buyers interviewed had either cancelled or postponed events following 'September 11th', while some 12 per cent of association buyers had done so.

Other crises (epidemics, wars, agricultural disasters, such as the 'foot and mouth' outbreak that affected the UK in 2001, for example) also have a negative impact on the demand for conferences in the countries and regions where they break out. Sometimes the impact will be short-lived, sometimes it may be more prolonged.

Paradoxically, crises and disasters can also stimulate demand for meetings, training courses and international conferences. 'September 11th', for example, heightened awareness of the need for security and crisis management strategies as an integral part of a conference management strategy, and generated seminars to address this need. Wars and threats of wars lead to international meetings and conferences in an attempt to find a peaceful solution to the causes of conflict.

Technological influences

Another factor affecting demand for conference facilities is the advent of satellite, video and teleconferencing technology. Evidence of the effects of these new technologies is still limited but it is clear that their usage is steadily increasing. The *UK Conference Market Survey 2002*, for example, found that, among corporate organizations, video conferencing was used by 61.7 per cent of *Survey* respondents in 2001 compared with 55.7 per cent in 2000. Similarly, the use of teleconferencing grew from 60.3 per cent in 2000 to 71.7 per cent in 2001. The same research revealed, however, that only 6 per cent of organizers admitted that these technologies were being used instead of face-to-face meetings (although 43 per cent said they were not sure!).

In the USA, teleconferencing was being used by 50 per cent of associations in 2001, compared with just 29 per cent in 1995. In the same period, the use of video conferencing experienced much more modest growth: from 14 per cent in 1995 to 18 per cent in 2001 ('Meetings Market Survey 2002' published by *Convene* magazine, March 2002).

More venues have invested in the installation of video and teleconferencing facilities in an effort to win these new niche markets.

Webcasting, the technology that allows someone to attend a conference as a 'virtual' delegate by sitting at their computer screen and listening to speaker presentations through an electronic link, is expected to widen conference attendance by making an event affordable and accessible to a much greater, global audience, rather than reduce the numbers of delegates wishing to attend an event in person.

Social factors and working patterns

Social factors must have some effect on people's interest in conferencing, although no research has been undertaken to quantify these. Predictions that, for example, many more people would be working from or at home by the end of the last millennium have not proved to be correct. However, if the 'office-in-the-home' should become a more common feature of everyday life in the future, its end result might well be an increased demand for conferences, as people respond to their gregarious instincts by coming together in regular meetings.

Changes in a country's industrial and commercial structures can also have an impact on the demand for conference facilities. In the UK, for example, reductions in trade union membership since 1980 have led to trade unions merging, which, in turn, has meant fewer trade union conferences (particularly affecting seaside conference destinations) but with larger numbers of delegates than previously. Some resorts, the traditional hosts of many trade union conferences, have found that their conference venues are no longer large enough to accommodate their former clients.

Finally, it should be noted that fluctuations in conference demand are more noticeable in the corporate sector than in the association sector, often because of factors such as lead times. Corporate events, with relatively short lead times, can respond quickly to changing economic situations. Association conferences, with much longer lead times and frequently much larger delegate numbers, find it less easy to adapt, but can also take a longer-term view and avoid what may sometimes prove to be a panic reaction to a particular situation (while still retaining the ability to react to emergency situations such as that encountered after 'September 11th').

The inadequacy of the information base

Before looking at some of the available figures on conference tourism, it might be useful to understand why the information and intelligence base for the industry is incomplete.

The Economist Intelligence Unit, in a report entitled 'The European Conference and Meetings Market' published as long ago as 1994, listed the following four main reasons why not enough is known about business and conference tourism in quantifiable terms (with the author's comments on these shown in italics), reasons which were still largely valid in 2002.

1 Fragmentation of industry sectors (in terms of both geography and markets). Each sector has its own trade association, and often more than one. International associations and organizations have varying degrees of representation in their member countries. *In part this seems to be a reflection of the tourism industry as a whole; in part it may also be due to the immaturity of the conference industry, with some rationalization of the industry's representative bodies likely to take place, if only because the market cannot sustain such a diversity of organizations. There is also a genuine desire among the industry's leading associations to forge collaborative partnerships with like-minded bodies in order to achieve a more cohesive voice for the industry.*
2 Lack of consensus on terminology and definitions. Segmentation of the market makes it difficult to produce a clear definition of each sector.
3 Certain segments of business and commercial tourism are difficult to measure. *This is particularly true of 'business travel', but similar problems can arise with incentive travel and conferences.*
4 Information about certain activities is sensitive and closely guarded. *This can apply to buyers and suppliers alike, with hotels enjoying special notoriety for their reluctance to release information on their bookings lest they give a competitive edge to other hotels in the vicinity.*

One or two practical examples may make clear why statistics and intelligence are far from comprehensive. Many of the individuals and organizations that contribute to the conference industry do so as part of a wider role (see also Chapter 2). For example, a training manager will use the services/facilities of the conference industry to run a training course or seminar away from company premises, but may only do this once or twice a year. It would be inaccurate, therefore, to categorize him as a full-time conference/event organizer even though he is a buyer at certain times of the year. Public relations consultancies will often be involved in organizing conferences, product launches or corporate events on behalf of their clients, but they remain first and foremost public relations consultancies, and may also escape classification as 'conference organizers'.

Likewise, a hotel will hire out its function rooms to conference organizers, but may equally hire them out to someone staging weddings or other social events. In many cases, the hotel will not differentiate in its record keeping between the different types of client or function, making it impossible to build up an accurate picture of the amount of conference business compared with other categories of business.

Despite such shortcomings in the industry's information base, much greater recognition is now being given globally to the importance of research. Some of the results of this research are given in this chapter and elsewhere in this book. When aggregated, they provide compelling evidence of the economic importance and vitality of this key industry sector at both national and international levels.

The size of the global conference industry

At present, there is little information available that adequately describes the size of the conference and convention industry. In the medium to longer term, projects such as 'DOME' will, it is hoped, provide a more comprehensive dataset for use by any country or organization wishing to use such information. It is necessary, therefore, to use a variety of (mostly unrelated) data sources to help to construct the jigsaw. The following examples begin to give a feel for the size and scale of the industry.

- There are well over 100 countries now active in marketing their facilities and services to the conference and conventions industry. The Union of International Associations (UIA) has records of international conferences being staged in 188 countries in 2001.
- The International Association of Convention and Visitor Bureaus (IACVB) has 500 destination marketing organization members in 30 countries (July 2002).
- Meeting Professionals International (MPI) had over 18 000 (individual) members in 2001, a figure which had grown from 540 at the time of its first annual convention in 1976. MPI members comprise a 50/50 ratio of buyers and suppliers.
- The International Congress and Convention Association (ICCA) has around 650 member organizations in 76 countries (July 2002).
- In the UK, there are an estimated 5000 conference venues, 11 000+ individuals with a conference organizing role, 530 000 people employed in 'business tourism' and, in 2001 (according to the *British Conference Market Trends Survey*), an estimated 1.3 million conferences and meetings staged.
- In Australia, in 1996–1997, 232 000 off-site meetings of 15 or more people were held at venues associated with Australian convention bureaux. These meetings attracted 11.4 million delegates (*Meetings Make Their Mark*).

The value of the industry

Measurements of economic impact

Assessments of the value of the conference industry to most countries are at best only estimates, based on information drawn from national and local surveys. Calculations of the value, or economic impact, of conferences measure the net change in the local (or national) economy resulting from the hosting of conferences and business events, i.e. what difference have such events made to levels of expenditure, income and employment. Such calculations must also take account of a number of factors, outlined by Cooper *et al.* (1993), which apply to the tourism industry as a whole:

> Tourists spend their money on a wide variety of goods and services. They purchase accommodation, food and beverage, communications, entertainment services, goods from retail outlets and tour/travel services, to name just a few. This money may be seen as an injection of demand into the host economy: that is, demand which would otherwise not be present. However, the value of tourist expenditure represents only a partial picture of the economic impact. The full assessment of economic impact must take into account other aspects, including the following:
>
> - indirect and induced effects
> - leakages of expenditure out of the local economy
> - displacement and opportunity costs.

Cooper *et al.* refer to the 'cascading' effect of tourist expenditure, with the benefits of tourist spending being felt in hotels, restaurants, taxi firms and shops, and then permeating through the rest of the economy. From this total direct impact, however, must be subtracted the cost of 'imports necessary to supply those front-line goods and services . . . for example, hotels purchase the services of builders, accountants, banks, food and beverage suppliers, and many others.' These suppliers will, in turn, purchase goods and services from other suppliers, generating further rounds of economic activity, known as the indirect effect.

> The indirect effect will not involve all of the moneys spent by tourists during the direct effect, since some of that money will leak out of circulation through imports, savings and taxation. Finally, during the direct and indirect rounds of expenditure, income will accrue to local residents in the form of wages, salaries, distributed profit, rent and interest. This addition to the local income will, in part, be respent in the local economy on goods and services, and this will generate yet further rounds of economic activity. It is only when all three levels of impact (direct *plus* indirect *plus* induced) are estimated that the full positive economic impact of tourism expenditure is fully assessed.

Cooper *et al.* also make reference to certain 'negative economic impacts' of tourist expenditure. These include opportunity costs and displacement effects. Opportunity costs refer to the use of resources, such as labour and capital, for the benefit of one industry rather than another. Decisions to invest limited capital resources in tourism infrastructure, for example, will have negative impacts on other industries that failed to attract that investment.

> Where tourism development substitutes one form of expenditure and economic activity for another, this is known as the displacement effect. Displacement can take place when tourism development is undertaken at the expense of another industry, and is generally referred to as the opportunity cost of the development. However, it is more commonly referred to when a new tourism project is seen to take away custom from an existing facility. For instance, if a destination finds that its all-inclusive hotels are running at high occupancy levels and returning a reasonable yield on investment, the construction of an additional all-inclusive hotel may simply reduce the occupancy levels of the existing establishments, and the destination may find that its overall tourism activity has not increased by as much as the new business from the development. This is displacement.

Figure 3.1 illustrates the measurement of net economic impact arising from tourist expenditure in an area through the application of the tourism multiplier concept.

The use of multipliers

Measurement of the economic impact of tourist spending is effected by using multiplier analysis. Various types of multiplier exist, and it is important to use the correct multipliers for specific functions, such as those measuring the additional revenue or employment for an area arising from tourist expenditure. However, the formulas used to calculate the net impact of conferences and similar events are complex and resource-intensive to administer. For these reasons, many industry professionals, required to give account of the value of conference and business tourism to their city or area, tend to use the 'gross' figures rather than the 'net' impact figures, i.e. the total gross expenditure calculated by multiplying:

- number of delegates/attendees;
- delegate spending (which varies by origin and type of event – see Figure 3.2 and Table 3.1 as examples of such variations);
- number of days' duration of the event;

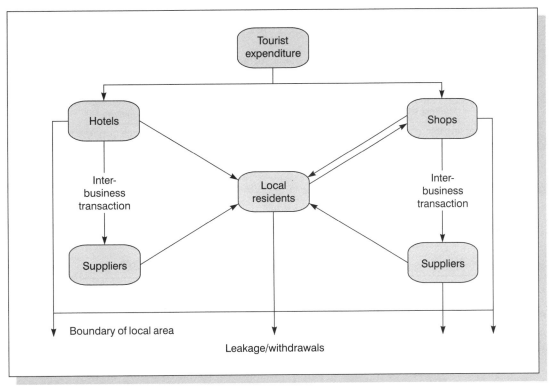

Figure 3.1 The tourism multiplier concept. Source: Dr John Heeley, University of East Anglia.

- any additional days (i.e. for delegates staying on after the event or arriving early before the event starts);
- additional members of the group (e.g. spouses/partners);
- organizers' (and others') spending.

The totals arrived at only measure the direct expenditure to a destination and do not, therefore, take into account the negative effects (opportunity costs, displacement and leakages) referred to above. As an example of this practice, the London Convention Bureau uses 'Conference and Convention Daily Spend Multipliers' to assess the value of business to London, based on research undertaken for the *Conference Delegate Expenditure Survey* (research commissioned by the National Tourist Boards of England, Northern Ireland, Scotland and Wales, 1998) and the *International Passenger Survey* (IPS) estimates for London (see Figure 3.2)

Average expenditure by delegate per trip and per day

An illustration of how and where different types of conference delegates spend money is shown in Table 3.1. The figures are based on a survey undertaken in the UK in 1997, updated to 2001 prices by Bournemouth University. Some 48 conference venues

---

LONDON CONVENTION DELEGATE SPEND MULTIPLIERS

a) Visitors to London from Key Foreign Markets, All Sectors (Residential)

Estimated daily expenditure rates by delegate/attendee are calculated as:

$$\frac{\text{Market's total expenditure in London on convention and conference business}}{\text{Market's total number of nights spent in London on convention and conference business}}$$

Foreign Market Supplying Convention Attendees to London	Market Figures	Outcome in Spend Per Delegate Per Day
USA	£73,288,000 / 358,849	£240
FRANCE	£16,970,000 / 74,769	£166
GERMANY	£29,239,000 / 158,629	£224

The preeminent importance of the inbound US market for London is clear from the above figures.

b) All Other Domestic and Foreign Markets (Residential)

The average daily expenditure figures for UK conferences summarized in the 'Conference Delegate Expenditure Survey' (1998) are used for all other foreign markets and for domestic conference market sectors. These figures have been multiplied by 1.034 and then 1.015 as inflation figures for 1999 and 2000. These result in spend figures as shown below:

Year	Corporate market	National association market	International association market	Other
	£ per delegate per day	£ per delegate per day	£ per delegate per day	£ per delegate per day
1998	£127 (Median)	£123 (Mean)	£182 (Mean)	£116 (Mean)
1999	£131	£127	£188	£120
2000	£133	£129	£191	£122
2001	£140	£136	£201	£128

c) Non-Residential Conferences, All Markets and Sectors

The average daily non-residential delegate rate for London calculated by the 'British Conference Market Trends Survey 1999' is applied to all non-residential conferences: £42. This figure has been multiplied by an inflation figure for 2000 of 1.015, giving a daily spend per delegate figure of £42.60.

Figure 3.2 London convention delegate spend multipliers. Source: London Convention Bureau.

throughout the UK were recruited to take part in the study, and over 4200 face-to-face interviews with delegates were undertaken in these venues. In addition, 1800 post-event questionnaires were also completed along with 116 questionnaires from conference organizers.

Expenditure category	Corporate	National association	International Association/ Academic	Public and Voluntary Sector
Registration fee	333	159	201	133
Overnight accommodation at the conference	226 (105)	155 (58)	151 (57)	128 (47)
Overnight accommodation before or after the conference	174 (86)	116 (44)	88 (46)	113 (45)
Travel to UK	511	489	574	455
Travel in UK to conference	72	46	73	36
Local travel at destination	6	4	3	3
Food and drink	39 (20)	40 (15)	40 (13)	33 (13)
Evening events and entertainment	4 (2)	9 (3)	18 (13)	7 (3)
Shopping and gifts	18 (7)	34 (12)	28 (6)	24 (9)
Day trips and/or pre/post-conference tours	3	2	3	1
Total expenditure/trip (excluding travel to and from destination)	**355**	**400**	**548**	**354**
Total expenditure/day (excluding travel to and from destination)	**140**	**136**	**201**	**128**

Source: 'Estimating the Direct Expenditure Benefits of Conferences to a Local Area'.

Table 3.1
Average expenditure (£) by delegate per trip and per day in the UK (per day figures are shown in brackets)

Davidson describes a similar approach to data collection in France, where:

the national association of conference towns, France Congrès, in 1998 developed a model which enables conference centres to calculate the economic impact they have on the cities in which they are situated. Based on the calculation of delegates' spending, the use of the model produces estimates of the revenue created by conferences in each city and the number of jobs created or supported by them, taking into account the direct, indirect and induced economic impacts of such events (Gazette Officielle, 1998). When the first results were published in 2000, it was shown, for example, that, in Cannes, 10 per cent of the population were employed in that town's meetings industry.

Negative impacts of convention activity

Before looking at other current features and trends in the global conference industry, it is important to give consideration to the negative impacts of convention business on a destination.

Reference was made in Chapter 1 to the harmful effects of business tourism (part of which comprises conference tourism) on the environment because of the volume of trips undertaken, and the demands of business tourists for high-quality accommodation and facilities. There are also issues concerning CO_2 emissions by venues and the levels of waste generated by exhibitions/expositions (which are often staged alongside a conference). A number of tentative steps are being taken to address these environmental factors (such as the development of quieter aircraft to reduce noise pollution, the work of the International Hotels Environment Initiative, the adoption of waste management and recycling strategies, more energy-efficient systems in conference venues, the use of email and electronic communications to reduce paper waste) but it is clear that much more needs to be done before the industry can claim genuine 'green' credentials.

Not all expenditure on a conference is retained in a destination. As explained earlier in this chapter, some of the money leaks out through indirect and induced effects, opportunity costs affect other industry sectors in a negative way, and displacement simply moves existing business around without creating new additional income for the locality. While these are not necessarily all negative impacts, they do mean that the positive impacts may not always be as great as are portrayed.

Social disruption to the local community is inevitably caused when a major convention comes to town, especially where there is a need for high levels of security. This can mean that the area surrounding the convention centre is cordoned off during the convention and often for some days in advance, making it a 'no-go area' for local residents, and reducing trade for shops and other businesses in the vicinity. Similarly, restaurants may be full with delegates eating out, traffic may be congested and public transport overloaded. While most local communities now recognize that such inconveniences are a price worth paying because of the wider economic benefits, there is often still a minority of residents who voice criticisms.

Research findings

The following research findings have resulted from the application of economic impact studies and multiplier analysis to the conference and business tourism sector. In their totality they underline the importance of this tourism sector at the high-quality, high-yield end of the tourism spectrum. The research also summarizes some of the current trends and characteristics of the industry.

DOME research

Brief reference has already been made to DOME (Data on Meetings and Events) in Chapter 1 and its overall objectives. One of its specific goals is to provide accurate real-time data on conventions, including hotel rooms used by property and by night, and air seats used by airline, flight segments and class of service. Such data will prove invaluable to a variety of end users, such as the organizers of the convention, destinations seeking to host the convention in the future, hotel chains and airlines, among others.

The methodology and online systems for collecting such data are still being developed and tested, but a summary of the results from one such test carried out among attendees to the Asia Pacific Incentives and Meetings Exhibition (AIME) held in Melbourne in February 2002 gives a feel for the type of data being captured. Data were captured on 651 attendees (out of a potential total of

Origin of attendees	Number of attendees	Number of accompanying persons
Europe	78 (12%)	4
North America	10 (2%)	0
South America	3 (0.5%)	0
Australia/New Zealand	466 (72%)	79
Asia	86 (13%)	7
Africa	8 (1%)	4
Total	651	94

Table 3.2
Origin of AIME 2002 attendees (non-local) included in the DOME test

Pre-exhibition	232
February 17	367
February 18	540
February 19	538
February 20	306
Post-exhibition	419
Total	2402

Table 3.3
Total hotel room nights consumed (2402)

Holiday Inn Melbourne	297 (12%)
Melbourne Crown Towers	225 (9%)
Grand Hyatt Melbourne	184 (8%)
Sheraton Towers Southgate	166 (7%)
Hilton on the Park	124 (5%)
Novotel on Collins	107 (4.5%)
Duxton Hotel Melbourne	96 (4%)
Saville on Russell	92 (4%)
Quay West Suites	91 (4%)
Le Meridien at Rialto	70 (3%)

Table 3.4
Room nights by hotel (top ten)

Qantas	616 (58%)
Virgin Blue	86 (8%)
Malaysia	72 (7%)
Singapore	30 (3%)
Thai	29 (3%)
Cathay Pacific	28 (2.5%)
Austrian	26 (2.5%)
Emirates	25 (2%)
Air New Zealand	24 (2%)
Ansett	21 (2%)

Table 3.5
Airline seat sectors by top ten
carriers (inbound only)

non-local attendees of 1035, a capture rate of 63 per cent) (see Tables 3.2–3.5).

The DOME research also gathers information on the class of seats/type of flights booked, participants' airport of departure and airport hubs used.

Destination surveys

Australia ● ● ●

Peter van der Hoeven, Manager of the Adelaide Convention Centre, in an article entitled Australia's headlong rise in 25 years' published in *Tagungs-Wirtschaft* magazine (April–May 2002), writes:

> Twenty-five years ago the meetings industry in Australia was virtually non-existent. Ten years later, at the beginning of 1987, there was still not a purpose-built convention centre in any Australian city and, nationally, meetings-related business was worth less than AU$450 million. Today, fifteen years after the establishment of the

Adelaide Convention Centre in mid-1987 as Australia's first, this figure is AU$4.2 billion, and the estimate for ten years ahead is AU$10 billion.

He goes on to describe Australia as the 'new frontier' among conference destinations.

The only national study into the Australian conference and meetings market covered the period 1996–1997 and was published in 1999 as *Meetings Make Their Mark* by the Bureau of Tourism Research. A second study is being planned that will survey venues/delegates and trade show attendees/and organizers, but this new study is not expected to be published before late 2003. Some of the key findings from the first study are shown in Table 3.6. It should be noted that the study excluded:

- events held at venues not associated with convention bureaux;
- in-house events at business premises and training facilities;
- events with less than 15 people in attendance;
- incentives not incorporating a meeting or conference.

Other key findings from the study included the following.

- Delegates were most likely to be male, aged 40–49, and employed as either professionals or managers and administrators.
- 3.3 million delegates took overnight trips to attend a meeting, while 3.5 million delegates took day trips.

	Single-day or part-day meetings	Meetings of more than one day	Total
Number of meetings			
Corporate	81 099	44 674	125 773 (46%)
Association	20 593	8 595	29 188 (21%)
Government	30 393	14 436	44 829 (17%)
Private	19 342	13 055	32 397 (16%)
Total	151 427	80 760	232 187
Number of attendees			
Corporate	3 167 872	2 073 835	5 241 707
Association	1 448 998	949 122	2 398 120
Government	1 324 427	575 348	1 899 775
Private	1 108 856	735 475	1 844 331
Total	7 050 153	4 333 780	11 383 933

Table 3.6
Number of meetings and attendees, Australia, 1996–1997

- Delegates contributed AU$6 billion to the Australian economy in 1996–1997. About AU$1 billion could be considered export earnings, as it resulted from expenditure by international delegates.
- On average, each delegate spent AU$529 within Australia, but this differed significantly by delegate type:
  - local delegates spent AU$ 138;
  - domestic day trip delegates spent AU$ 250;
  - domestic overnight trip delegates spent AU$ 1143;
  - international delegates spent AU$ 4429.
- People attending conferences, conventions and exhibitions (and those accompanying them) accounted for 212 000 visitors, or 5.5 per cent of all international visitors, to Australia in 1996–1997. Between 1990 and 1996, this market grew by an average 11 per cent per year. Asia was the source of 36 per cent of all international conference visitors, and New Zealand (22 per cent), Europe (22 per cent) and the USA (15 per cent) were also important sources. These visitors accounted for approximately 4.7 million visitor nights, or 5.2 per cent of all international visitor nights. On average, conference and exhibition visitors had a shorter duration of stay than other international visitors, but a higher per night expenditure (International Visitor Survey, 1996).

Within Australia, the city of Sydney, through the Sydney Convention & Visitors Bureau, has undertaken a regular annual or biennial 'Convention Delegate Study'. The 2001 Sydney Convention Delegate Study includes information from a total of 3024 delegates (2416 international delegates, 608 domestic) who attended 14 conventions held in the city. The findings 'confirm the high yield nature of conventions and their ability to create incremental revenue and repeat visitation to the host city. The Study identifies why the business tourism market is the fastest growing tourism sector.'

The 2001 Study revealed an average length of stay in Sydney of 6.6 nights compared to 7.6 in 1999, and 6.9 in 1997. Analysis of the duration of conventions in 1999 (5.1 days) compared to 2001 (4.3 days) indicates one day less on average, which might account for the reduced stay in Sydney.

Table 3.7 gives a breakdown of delegate expenditure, based on responses provided by 1838 delegates.

Canada

The Canadian Tourism Commission (CTC) has collated information from various sources – National Tourism Indicators, International Travel Survey, Canadian Economic Observer (Statistics Canada), and the World Tourism Organization – on the economic characteristics of business and conference travellers to Canada. While individual cities also collect data through their convention

Expenditure items	Total expenditure per delegate 2001 (AU$)	1999/2001 % change	Total expenditure per delegate 1999 (AU$)
Registration fees	1131	+34	844
Shopping	655	+21	540
Hotel accommodation	1286	+7	1205
Convention social functions	323	+37	236
Local ground transport	162	+30	125
Restaurants	447	+10	405
Domestic air transport	1229	+87	658
Theatre/concerts/cinema	210	+33	158
Telephone/fax	101	+12	90
Recreational facilities	329	+37	240
Tours	498	+78	279
Star City Casino	286	+49	192
Other expenses	736	+38	535

Source: Sydney Convention Delegate Study 2001 (Sydney Convention and Visitors Bureau).

Table 3.7
Total itemized expenditure per delegate

and visitor bureau (see Case study 4.2 – Vancouver), the methodologies and types of data vary, making any comparisons invalid. CTC information is given below:

Meetings, conventions and incentive travel market visitors from the USA

Although business travel was steady in the three years prior to 2001, it fell 11 per cent to 1.9 million person-trips in 2001. While some of the decline can be attributed to September 11th, business travel had dropped off by the second quarter (–9 per cent) over the same quarter in 2000.

After climbing for three years, overall US overnight business spending declined by 3 per cent in 2001 to $1.57 billion, attributable to the significant drop in the number of business trips. While total business travel spending decreased due to lower traveller numbers, average spending per night in Canada increased, as it had done over the past few years. Over 2000, spending per night increased 10 per cent from $238 to $255. Spending per trip also increased from $754 in 2000 to $811 in 2001.

Details of travel:

• out of total business travel in 2001, 59 per cent of US visitors came to Canada for meetings, staying on average 2.5 nights, with an average spending per night of $275;

- 29 per cent of US visitors came to Canada for conventions, conferences, trade shows and seminars, staying an average of 4.0 nights, with an average spending per night of $215;
- 12 per cent of US business travellers came to Canada for 'other work' reasons, staying on average 4.2 nights, and spending $199 per night.

Demographics:

- 68 per cent of US business travellers are male with over half of total travellers being between the ages of 35 and 54.

Provincial markets:

- four provinces captured 94.3 per cent of total US business travel into Canada. The most frequently visited provinces are Ontario (53.5 per cent), Quebec (17.5 per cent), British Columbia (15.7 per cent) and Alberta (7.6 per cent).

Destinations and origins:

- Toronto remains by far the most popular destination among business travellers, and welcomed 697 500 US business person-trips in 2001 (although this was down substantially from 831 200 in 2000). Montreal (295 000 business trips in 2001 and 319 000 in 2000) continued to be the second most popular city, although by substantially less than Toronto. Toronto, Montreal, Vancouver (246 000 trips), Edmonton (86 000) and Ottawa–Hull (85 000) made up the top five, although there was a 34 per cent decline in business travel to Ottawa.
- California remained the top originating state of business travellers, although trip numbers were down 7 per cent (to 168 000). With a 4 per cent rise in business travel, Washington State (154 000 trips) overtook New York State (down 9 per cent to 146 000 trips) as the second most frequent originator of business travellers.

Business versus leisure spending:

- on average, a US business traveller spends $213 more on accommodation per trip than a US leisure traveller, and $63 more on food and beverages.

Quarterly travel:

- the majority of business travellers arrive in Canada between April and September, during the second and third quarters of the year.

Air flight influences:

- According to the Business Travel Coalition (BTC), which represents the interests of US corporate travel buyers in public policy and industry affairs, the 77 per cent increase in business air fares since 1996, and passenger service problems have led to a long-term strategy within US business to reduce overall travel budgets and to a decline in US business travel.

- Air travel continued to be significantly more important for business travel than for leisure travel with 69 per cent of 2001 business travellers using air (down from 73 per cent in 2000) as their primary mode of transport and 29 per cent using auto (non-business travellers used air only 18 per cent of the time and drove 69 per cent of the time).
- Business person-trips by auto remained steady from 2000 to 2001 although there was a significant decline in business air travel (–18 per cent) from 1.7 million air trips to 1.4 million air trips in 2001. Business air travel decreased in all four quarters of 2001 over the same periods of 2000, most significantly in the third (–27 per cent) and fourth quarters (–32 per cent).

Overseas meetings, conventions and incentive travel market visitors to Canada

Overseas business trips to Canada (for visitors from outside North America):

- After climbing steadily for several years, overseas business travel fell by just over 20 per cent from 783 000 person-trips in 2000 to 622 000 person-trips in 2001.
- Overseas markets supplying the most business travellers to Canada in 2001 were the UK, Japan, Germany, Mexico and then France. Business travel from France and Japan experienced the sharpest declines – both dropped by over 50 per cent while business trips from the UK declined by 10 per cent. Business travel from Germany and Mexico, however, showed extremely strong growth (46 per cent and 71 per cent, respectively). The increase in business travel from Germany was particularly positive, since overall travel to Canada from Germany declined.
- Total overseas business travel spending was down 20 per cent, at $829 million. Japanese business travellers spent the most in 2001 ($86 million), despite the fact that business travel spending from the Japanese market declined the most substantially (–49 per cent) of the main overseas markets. Canada's second most important overseas market in terms of spending in 2001 was the UK ($80 million).

Reason for travel:

- Meetings were the main trip reason for 55 per cent of overseas visitors, while 30 per cent came for conventions, conferences, trade shows and seminars. Fourteen per cent travelled to Canada for 'other work' reasons.

Demographics:

- 64 per cent of overseas business travellers to Canada are male and over 54 per cent are between 35 and 54 years.

Spending and activities:

- Of the main overseas business travel markets, business travellers from France and Mexico spent the most per trip in 2001 ($1307 and $1303, respectively), followed by Japan, the UK and Germany.
- Shopping, sightseeing and fine dining were the main activities enjoyed by overseas business travellers.

Quarterly travel:

- In 2001, 60 per cent of overseas business travellers arrived in Canada between the months of April and September, during the second and third quarters.

Total tourism expenditures and employment in Canada

In 2001, total tourism expenditures in Canada reached $54.6 billion, up marginally by 0.9 per cent from 2000. The US and overseas MC&IT market captures 5.2 per cent of total tourism expenditures at a combined $2.8 billion.

In 2001, tourism employed 563 500 people, up 3.1 per cent (17 100) over 2000. Tourism employment growth outpaced the 2.3 per cent rate of growth in both business sector employment and in total employment.

The 1998, the IACVB 'Convention Income Survey' found an average expenditure by associations on events in Canada of $118 863 (Canadian dollars). Such events had an average attendance of 784 delegates and an average duration of 3.21 days. (Updated figures from the same Survey for the USA can be found later in this chapter on page 94, but it should be noted that these take account of US and not Canadian inflation rates.)

Research carried out by the International Congress and Convention Association, published as 'The International Meetings Market 1994–2003' in June 2002, positioned Canada as 13th for international meetings in 2001, with 77 qualifying meetings attracting 71 874 delegates.

A survey of the 2002 corporate meetings market in Canada for *Meetings & Incentive Travel Magazine* found an increased trend for Canadian corporations to hold their events in Canada rather than abroad: 95 per cent of the 156 corporate buyers responding said that they held some or all of their meetings in Canada in 2001, an increase of 9 per cent over 2000. Only 10 per cent of respondents expected to hold more events outside Canada in 2002, compared with a figure of 40 per cent in the previous survey. However, the total number of meetings organized remained at similar levels to previous years, despite greater usage of video conferencing and 'webinars' (i.e. online seminars). Almost half (48 per cent) of the corporate planners surveyed organized at least eight meetings away from the office in 2001 and, of these, 34 per cent had at least 12 off-site meetings.

The Canada-based *Meetings & Incentive Travel Magazine* also surveyed associations and not-for-profit organizations in Canada, generating responses from the meeting planners of 219 such organizations. The survey found a fall in the number of meetings held in 2001: 56 per cent of respondents planned less than seven meetings, compared with the findings for 2000 when 50 per cent reported planning more than eight meetings each year. However, while the number of meetings held has reduced, their size has remained constant: 64 per cent of respondents have an attendance of 'less than 50' for their smallest meetings, while an average of between 100 and 399 participants is the most frequent for larger meetings (cited by 36 per cent). Canadian associations spent an estimated $70 million on meetings in 2001; 60 per cent of respondents had a similar budget for 2002, while 25 per cent reported an increased budget and only 10 per cent a decrease.

Germany ▫ ▫ ▫

'The German Meetings and Convention Market 1999–2000' is the title of a report commissioned by the German Convention Bureau, looking at the size, value and other characteristics of the market in Germany. Contributors to the research included suppliers, delegates/participants at events, and buyers/planners. Among its principal findings are the following.

- The supply side of the market included 10 729 meeting venues, of which 9982 (93 per cent) were hotels, 400 (4 per cent) were convention centres (including municipal and multipurpose halls), 317 (3 per cent) universities and 30 (0.1 per cent) airports. To qualify, a meeting venue needed space for at least 20 people, theatre-style, in the largest room.
- These venues staged 1.15 million meetings and conventions in 1999–2000, involving approximately 63 million participants, with a total industry value of some 43 billion euros (approximately 26.5 billion pounds sterling). A total of 8.7 million participants were from overseas.
- 79 per cent of these events lasted no longer than 2 days, 11 per cent lasted for 3 days, and 10 per cent lasted for 4 days or longer. The average duration was 1.9 days. Nearly two-thirds of all events had 30 or fewer participants.
- 5 per cent of events had an accompanying exhibition or exposition.

- The peak seasons of the year for holding events were spring (with March being the busiest month) and autumn (especially October–November). Demand is also heaviest in mid-week, with Tuesday, Wednesday and Thursday being the most popular days.
- Factors influencing the choice of location for an event were (in ranking order): 1, recommendations; 2, internal structure of the organization; 3, recognition level of the destination; 4, internet; 5, printed media.
- Average daily budgets for event expenditure were (per participant): 224 euros for corporations (139 pounds sterling approx.), 96 euros for associations (60 pounds sterling approx.). There was a clear expectation among German planners that the number of events would increase but that their budgets would remain the same.
- The most popular meeting and convention cities in Germany were: Berlin, Cologne, Dresden, Düsseldorf, Frankfurt, Hamburg, Heidelberg, Munich, Stuttgart and Weimar.
- 32 per cent of participants were female and 68 per cent male. Two-thirds of participants were under 45 years of age, and 44 per cent were university graduates.
- In the five years prior to 1999–2000, the following trends were noted:
  - the supply side of the market grew significantly, more than the demand side;
  - the average duration of events reduced;
  - the number of events grew more than the number of participants;
  - the proportion of overseas participants increased;
  - the number of participants bringing a companion and extending their stay as leisure visitors increased in significance.
- Forecasts for the next 5-year period included:
  - a slowdown in the supply side of the market, with supply being more closely matched to demand;
  - a reduction in the average duration of events, but an increasing willingness by participants to attend more events;
  - an increase in the number of events, although with budgets remaining the same and more events being held outside Germany.

A more detailed executive summary of the report is accessible on the German Convention Bureau website: www.gcb.de ('Press/ News' section, 'Archives').

Ireland

In the year 2000, 113 000 overseas conference delegates attended association conferences in Ireland (Republic of), spending 100

Origin	1993	1994	1995	1996	1997	1998	1999	2000
Britain	25	24	38	27	31	42	39	57
Mainland Europe	10	13	27	27	37	31	33	36
North America	2	10	10	10	13	18	11	13
Other overseas	3	5	7	4	5	4	10	7
Total	40	52	82	68	86	95	93	113

Source of information: Convention Bureau of Ireland (Bordfailte) – www.conference-ireland.ie.

Table 3.8
Overseas conference visitors to Ireland (000s)

million euros. Dublin staged 70 per cent of these events, followed by Cork, Galway, Limerick and Killarney. Projections were for visitor numbers to rise to 133 000 by 2002, with revenue rising to 130 million euros.

A steady growth in overseas conference visitors was experienced from the mid-1990s onwards, as shown in Table 3.8.

New Zealand

In the year ending 31st July 2002, approximately 45 000 international visitors went to New Zealand to attend a conference. Table 3.9 gives an analysis of their countries/regions of origin.

Estimates compiled by Ernst and Young for Conventions and Incentives New Zealand put the total value of conference expenditure by international delegates at NZ$ 260 million. Such delegates spent an average 3.5 days attending a convention, and

Country of origin	% share	Average spend per day: conference	Average spend per day: pre/post-tours	Total average spend per day
Australia	61%	$411	$184	$297
North America	12%	$384	$368	$373
UK/Europe	8%	$492	$150	$241
Asia	13%	$534	$395	$442
Other countries	6%	$377	$200	$255
Total	100%	$428	$246	$320

Source: Ernst & Young survey commissioned by Conventions & Incentives New Zealand.

Table 3.9
Estimated impact of international convention delegates on New Zealand economy in the year to 31st July 2002

a further 5.5 days on pre and post-conference tours, a total of 9 days per visit spending an average of NZ$320 per day. Table 3.9 also provides a breakdown of visitor spend by country/region of origin.

South Africa

Case study 3.1 provides an analysis of the economic impact and benefits to accrue to Cape Town and to Western Cape Province from the construction of Cape Town International Conference Centre, due to open in July 2003.

United Kingdom

Information has already been given on the demand side of the UK conference industry (Chapter 2 – key findings of the *UK Conference Market Survey 2002*). Supply side data are collected annually through research carried out among conference venues, which is published as the *British Conference Market Trends Survey*. The main results of the *2001 Survey*, based on data provided by 314 venues across the UK, include the following.

- An estimated 1.4 million conferences and meetings (eight or more delegates) took place at UK venues during 2001. About one in five meetings and conferences (19 per cent) involved delegates having an overnight stay at the venue.
- Over two-thirds (71 per cent) of all meetings and conferences took place in urban/airport hotels, while a tenth (11 per cent) took place in rural hotels.
- The average duration of non-residential conferences was estimated to be 1.4 days, while residential conferences lasted an estimated 2.4 days.
- The average number of delegates attending non-residential conferences was 46, while an average of 50 delegates attended residential conferences.
- Non-residential conferences were more likely to be held in March (11 per cent), September (10 per cent) and October (11 per cent). Residential conferences were most likely to take place in September (11 per cent) and October (11 per cent).
- 20 per cent of residential conferences were attended by overseas delegates compared to 13 per cent of non-residential conferences.
- Overall, a third (34 per cent) of all conferences were booked through a professional conference organizer or venue-finding agency.
- Venues were asked to indicate their maximum conference capacity (i.e. single largest room, theatre-style). Just over half of venues (56 per cent) had a maximum capacity of between 101

and 500 delegates. Overall, the average maximum capacity was 391 delegates, slightly less than the average recorded in the *2000 Survey* (410 delegates).

- Around a third (32 per cent) of venues had dedicated exhibition/exposition space available. Venues most likely to have such space included multipurpose venues (64 per cent) and purpose-built venues (62 per cent).
- During 2002, an estimated 5 per cent of conferences held were organized in conjunction with an exhibition (defined as five or more staffed stands).
- Venues were asked to estimate the average daily delegate rate achieved during 2001 (including VAT). Nearly half (48 per cent) of venues achieved an average of between £26 and £50, while a third charged less than £26. Overall, the average daily delegate rate achieved was £35. The average 24-hour delegate rate achieved was £123.
- Estimates for the different types of conference venue used as the basis for the *2001 Survey*, out of an estimated 'universe' of 5000 UK venues, were as follows: purpose-built conference centres, 3 per cent; multipurpose civic and municipal halls, 3 per cent; educational establishments (mostly universities), 3 per cent; urban/airport hotels, 41 per cent; rural hotels, 20 per cent; residential centres, 2 per cent; unusual/unique venues (e.g. castles, sporting venues), 25 per cent.

Table 3.10 gives details of the key characteristics of non-residential and residential conferences in the UK in 2001. It is interesting to note that, in 2001, business visitors to the UK had a higher level of spend than holiday (leisure) visitors for the first time ever, according to figures taken from the *International Passenger Survey* and published by the British Tourist Authority in June 2002. Business visitors spent a total of £3.585 billion, compared with a spend by holiday visitors of £3.138 billion.

Characteristic	Non-residential conferences	Residential conferences
Estimated volume in UK, 2001	1.0 million	0.3 million
Average duration	1.4 days	2.4 days
Average size	46 delegates	50 delegates
Average day/24-hour delegate rate	£35	£123
Estimated value in UK, 2001*	£2300 million	£5000 million

* Based on average achieved delegate rates.
Source: *British Conference Market Trends Survey 2001.*

Table 3.10
Key characteristics of UK non-residential and residential conferences

Birmingham

NEC Ltd, the company responsible for managing Birmingham's National Exhibition Centre (NEC) – including the NEC Arena, International Convention Centre (ICC) (including Symphony Hall), and the National Indoor Arena (NIA) – commissioned management consultants KPMG to conduct a study of the economic impact of these venues on the City of Birmingham and the West Midlands region. The study was carried out during the period September 1998 and August 1999, and was based on a survey of visitors, exhibitors, organizers and promoters. As well as conferences and exhibitions, the venues stage a variety of other events, including rock and classical concerts, dog shows and sporting events.

The study found a total direct expenditure of £711 million in the 12-month period: 52.7 per cent personal spending by the venues' visitors; 44.7 per cent business expenditure by organizers, promoters and exhibitors; and 2.7 per cent other. This is expenditure that was truly additional in that it would not have been generated without the venues and their events.

The study breaks down the income generated by the venues through direct, indirect and induced expenditure. This analysis is shown in Table 3.11.

Table 3.12 breaks down the employment generated by the venues through direct, indirect and induced income.

Since an earlier study carried out in 1993, net direct expenditure into the region had increased by over 40 per cent (from £504 million to £711 million), while economic impact in terms of retained income had increased by 55 per cent (from £194 million to £310 million) and employment by over 40 per cent (from 15 500 jobs in 1993 to 21 844 in 1998–1999).

In 1997, Birmingham's International Convention Centre hosted the annual congress of the World Small Animal Veterinary

Venue	Direct expenditure	Indirect expenditure	Induced expenditure	Total
NEC	150.4	61.6	34.3	246.3
ICC	18.6	7.7	4.3	30.6
Symphony Hall	3.6	1.7	0.9	6.2
NIA	4.9	2.3	1.1	8.3
NEC Arena	5.7	2.3	1.3	9.3
Total	**183.2**	**75.6**	**41.9**	**300.7**

Source: KPMG Economic Impact Study for The NEC Group, Birmingham.

Table 3.11
Total income by venue at NEC group of venues, Birmingham, 1998–1999 (£m)

Venue	Direct	Indirect	Induced	Total
NEC	10 923	4 475	2 494	17 892
ICC	1 353	560	310	2 223
Symphony Hall	262	127	63	452
NIA	354	163	84	601
NEC Arena	410	172	94	676
Total	**13 302**	**5 497**	**3 045**	**21 844**

Source: KPMG Economic Impact Study for The NEC Group, Birmingham.

Table 3.12
Total employment generated by NEC group of venues, Birmingham, 1998–1999

Association (WSAVA), an event which attracted over 6700 delegates from 49 countries (over 1100 of them were from overseas). Some 13 000 bed-nights were booked during the event, both in city centre hotels and at hotels throughout the region. Total delegate expenditure was estimated at £2 million, covering accommodation, travel, eating out, entertainment and shopping (based on an average expenditure of £130 per day). In reality, the full economic impact was even higher than this, as the expenditure estimate was only based upon congress delegates. Many delegates were accompanied by partners and some by their families, but this spending was not included in the figures.

Glasgow

The Scottish Exhibition and Conference Centre (SECC) is the largest purpose-built centre in Scotland with a seating capacity of 3000 in the Clyde Auditorium and larger capacities in its other multi-purpose halls. In the year 2000–2001, the events staged at the SECC injected £83.7 million into the Glasgow (and wider Scottish) economy and directly supported over 3300 jobs. Some £28.6 million was income derived from a total of 79 conferences and conventions, which brought around 50 000 delegates to Glasgow generating 185 000 delegate days. £20.6 million of income came from 61 exhibitions/expositions, and £34.5 million from concerts and events. For further information, see the website: www.secc.co.uk/corporate/economic/.

Conference catering – Bournemouth

An examination of the eating habits of a major convention can perhaps help to make real its benefits to a local economy (although maybe not to a delegate's stomach!). In 1999, the British Labour Party held its centenary conference in Bournemouth, on England's south coast. In total, the conference attracted around 20 000 visitors to the town, including delegates, visitors, journalists, exhibitors and technicians. During the week-long conference, approximately 35 000 cups of tea and coffee were served, with 900 doughnuts and 3200 biscuits; 3000 baguettes were prepared with 500 eggs, 650 lb of cheese and 500 lb of fresh meat.

Bournemouth estimates that conference and exhibition tourism was worth £72 million to the town in 2001–2002. The Labour Party conference alone, due to be held in Bournemouth in Autumn 2003, will inject about £10 million (including an estimate for the value of PR and media coverage generated by the event) into the local economy and further boost an industry that directly supported 3371 jobs in 2001 out of a total of approximately 15 000 jobs in tourism overall.

United States of America

Convene, the magazine published by the Professional Convention Management Association (PCMA), undertakes an annual 'Meetings Market Survey'. The Survey covering 2001 was published in March 2002, and the findings (based on replies from over 200 PCMA members of US associations) are inevitably coloured by the 'September 11th' factor. Here are some of the key results (see also www.pcma.org/convene):

- The average convention/meeting budget for associations in 2001 was US$1.49 million, representing an increase of 9 per cent over the previous year. The single largest item of increased expenditure was for audiovisual expenses, which revealed a 25 per cent increase in the period 1999–2001.
- Strong growth in convention registrations via the Internet was noted. 74 per cent of associations were using online registrations in 2001 compared with just 13 per cent in 1995. 15 per cent of associations were using 'virtual trade show' technology in 2001, allowing browsers to 'visit' their exhibition or exposition electronically.
- The number of small meetings held by associations declined markedly, from an average of 35 to 30 a year. One reason for this was the almost complete elimination of face-to-face meetings in the weeks following 'September 11th'. Budget cuts also reduced the number of seminars and training sessions. However, projections from 41 per cent of respondents were for an increase in the number of small meetings in 2002 (with 32 per cent projecting 'no change' and 27 per cent a decrease).

The Convention Industry Council (CIC) is the principal body in the USA gathering and publishing economic impact data. At the time of writing, the author was advised that new research is scheduled for publication by the CIC in Summer 2003.

The International Association of Convention and Visitor Bureaus, via the IACVB Foundation, has updated CIC data from 1995 to take account of inflation. The IACVB Foundation's estimate for the total direct spending attributable to the convention, exposition (exhibition), meeting and incentive travel industry in 2001 was US$98.8 billion. 1995 data published by the CIC gave the breakdown for the different segments as follows: conventions and expositions, 63.1 per cent; meetings, 32.7 per cent; incentive travel, 4.2 per cent. It seems reasonable to assume similar, although not necessarily identical, percentages for 2001.

Table 3.13 shows the IACVB Foundation's updated figures for spending on events in the USA (and Canada) for the period 1998–2001.

Summary

- Conferences are a segment of business tourism, which is itself a sector of the wider tourism industry. Estimates suggest that, within developed economies such as the UK, business tourism may account for around a quarter of the total value of tourism. The conference segment of business tourism is worth hundreds of billions of pounds per annum on a global scale.
- Comprehensive statistics for the conference industry do not yet exist. There are many reasons for this, including the somewhat fragmented nature of the conference sector, the lack of consensus on terminology and the sensitivity of certain commercial information.
- Measurements of the size of the conference industry are possible, even though these are based on partial rather than fully comprehensive surveys. They point to an industry that is active and growing in both developed and developing countries around the world.
- Calculations of the economic impact of conference business must take into account a number of negative economic impacts, such as opportunity costs and displacement costs, as well as the cascade of positive benefits, in order to arrive at an accurate assessment of net beneficial effects.
- Measurement of the economic impact of tourist spending is achieved by the use of multipliers. Multipliers can be used to measure income generated and employment supported, among other things.
- National surveys and local studies confirm that conference tourism occupies one of the top places at the high-yield end of the tourism spectrum. It provides substantial economic benefits for those countries that have embraced it vigorously and invested in the necessary infrastructure to attract and retain conference business. It sustains jobs that are all-year-round and brings income through delegate expenditure, which benefits many sections of local communities.

	Spending generated per event				Spending generated per day			
	1998	1999	2000	2001	1998	1999	2000	2001
Delegate spending	$696	$716	$742	$748	$231	$238	$247	$248
Association (organizer) spending (*per delegate*)	$68	$69	$72	$74	$18	$18	$19	$20
Convention delegate total spending	**$764**	**$785**	**$814**	**$822**	**$249**	**$256**	**$266**	**$268**
Plus exhibitor spending (*per attendee*)	$300	$306	$317	$326	$83	$85	$88	$91
Trade show delegate total spending	**$1064**	**$1091**	**$1131**	**$1148**	**$332**	**$341**	**$354**	**$359**
Breakdown of delegate spending								
Lodging and incidentals	$343	$352	$369	$371	$114	$117	$123	$123
Hotel food and beverage	$93	$96	$98	$101	$31	$32	$33	$34
Other food and beverage	$86	$89	$91	$93	$29	$29	$30	$31
Tours/sightseeing	$14	$15	$15	$15	$5	$5	$5	$5
Admission to museums, theatres, etc.	$8	$8	$8	$8	$3	$3	$3	$3
Recreation	$7	$8	$8	$8	$2	$3	$3	$3
Sporting events	$2	$3	$3	$3	$1	$1	$1	$1
Retail stores	$74	$76	$76	$74	$24	$25	$25	$25
Local transportation (bus, taxi, limo)	$13	$13	$14	$14	$4	$5	$5	$5
Auto (car) rental (within event city)	$22	$22	$23	$22	$7	$7	$8	$7
Gasoline (petrol), tolls, parking (within event city)	$11	$12	$14	$14	$4	$4	$4	$5
Other	$23	$23	$24	$25	$8	$8	$8	$8
Total	**$696**	**$716**	**$742**	**$748**	**$231**	**$238**	**$247**	**$248**

Average length of stay: 3.01 nights (delegates); 3.74 days (association); 3.59 days (exhibitors).
1999–2001 numbers inflated based on applicable Travel and Consumer Price Index categories (Travel Price Index).
Sources: IACVB Foundation, Travel Industry Association of America, US Department of Labor, Bureau of Labor Statistics (Consumer Price Index).

Table 3.13
USA and Canada: convention income survey – 2001 update. Expenditure on all events (overall average)

Review and discussion questions

1 If you were responsible for marketing an entire destination, what arguments would you put forward to the hotels you are representing to encourage them to disclose to you information on their client groups and bookings? What might be the benefits to them of so doing?

2 List the main arguments for and against the establishment of a comprehensive national database of conferences and similar events.

3 Develop your own questionnaire for measuring the economic impact of convention delegate/attendee expenditure in a specific destination.

4 You have been asked to make the economic case for public funds to be committed for the construction and marketing of a new convention centre. What arguments would you put forward? Illustrate your answer with data/statistics from comparable developments in other locations.

5 As a restaurant owner, whose restaurant is situated close to a major convention centre, suggest the practical steps you might take to ensure that you gain maximum benefit from having this facility on your doorstep.

Notes and references

Australian Tourist Commission International Visitor Survey (1996).

British Conference Market Trends Survey 2001. Carried out by NFO System Three on behalf of the British Tourist Authority, British Association of Conference Destinations, CAT Publications, International Congress and Convention Association (UK Chapter), Meetings Industry Association, Northern Ireland Tourist Board, VisitScotland and Wales Tourist Board (2002).

British Tourist Authority. International Passenger Survey (2002).

Convene. Meetings Market Survey 2002. *Convene Magazine* (March 2002).

Cooper, Chris; Fletcher, John; Gilbert, David and Wanhill, Stephen. *Tourism Principles and Practice.* Addison Wesley Longman Ltd (1993).

Davidson, Rob and Cope, Beulah. *Business Travel.* Pearson Education (2002).

German Convention Bureau. The German Meetings and Convention Market 1999–2000 (2000).

Heeley, J. *Tourism and Local Government, With Special Reference to the County of Norfolk*, Volume 1, page 72. University of East Anglia (1980).

International Association of Convention and Visitor Bureaus. Convention Income Survey (1998). International Congress and Convention Association. The International Meetings Market 1994–2003 (2002).

Meetings Make Their Mark. Bureau of Tourism Research (1999).

Rockett, G and Smillie, Gill. *The European Conference and Meetings Market.* The Economist Intelligence Unit (reprinted from *Travel & Tourism Analyst*, Issue 4, 1994).

The UK Conference Market Survey 2002. Research carried out by The Right Solution on behalf of the Meetings Industry Association (June 2002).

CHAPTER 4

Conference industry marketing activity

Location has always been one of the key factors in
decisions over the choice of conference venues. Its
importance has led to the creation of marketing
organizations whose prime focus is that of location or
'destination' promotion, operating at national,
regional or city level. Following a summary of
general marketing principles and their application to
the conference industry, this chapter will look at the
role of destination marketing organizations. It will
also examine some of the other ways in which
individual venues, or groups of venues, bring their
product to the marketplace through branding and the
establishment of consortia. The key aspects of
marketing conferences and events will be covered in
Chapter 5.

Specific sections in this chapter include:

- marketing principles;
- relationship marketing and customer relationship
management;
- a definition of destination;
- the branding of cities and other destinations;
- destination marketing organizations;
- conference venue marketing;
- the branding of hotel venues;
- overseas marketing.

Marketing principles

Before looking at conference venue and destination marketing activities, it will be useful to summarize some of the general principles of marketing, and how they apply to the conference and tourism industry.

Customer focus

There are many definitions of marketing. One of the more straightforward ones is that adopted by the (British) Chartered Institute of Marketing, which defines marketing as: *'The management process responsible for identifying, anticipating and satisfying customers' requirements efficiently and profitably'*.

This focus on customers' needs is the key to all successful marketing activity. There are alternative philosophies, which are well described by Cooper *et al.* (1993) and reproduced in Figure 4.1:

> Examples 1 and 2 [in Figure 4.1] can be ineffective due to problems encountered in having the wrong product for the market, and therefore having to devote more resources to promotion and selling in order to achieve sales. In these examples it is normal to find companies

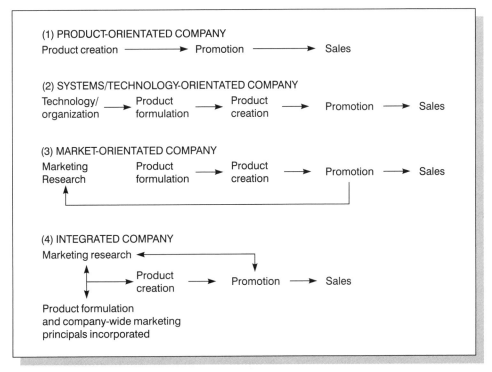

Figure 4.1 Four possible business philosophies. (*Source:* Cooper *et al.* (1993) *Tourism: Principles and Practice*).

which believe their products are acceptable, and all that is required for sales to occur is the identification of prime markets and methods of selling.

The emphasis is on the product, and in tourist promotional literature it is often characterized by photographs of empty bedrooms or conference rooms, of buildings and views of the destination. It is selling 'features' rather than the 'benefits' the consumer is seeking, and fails to show pictures of tourists and delegates enjoying themselves and receiving good service.

On the other hand, examples 3 and 4 in Figure 4.1:

> offer the ideal approach to organizing business in today's tourism marketplace. They are driven by research which creates an understanding of the consumer, the business and the marketplace . . ..The tourism industry is spending vast sums of money on developing new attractions, improving products, building hotels and investing in technology. The only way for the risk level to be kept to a minimum is through adoption of a marketing philosophy which provides products related to the needs of consumers.

The establishment of a customer orientation, which permeates through every department of a conference venue or conference marketing organization, is essential to its success. This provides the basic building blocks upon which marketing strategies can be constructed. It will ensure that the physical product is suited to market needs: the multipurpose hotel function room, for example, is less and less able to meet the increasingly sophisticated needs of today's conference planners. It will also ensure that the people servicing a venue have a proper understanding of the specific needs of the conference organizer and his delegates, and that they are equipped with the personal and technical skills to meet such needs in ways which will encourage the customer to return again and again.

Marketing plan

The practical steps involved in preparing to approach the marketplace include development of a marketing plan or strategy. The plan will need to set out what an organization is trying to achieve, in other words its corporate mission and goals, and include an analysis of where it is at the present time, sometimes referred to as an internal and external audit. The plan must also assess the general business situation and make projections for the organization's likely performance. It should set out clear objectives, create an appropriate marketing mix strategy, and determine effective monitoring systems and performance measures. The process is likely to include a PEST analysis, looking at the political, economic, social and technological changes, which may affect the organization and the market, and a SWOT analysis, assessing the major strengths, weaknesses, opportunities and threats facing the company.

Tables 4.1 and 4.2 show extracts taken from the 'Convention Bureau Business Plan 2002–2003' of Australia's capital city, Canberra. They show how the Plan is structured, and set out the principal objectives and targets to be met, together with appropriate performance measures. Canberra Convention Bureau (CCB) also produces a three-year corporate plan setting out longer-term strategic objectives.

The Convention Bureau's *vision* is: '*For Canberra to be recognized as a leading business events destination shaped by its competitive advantages*'.

Its *mission* is: '*As the key business events marketing body, the CCB is committed to increasing meetings, incentives, conventions and*

Contents	Page
1. Introduction	3
2. Summary of key result areas – targets for 2002–2003	4
3. Competitive analysis and competitive advantages	5
Our competitive advantage	5
4. Key result area one: promotion of Canberra	6
Strategic objective	6
2002–2003 target objectives	6
Sales/business development activities	6
Cooperative promotions	7
Advertising	8
Publications	9
Public relations	9
Web marketing	10
5. Key result area two: providing quality services to our clients	11
Strategic objective	11
Clients	11
Members	11
6. Key result area three: good business management	12
Strategic objective	12
2002–2003 target activities	12
7. Key result area four: industry leadership	13
Strategic objective	13
2002–2003 target activities	13
8. Canberra Convention Bureau contact details	14
9. CCB promotion activity calendar 2002–2003	15
10. Registration of interest	16
11. Terms and conditions of cooperative marketing	20

Table 4.1
Canberra Convention Bureau Business Plan 2002–2003 'table of contents'

Key result area	Strategic objective	Performance measurement	Target for 2002–2003
1. Promote Canberra	Secure return on stakeholders' investment through promotion of Canberra and its competitive advantages to key target markets	1. Secure high-yield, measurable business events for Canberra	Convert AU$27 million worth of business events for ACT
		2. Execute new Showcase Program in Sydney	Secure minimum of 50 buyers to attend
		3. Execute Top Secret 2003 program	Secure minimum of 40 qualified buyers to attend program
		4. Upgrade website to enable improved membership access to benefits, e.g. MICE calendar	By January 2003
2. Provide quality service to our clients	Satisfy the expectations and needs of our business events clients, industry members and government	1. Execute independent survey of our business clients	That 80% of respondents rate our services to be good or excellent
		2. Execute independent survey of our CCB members	That 80% of respondents rate the CCB as being effective (in each of our key result areas)
3. Good Business Management	Achieve better practices in managing our business effectively in a productive and supportive work environment	1. Review and analyse business processes in line with provisions of the Privacy Act	That the CCB is fully compliant with new Privacy Law by 31/12/2002
		2. Implement an internal Team Scorecard to measure effectiveness and supportiveness	That staff rate the CCB as being a supportive work environment by passing 80% of key elements of successful workplace
4. Provide leadership for business events industry	That the CCB is considered to be the one-stop-shop for clients, stakeholders and media in relation to business events industry issues in the ACT	That the CCB is actively involved in issues related to our sector locally and nationally	That our members rate us as being effective or highly effective

ACT, Australian Capital Territory.

Table 4.2
Canberra Convention Bureau Business Plan 2002–2003: summary of key result areas – targets for 2002–2003

exhibition activity for the economic benefit of Canberra and our key stakeholders.'

The CCB website address is: www.canberraconvention.com.au.

Marketing mix strategy

Through a process of market research, target markets of current and potential customers must be identified, whether in broad terms (e.g. corporate conferences for up to 100 delegates or professional association conferences for 500 to 1000) or in more specific niche and segment terms (e.g. very high-spend pharmaceutical conferences for 20–40 delegates, or residential educational sector conferences for 50–100). Once this has been done, an appropriate marketing mix strategy can be developed.

The marketing mix is frequently defined as comprising the four Ps: product, price, promotion and place (distribution). Other marketing gurus would extend these traditional four points to eight, to include packaging, planning, the prospect and post-sale.

In the marketing of a conference destination or venue, these terms signify:

- *Product* is the destination/venue and its facilities and resources. To conference organizers and meeting planners, it means a destination/venue that can handle the convention, meeting or exhibition requirements. It covers such issues as service, quality, branding, and those unique features that differentiate it from competitors (USPs or unique selling propositions).
- *Price* may cover a variety of issues including conference centre/venue hire charges and delegate rates, hotel or guesthouse accommodation costs, and transport costs. Pricing policies must take account of many factors, including projected future demand and any seasonal fluctuations expected; the need to maximize yield (see Chapter 6); the perishable nature of the product (it is something that cannot be stored for future use, like a conference room that is unused on a particular day and brings in no revenue and that potential revenue is lost forever); the psychological impact on clients of raising or lowering prices; the activities of competitors; and the wider economic situation.
- *Packaging* relates to the way in which the product and price are offered in the market. Special delegate packages may be offered in conjunction with local tourist attractions, or between conference venues and hotels. Most venues, both residential and non-residential, promote their own delegate packages: Bodysgallen Hall and Spa, Llandudno, North Wales, offers 'residential' and 'daily' delegate packages (see Table 4.3). Some convention centres will offer their meeting rooms rent-free to certain types of not-for-profit organizations

Residential delegate rate (£140 per person for 24 hours) includes:

Single accommodation
Cooked breakfast
Morning coffee and biscuits
An allowance of £14.50 towards luncheon
Afternoon tea and biscuits
An allowance of £27.50 towards dinner
Hire of meeting room and equipment hire, to include overhead projector and screen, one flip
  chart, direct telephone
Full use of the hotel's health and leisure spa

Daily delegate rate (£45 per person for 8 hours) includes:

Hire of the meeting room
Morning coffee and biscuits
An allowance towards luncheon
Afternoon tea and biscuits

Delegate rates are only available for parties of eight or more.
www.bodysgallen.com

Table 4.3
Residential and daily delegate rates – Bodysgallen Hall and Spa, Llandudno, Wales

whose events meet specific economic benefit criteria. The New Zealand Convention Association has developed its Conference Assistance Programme (CAP) to assist the country to win more international association conferences. The CAP initiative helps a New Zealand (national) association to bid for the international conference to which it is linked by undertaking an initial feasibility study on its behalf free of charge. It then assists with compilation of the bid in conjunction with a professional conference organizer. As at October 2001, the CAP initiative had secured more than NZ$123 million worth of business over the previous six years.

- *Place (or distribution)* focuses on the activities used by a destination or venue to make its product available and accessible to prospective clients. Such distribution channels include trade shows, destination or venue guides and brochures, CD-ROMs or videos and websites.
- *Planning* is the strategic process of analysing markets, assessing the competition, identifying programmes and selecting appropriate marketing strategies.
- *Promotion* communicates information about the destination/venue and its products to prospective clients. There is a need to inform and persuade current customers to remain loyal, potential future customers to experience the product, but also

journalists and other key people (e.g. leading figures in the local community and politicians) who may in some way influence business activity levels. Advertising, public relations, direct marketing, selling and familiarization visits are some of the promotional activities undertaken.

- *Prospect* (or client/customer) is the sole reason for, and the object of, all the destination or venue's marketing endeavours. The Body Shop retail company expressed the importance of the customer in its mission statement as follows:

> A customer is the most important visitor on our premises. She is not dependent on us. We are dependent on her. She is not an interruption to our work. She is the purpose of it. She is not an outsider in our business. She is part of it. We are not doing her a favour by serving her. She is doing us a favour by giving us the opportunity to do so.

It is this same customer orientation that is crucial to the success of all venues and destinations seeking to attract conference delegates.

- *Post-sale* processes address the continuing need to provide service to and for prospects and to ensure that the sense of expectation generated at the sales meeting is not just met but exceeded in the run-up to an event and, indeed, in the provision of service during and after it. Client retention is not always possible within the conference industry because of the buying patterns of certain organizations, especially within the association sector, but keeping satisfied clients is a much more cost-effective way of maintaining and building market share than having constantly to find and attract new clients. Recommendations by colleagues/peers of venues and destinations are frequently found to be a key way in which these are sourced, as a satisfied customer becomes an unpaid ambassador (or 'distribution channel') whose value should never be underestimated.

Other marketers suggest further Ps be added to the marketing mix, such as *people* – those who are between the product and the prospect, delivering the product/services to the client including convention bureau staff, venue personnel, destination management companies, professional conference organizers, restaurateurs, and shop and visitor attraction staff.

There is clearly some overlap between these different marketing mix tools, but in total they provide the essential ingredients for bringing a conference venue or destination to the marketplace in a way that is professionally planned and likely to enjoy the greatest success.

Relationship marketing and customer relationship management

One of the key features of conference venue and destination marketing is the forging of relationships between suppliers and buyers, the building of trust between those offering facilities and services and those looking to make use of them to stage events. Gartrell (1991) suggests that:

> though a convention bureau is a sales organization, its premise of operation is the development of a relationship with planners that cultivates understanding and trust. Though such a relationship may not initially appear mutually supportive, the reality is that the bureau and planner have common goals and in essence need one another.

The meeting planner or conference organizer needs, for example, to carry out familiarization or inspection visits to a destination and its venues, to assess its appropriateness for specific events. The convention and visitor bureau is the ideal vehicle through which such visits can be organized because: the bureau can provide a comprehensive overview; pull together all the necessary information; arrange a schedule of visits to venues and attractions, and usually escort them as well; and then advise on the availability and accessibility of all the other components of a given conference package. PCOs and DMCs can also be involved in this process in a similar way. For the individual conference organizer to plan such a visit using his own resources, possibly from hundreds or thousands of miles away, would require a huge investment in time and resources.

Trust and understanding are also of critical importance between the venue that is to stage the conference and the conference organizer. A chain of relationships is formed, initially between the venue sales manager and the conference organizer, and then between the conference and banqueting manager/event coordinator and the organizer. All need to have confidence in each other: the conference organizer needs to trust the venue staff to deliver what has been promised within agreed budgets, and the venue staff need to feel comfortable that their client will keep his side of the deal (e.g. in numbers of delegates, in the conference programme, and in any specially planned arrangements). When such strong and trusting relationships exist, there is a much greater prospect of successful events and of future repeat business. When relationships are less strong, often because of high staff turnover in the venue, poor communications between client and venue, or because of insufficient planning time allocated by the conference organizer, problems are much more likely to occur.

In the author's experience, one of the real attractions of the conference industry is the many opportunities it affords for the development of relationships between buyers and suppliers, between buyers and buyers, and between suppliers and suppliers. It is very much a people industry and, while there may be fierce competition for business, this takes the form of friendly rivalry rather than cut-throat aggression. Formal and informal networks are established, and it is quite common for one destination to pass on information about a client or an event to the destination that will play host to them next. Similarly, buyers will exchange their experiences of venues and destinations, and peer recommendation is one of the most important ways in which future venues are sourced.

'Relationship marketing' and 'customer relationship management' (and also 'key account management') are the terms used to describe the establishment and nurturing of relationships with clients. 'Relationship marketing' focuses on the initial identification and building of contacts with potential clients, while 'customer relationship management' concentrates on the fostering and strengthening of such relationships.

A crucial tool in customer relationship management is the development of customer profiles in a client database, which is normally computerized but could also take the form of a card-index system. Such databases are built from a core record giving full contact details (client name, job title, company name and address, telephone and fax numbers, and email address as a minimum), but will then go on to establish a profile of the client's buying requirements (e.g. kinds of conferences organized, types of venues used, sizes of events, locations considered). Customer Relationship Management facilitates direct contact with customers in ways that should generate real response. The more sensitive and creative the use of the data, the better the reaction (or 'response'). Frequently, direct marketing is linked with some form of incentive to encourage recipients to respond. Relationship marketing and customer relationship management are about one-to-one contact with an organization's clientele, involving strategies for customer retention and a more targeted approach to the creation of customer value. They provide a complementary approach to conventional marketing strategy by focusing upon the search for mutually beneficial partnerships with customers.

It is easier to put such approaches into practice within the conference sector than, for example, the leisure tourism sector because the number of clients and potential clients is much more restricted. This is not mass leisure tourism. It is, as mentioned earlier in this chapter, about identifying specific markets and building a rapport with individual decision-makers within these defined markets

A definition of destination

'Location, location and location' is a commonly heard expression within the conference industry. When it comes to choosing a conference venue, the most important initial consideration for event organizers is its location. This factor often assumes greater importance than factors such as price, type of venue, quality of facilities and proximity to tourist attractions, as confirmed by the *UK Conference Market Survey 2002'* research (see Chapter 2, Table 2.4). Buyers purchase location first and foremost.

Location can mean a number of different things: a town, a city, a county, a region, an island, a rural area, a city centre, even a country in the context of high-profile international conventions. In some cases, an organizer will express location in terms of 'proximity to an international airport', 'within a 20-mile radius of a certain town' or 'somewhere between two named motorways'.

Where the reference is to a discrete area, the term most frequently and aptly used to describe this area is 'a destination'. Gartrell (1994) defines destinations as follows:

> From the perspective of the consumer, destinations are perceived as those geographic areas that have attributes, features, attractions, and services that appeal to the prospective user. How the consumer defines a geographic area varies greatly and may or may not include specific geographic boundaries.

The key phrase here is 'areas . . . that appeal to the prospective user'. The marketing of conference venues and destinations must be driven by what makes sense to the consumer: in this case, the conference organizer and the delegates he is seeking to attract. It cannot be undertaken successfully by the artificial 'destinations' which are sometimes created to satisfy bureaucratic or political whims, a criticism that may justifiably be levelled at some of the current regional tourism structures within Britain.

The branding of cities and other destinations

The branding of consumer products (e.g. cars, washing machines) has played a major part in their promotion for many years. More recently, branding theory has been applied to the practice of marketing destinations, and is now seen as a key component or tool in any successful promotion of cities, regions and countries.

The classical definition of a 'brand' is: 'A name, term, sign or design, or a combination of them, which is intended to identify the goods or services of one seller or group of sellers and to differentiate them from their competitors' (De Chernatony and McDonald, 1998).

However, this is very much a supply-side perspective. It is also necessary to consider the consumer's role in branding and to take account of the messages the consumer receives. More modern definitions of a brand that acknowledge this two-way process are the following:

> A brand is a simple thing: it is in effect a trademark which, through careful management, skilful promotion and wide use, comes into the minds of consumers, to embrace a particular and appealing set of values and attributes, both tangible and intangible' (Interbrand, 1990). A brand is a 'product or service made distinctive by its personality and its positioning. Its personality is a unique combination of tangible/physical attributes (i.e. what do I get?) and intangible/symbolic attributes (how do I feel?). Its positioning defines the point of reference with respect to the competitive set, and occupies a unique space in the consumer's mind (Hankinson, 2001).

Brands work by:

> facilitating and making the customer's choice process more effective. The objective of branding is to provoke a positive action in customers by facilitating the decision-making process. The development of a name and logo, and the presentation of an attractive and (both physically and emotionally) feasible proposition for the brand validated by consumers and deliverers are basic branding procedures (Doyle, 1989).

To achieve really successful destination branding, the brand must come alive for tourists. Marketers must 'be in the business of delivering impactful experiences, not merely constructing a clever brand identity on paper with slick slogans and brand logos' (Morgan et al., 2002). Today many destinations have (or at least claim to have!) superb venues and hotels, easy accessibility, diverse visitor attractions and a unique cultural heritage. But their future success in attracting visitors will depend on their ability to create a unique identity for themselves, to differentiate themselves from their competitors (see the example of Vancouver in Case study 4.2). 'In this marketplace, what persuades potential tourists to visit (and revisit) one place instead of another is whether they have empathy with the destination and its values. The battle for customers in tomorrow's destination marketplace will be fought not over price but over hearts and minds – and this is where we move into the realm of branding' (Morgan et al., 2002).

There is not space here to explore fully the theory and practice of destination branding, but it is worth emphasizing that, 'whatever branding proposition is used, it must have the potential to last, to grow old and to evolve in a long-term branding campaign, so it is essential to get it right. However, the point of differentiation must reflect a promise which can be delivered and which matches expectations. Good destination branding is, therefore, original and different, but its originality and difference needs to be sustainable, believable and relevant' (Morgan *et al.*, 2002).

A more unusual example of a newly developed conference destination brand is 'BestCities.net', a global convention and visitor bureau alliance that 'delivers the world's best service experience for the meetings industry'. The alliance, which currently comprises the convention bureaux of five cities (Boston, Copenhagen, Edinburgh, Melbourne and Vancouver) and will be looking to add 5–7 more cities over the next three years, claims 'consistently high service standards and close cooperation through information exchange, which enable five convention bureaux on various continents to offer a totally unique product'. In an industry known for its wide range of differing services and standards, BestCities.net promises 'an assurance of quality, expertise and professionalism to clients'. For further information, see the website: www.bestcities.net.

Destination marketing organizations

Destination or 'place' marketing is undertaken at both a local level (city or county, for example) and a national level (by a national tourism organization). This section looks at a number of models of destination marketing organizations at both levels.

Local destination marketing

Convention and visitor bureaux

A number of references have already been made to the role of convention and visitor bureaux in the formation of the conference industry (Chapter 1) and in the provision of services to that industry (Chapter 2).

In structure, conference or convention bureaux (variations on the name are to be found) are usually formed and financed as partnerships between public and private sector bodies. In Britain this can include local authorities/councils, chambers of commerce, local enterprise companies/agencies, hotels, venues and other private sector suppliers. They are set up as not-for-profit organizations, controlled by a management board, to fulfil a strategic marketing role and be the 'official' voice of the destination they represent. In most cases, the bureau is established at arms' length from the local authority or authorities that it represents, but in others (e.g. Blackpool Conference Bureau, or

Kent Conference Bureau) the bureau remains an integral part of the local authority structure.

Funding is derived from public sector contributions (usually the largest single source), private sector membership fees (members including venues of all kinds, accommodation providers, PCOs/DMCs, transport operators, audiovisual companies, and other kinds of suppliers), sponsorship, joint commercial activities with members, and, in some cases, commission, which is charged to venue members on business placed. Some bureaux prefer to have a high membership fee, which covers a full package of benefits and services to their members (with no or few hidden or extra charges). Other bureaux opt for a much lower membership fee, which provides a core of benefits, but they then invite their members to buy into additional activities and services on a partnership basis. Both models have their strengths and weaknesses.

1 *High membership fee.* For the bureau, the high membership fee, which can amount to as much as £5000 per annum for large hotels, enables longer term planning to be undertaken with greater confidence, provided of course that the bureau can also achieve a high retention level amongst its membership. The bureau knows that it should receive a certain membership income in ensuing years and can plan its activities and expenditure accordingly. The high membership fee model also means that the bureau does not have to go back to its members on a regular basis to seek their financial support for particular activities during the year, which can be time-consuming for the bureau and a cause of irritation to its members. The weakness, or perhaps more accurately the challenge, of this funding model is the need to guarantee significant returns to the membership for their high investment in the bureau.

2 *Lower membership fee* – this would typically be a membership fee of several hundred pounds (£500–£1000 is the normal range). For the bureau, this can make it easier to 'sell' bureau membership to potential members because the initial outlay for them is much smaller. For bureau members, there is greater flexibility in buying into those activities of the bureau (e.g. a stand at a trade exhibition or an entry in a piece of promotional print), which are of most interest to them and which match their budgets. They do not have to buy into a full package of benefits, some of which they may not require. On the down side, there are significantly higher administrative costs with this model. It can also be argued with some justification that those members paying a lower membership fee are likely to be less committed to the bureau than those who have paid a high fee and need to see the bureau succeed to justify their investment.

There is no right or wrong model. Each destination and the suppliers within it must agree what is appropriate for them and then develop and fine-tune the model in the light of experience. Bureaux are dynamic entities that must continue to evolve in the light of local circumstances, changes in market trends, the demands of clients and a multitude of other factors (see also Chapter 9).

In the British Isles, there are around 40 conference bureaux. 'Bureau' is a generic term, which, as has been seen, disguises a variety of models in terms of their staffing, funding and operations, although all share the same fundamental mission, which, in the words of Gartrell (1994), is to 'solicit and service conventions and other related group business and to engage in visitor promotions which generate overnight stays for a destination, thereby enhancing and developing the economic fabric of the community'.

British conference bureaux have an average of two or three staff (typically a general manager, a sales executive and an administrative assistant with computing skills), but the range is from just one member of staff up to 12. Case study 4.1 describes the structure, resources, objectives and activities of Aberdeen and Grampian Convention Bureau.

The concept of a convention and visitor bureau (CVB) is now widely adopted around the world. Bureaux in North America, for example, operate on a vastly different scale from the UK, largely because there is a longer tradition of CVBs (even relatively small towns have a CVB), with the world's first visitor and convention bureau, Detroit (or Metropolitan Detroit Convention and Visitor Bureau as it is now known) being established in 1896. In the USA, bureaux are also funded differently, principally through a system of *hotel transient occupancy tax* (or bed tax), which means that hotel guests pay a tax that goes to the local city or town council, and can be added to the resources available to market the destination. In North America, CVBs also play a prominent role at the centre of community life, being involved in a wide spectrum of community development issues that may impact on the future prosperity of the visitor industry. Case study 4.2 gives details of the convention marketing activities, structure and funding of Tourism Vancouver, the body established in Canada's leading Pacific seaboard destination to generate business and leisure visitors for the city.

The International Congress and Convention Association (ICCA) has a category of membership specifically for CVBs. It carries out research into this category on a three-yearly basis. The last such research was undertaken in 2000, covering 146 members around the world, and it found that 40 per cent of these CVBs operated at a local city level, 12 per cent at a regional level and 48 per cent at a national level (see later in this chapter for examples of a number of national bureaux). The research also found the average city convention bureau in Europe had six staff, compared with an average of 18 in non-European bureaux. Budgets for European city bureaux averaged less than half a million US dollars, whereas non-European city bureaux had average budgets of over US$5 million. Case study 4.3 profiles Vienna Convention Bureau, one of the best-resourced and most successful bureaux in the world.

Convention and visitor bureaux provide a range of services, many free of charge, to conference organizers and meeting planners. They aim to offer a 'one-stop' enquiry point for their destination, with impartial advice and assistance (although there is increasing debate over whether their role should now be focused on steering customers towards the suppliers best able to meet their needs, rather than seeking to represent all of their suppliers in a comprehensive, unbiased way). Such CVB services are likely to include some or all of the following.

1 Pre-booking the event
 • literature and website information
 • venue location and selection advice
 • availability checks
 • rate negotiation
 • provisional booking service
 • familiarization/inspection visits
 • preparation of bid documents
 • assistance with bid presentations to a selection committee/board
 • assistance with civic hospitality requests.
2 Preparing for the event:
 • block accommodation booking service for delegates
 • coordination of the full range of support services including transportation, registration, translation, office support; in some cases, these will be provided in conjunction with a professional conference organizer (PCO) or destination management company (DMC)
 • provision of 'welcome desks' for delegates at major points of entry
 • promotional and PR support to maximize delegate numbers and increase awareness of the event in the host destination
 • supply of delegate information
 • planning partner programmes, social programmes, and pre- and post-conference tours
 • arranging contact with local conference service companies and event organizers.
3 During the event
 • civic welcome and recognition
 • PR support
 • provision of tourist information.

4 After the event
  • post-event evaluation and follow-up research
  • consultancy support to the destination that will next host the conference.

Many of a bureau's marketing activities are implicit or explicit in the list of services it offers to conference organizers. A typical portfolio of activities for a British convention bureau will include some or all of the following, dependent upon staff and financial resources.

• *Direct marketing* – particularly direct mail, but also telesales and, occasionally, with a sales person 'on the road'.
• *Print and audiovisual production* – compiling conference destination guides and other promotional print, as well as videos, CD-ROMs and websites.
• *Exhibition attendance* – taking stands at trade shows such as International Confex, Confer, Meetings & Incentive Travel Show, National Venue Show, EIBTM, IMEX.
• *Overseas trade missions* – participation in overseas roadshows and workshops, often organized by the British Tourist Authority.
• *Familiarization visits* – organizing visits for groups of buyers and press representatives.
• *Receptions* – coordinating receptions, lunches, occasionally small workshops to which key clients, existing and potential, are invited.
• *Advertising* – in local and national press.
• *Public relations* – circulating information and releases to the media and often to influential community organizations.
• *Ambassador programmes* – identifying, recruiting, training and supporting key individuals in the local community (university academics, hospital professional staff, leading industrialists, members of the business community, trade unionists) as 'ambassadors' for the destination, assisting them to bid for and attract the annual conference of the professional institution or trade union to which they belong. Other variations of ambassador programmes, like that operating in London, aim to recognize and publicly acknowledge particular initiatives undertaken by companies and organizations designed to attract more conference business to the destination, while Ireland's 'Conference Ambassador' partnership (see pages 124–5) is different again.

Conference offices and conference desks • • •

Conference offices (or conference desks) are normally established as part of a local authority's tourism marketing activity, where there is no convention bureau in operation. The staff, typically a conference officer with one assistant, are directly employed by the local authority/council and will usually be located in a department involved with economic development or leisure services. In some cases, they can tap into other staff resources (computer and administrative services, marketing, inward investment) available within the broader local authority structure.

Conference offices undertake many of the same marketing activities as convention bureaux, and offer similar services to conference and event organizers. The main differences between a conference office and convention bureau relate to structure and funding. A conference office does not have a formal membership, but it may coordinate the activities of a conference or tourism association within the destination, bringing together the main conference players to collaborate in joint marketing activities, for which financial or in-kind contributions are required. The conference office staff do not report to a management board, but to managers and councillors within a local authority department, although where a conference association has been established there is also a need to report back to them as well on the success of the marketing programmes. The budget for the conference office is determined by the appropriate council committee but is often supplemented by private sector contributions. Not infrequently, the conference officer may also have direct responsibility for the promotion of one or more civic buildings as conference venues. In the UK destinations such as Cambridge, Eastbourne, Guildford and Swansea operate with a conference office or desk.

National destination marketing

The role of national conference destination marketing is undertaken by a variety of bodies that differ from country to country. In some cases, these bodies equate to a national convention bureau – and frequently contain the words 'convention bureau' in their name – and have many features in common with the city convention bureaux described earlier in this chapter. In other cases, they are fully public sector organizations funded and administered within the central government structure.

The examples that follow, summarizing some of the leading national conference destination marketing organizations, highlight the variations that exist but also point to a number of common characteristics.

Australia: Team Australia

Team Australia is an alliance of tourism leaders who combine the forces of the Australian Tourist Commission and Australia's leading convention bureaux, i.e. the 13 city and regional convention bureaux that are members of the Association of Australian Convention Bureaux (AACB). It was formed (and formally launched in 1999) in the absence of a national convention bureau for Australia to assist in national marketing activity. At the time of writing (September 2002), the Federal Government was considering the creation of a national convention bureau as a component of its new Tourism Strategy Plan, based on strong recommendations from both the AACB and the Meetings Industry Association of Australia (MIAA). If the recommendations are adopted, it is likely that a national convention bureau would reflect the needs of the whole business events (i.e. the term used in Australia for MICE) sector for a stand-alone marketing entity, not just the traditional conventions sector.

Team Australia's objective is to encourage international corporations, associations and organizations to choose Australia as a destination for their meetings and events, and to do so through enhanced collaborative marketing for specific business events marketing projects. It involves branding Australia as a business events destination, using imagery based around the strapline of the 'Best Events Under The Sun'.

Team Australia was, therefore, formed to:

• brand Australia as a business events destination;
• identify additional opportunities to grow the international market for Australia;
• identify the gaps in the current international marketing activities and resource activities to fill these gaps;
• improve dispersal of international business throughout Australia;
• increase the effectiveness of Australia's business events marketing efforts by collectively planning and resourcing projects;
• increase the resources being allocated to Australia's business events marketing efforts.

Some current (i.e. as at September 2002) Team Australia projects, proposed and actual, include:

• participation in 2002/3 Asian MICE seminars;
• 2002/3 European & North American awareness campaigns;
• participation in PRIME 2002 (the 'Pacific Rim Incentives and Meetings Exchange', a relatively new trade show focusing on the business events industry in the Pacific Rim – www.prime-aloha.com);
• production of delegate-boosting collateral;
• updating the 'Case for Australia', a marketing tool directed to the corporate end user (see www.businesseventsaustralia.com).

While the Team Australia marketing budget was not available, the value of joint venture marketing projects by AACB members for 2002/3 was at least AU$883 thousand.

General management for projects is by the Team Australia Coordination Unit, based at the Australian Tourist Commission's Business Tourism Division (contact: myeates@atc.gov.au). Further information on AACB is given in Chapter 8.

Canada: Canadian Tourism Commission ● ● ●

The Canadian Tourism Commission (CTC) is a joint government-industry organization based in Ottawa that markets Canada as a four-season destination to Canadian and international business and leisure travellers. The federal government created the CTC in 1995, replacing Tourism Canada, a government department, in response to the Canadian tourism industry's call for direct involvement in marketing Canada as a tourist destination. The CTC brings together people and resources from all levels of government – federal, provincial/territorial and local – with the private sector and various local and regional tourism associations.

The Government of Canada contributes $83.7 million annually to the CTC. Private-sector partners are expected to match this contribution, and have consistently done so, in some cases exceeding the Government contribution. The budget for the Meetings, Conventions and Incentive Travel (MC&IT) Program is approximately $8 million, of which $4.2 million is core CTC support and over $4 million is industry partnerships. Two full-time staff support the Program in Ottawa; a further 12 in-market (on territory) MC&IT sales staff are dedicated to the US market, while in Europe, Asia and Latin America staff based in the CTC offices share their time also with the leisure market.

The MC&IT sector is one of the CTC's priority markets for several reasons:

- it provides an opportunity to attract a large number of visitors from a single organization;
- it uses a wide variety of facilities and services, and consequently gives a destination the opportunity to showcase the best it has to offer;
- the year-round nature of the business enables Canadian venues and hotels to maximize occupancy levels throughout the year;
- the size, scope and number of organizations choosing Canada for meetings have meant that Canadian destinations have been able to expand their convention centres as well as the number and quality of hotel rooms.

The objectives of the CTC's MC&IT Program are:

- to continue to build awareness of Canada as a destination for meetings and incentive travel buyers;
- to influence consideration of Canada as a destination by building a relationship with qualified prospects;
- to provide buyers with Canadian product information and the opportunity to move into the sales cycle;
- to stimulate interest in lower-demand destinations during peak periods and shift demand for 'hot' destinations in the shoulder seasons.

Target markets are:

- corporate, association and incentive meeting/event planners;
- incentive houses;
- third-party planners (i.e. agencies);
- sports associations;
- the MC&IT industry itself.

European geographical market segments to be developed over the next few years include UK associations and incentives, French and German incentives.

Marketing activities include the following.

- *Advertising*: to build awareness of Canada among meeting planners, the CTC and its partners use direct-response advertising campaigns in key US and European publications.
- *Direct mail/e-marketing*: customized direct marketing programmes using print and web-based media are designed to generate responses and requests for information on Canada's meeting destinations, and to build the CTC MC&IT and partner databases.
- *Key account development*: creation and enhancement of working relationships with key meeting planners by the CTC's sales force, and familiarization tours and site inspections under the 'Visit Canada Program'.
- *Trade shows and special events*: a Canadian presence at all major industry trade shows (such as ASAE, IT&ME, Affordable Meetings, MPI, PCMA and EIBTM) and hosting special marketplaces where Canadian suppliers are featured exclusively.
- *PR and media*: through activities linked to the CTC Leisure Marketing programmes, levering increased unpaid media exposure and public relations.

The CTC has sales staff located throughout the world with the aim of assisting meeting and incentive planners in bringing their event to Canada. The staff can provide advice and suggestions on everything from customs to procedures, from site selection to conference facilities, and to a wide variety of meeting and incentive services. If the organization meets the qualifying criteria, CTS sales staff can help to arrange familiarization tours to allow planners to experience Canada's destinations and facilities at first hand.

For further information, see the websites: www.canadatourism.com (industry site) and www.travelcanada.ca (consumer site).

Denmark – Danish Tourist Board

Tourism is Denmark's third largest industry. The annual turnover is 46.8 billion kroner (approx. 6 billion euros) and more than 70 000 Danes are employed in tourism. The majority of the tourists in Denmark come from Germany, Sweden, Norway or Denmark, and more than 60 per cent of the Danish Tourist Board's marketing resources are allocated to these markets. It is also in these countries that Danish companies themselves use most resources for direct marketing.

Meetings, incentives, conferences and exhibitions provide a central field of activity for the Danish Tourist Board. In seven markets, staff have been assigned to persuade as many companies and organizations as possible to choose Denmark when planning the next venue for their meetings, conferences, incentives and study tours. Among the tools used are promotional visits to prospects and the organization of tours of Denmark for decision-makers and convention organizers. Three staff work full-time on the conference and incentive market at the Danish Tourist Board's head office.

The Danish Tourist Board's market offices take part in all-important foreign travel exhibitions and fairs. They also arrange regular 'Denmark' workshops, enabling foreign travel operators to meet Danish suppliers to make deals on accommodation, transport, etc. or simply keep up their knowledge on what the Danish tourist industry can offer. As part of their participation in fairs and workshops, the local market offices keep in close contact with the major airlines and tour operators, and follow closely the legislation and economic conditions that can affect tourism.

Press trips, arranged by the foreign market offices in cooperation with regional Danish tourism development companies, are a large part of marketing Destination Denmark. More than 300 such trips are organized every year (leisure and business tourism), which generate media coverage worth more than 260 million Danish kroner (35 million euros). The Danish Tourist Board's local market office is responsible for maintaining strong media relations, and for handling the planning and logistics of the press trip, which is often led by a market office staff member.

In cooperation with research companies, The Danish Tourist Board's research department analyses markets, economics, tourist behaviour, etc. These analyses are the basis for marketing and campaign briefs in the various markets, and are available for purchase. All market offices keep close watch on market developments and the tactics of the competitors so that they are better able to react quickly as attitudes and market conditions change.

Contact details are:

- Danish Tourist Board, Conference & Incentive Travel Department, Danmakrs Turistrad, Vesterbrogade 6D, DK-1620 Copenhagen V, Denmark (tel.: +45 33–11–14–15; fax: +45–33–93–14–16; email: dt@dt.dk; website: www.visitdenmark.com).
- Danish Tourist Board, Conference & Incentive Travel Department, 55 Sloane Street, London SW1X 9SY, UK (tel.: +44 (0)20–7201–3977; fax: +44 (0)20–7259–5955; email: jc@dt.dk: website: www.visitdenmark.com).

Finland: Finland Convention Bureau

Finland Convention Bureau (FCB) is a non-profit marketing organization promoting Finland as a conference destination. The activities of the Bureau are financed and sponsored by the Ministry of Trade and Industry, 19 major congress towns in various parts of the country and about 80 companies representing the congress and travel industry (PCOs, conference centres, hotel chains, travel agencies, transport companies, etc.).

The Bureau began operating in 1974 and, at that time, it was one of the first convention bureaux to be set up in Europe. Until January 2002, the name of the Bureau was 'Helsinki–Finland Congress Bureau'. The Bureau has seven staff.

The FCB:

- provides meeting planners with complimentary information on conference facilities and services in Finland;
- assists organizers to find suitable venues, accommodation/housing and transport;
- helps in preparing bid documents;
- makes preliminary reservations;
- provides promotional material, such as videos, slides and brochures.

The activities of the Bureau also include compiling information on international congresses and conventions taking place in Finland, making studies and surveys, and preparing statistics. It also publishes *Meet in Finland* magazine three times a year.

The FCB works closely with international organizations of the meeting industry and is at the moment a member of EFCT, ICCA and UIA.

Contact details are: Finland Convention Bureau, Fabianinkatu 4 B 11, Fin-00130 Helsinki, Finland (tel.: +358 (0)9–668 9540, fax: +358 (0)9–6689 5410; email: info@finlandconventionbureau.fi; website: www.finlandconventionbureau.fi).

France – Maison de la France

Maison de la France began life as the 'Office Français du Tourisme' (French National Tourist Office) in 1925. The French National Tourist Office became a 'Groupement d'Intérêt Economique' (GIE) in 1987 and took the name of Maison de la France. Placed under the authority of the Ministry of Tourism, it represented a partnership between the State, the professionals in tourism, and the different sectors of the economy.

Maison de la France's mission is to promote the destination 'France' abroad for leisure tourism, conference and incentive travel, seminars, product launches and exhibitions. In 2000, France received 75 million foreign visitors generating tourism revenues of 215 billion francs.

As each market is special, Maison de la France helps its partners to promote their products and adapt them to each market. Appreciating that clients are becoming more and more demanding and the international competition is growing stronger, Maison de la France has a network of 31 offices in 26 countries on five continents.

Promotional activity includes:

- information to the public;
- press and PR;
- commercial promotions: leisure tourism (with tour operators and agencies), conference and incentive agencies, and corporates;
- publicity campaigns.

The Conference and Incentive Department of Maison de la France has three full-time staff at its head office in Paris; while its London office has three full-time staff and a trainee. There are also dedicated conference and incentive staff at the offices in the USA, Italy, Germany, Belgium and Spain. The London office deals with the whole of England and helps the 160 members of the French Convention Bureau (which is their Conference & Incentive Club).

Maison de la France organizes two large events:

- 'Evènement France', which takes place in a region of France and is open to all the French partners. Between 80 and 100 conference and incentive agencies are invited to participate for two and a half days (team building, workshop, site visits, etc.);

- 'Evènement Paris – Ile de France', to which 40–50 agencies are invited, and is for Paris and Ile de France partners only.

Maison de la France has a large presence at trade shows such as 'International Confex' and 'EIBTM'. After the latter show a delegation of conference agencies is invited to participate in a tour to the Rhône Alpes region (Divonne, Annecy, Megeve, Grenoble).

It produces a newsletter for the British market, with special offers and promotions, and one for the French market giving information on the British market, including updates on changes in conference and incentive agencies. Maison de la France maintains a very detailed agency database, which is updated every year for the use of its partners. It also carries out research surveys and produces studies on the key conference/ incentive sectors (automotive, pharmaceutical, IT and financial services).

The Conference and Incentive Department receives a budget from Maison de la France and from the French Convention Bureau.

Contact details are:

- Maison de la France, 20 Avenue de L'Opéra, cedex 1, Paris, France (tel.: +33 1–42–96–70–95; fax: +33 1–42–96–70–71; email: christina.aagesen@mdlfr.com; website: www.franceguide.fr).
- Maison de la France, 178 Piccadilly, London, W1L 9AL, UK (tel.: +44 (0)20–7399–3521; fax: +44 (0)20–7493–6594; email: rachel.sobel@mdlf.co.uk).

Germany: German Convention Bureau • • •

The German Convention Bureau (GCB) is the marketing, not-for-profit organization for the solicitation of international meetings for Germany's congress and convention industry. Founded in 1973, the GCB was established to provide impartial advice and suggestions to meeting planners concerning facilities, sites, accommodation, and programmes in Germany.

The GCB, based in Frankfurt with 11 staff and with an overseas office in New York, is a single umbrella organization representing the leading companies in the German meetings industry. Its 200 or so affiliate members include the principal congress cities, convention centres and hotels, professional conference/congress organizers (PCOs) and other convention service providers, Lufthansa German Airlines, German Railways and the German National Tourist Office.

The GCB arranges conference services in Germany for clients around the world. It also works in close cooperation with German representatives of international associations and organizations, and with meeting planners of associations, agencies and companies from abroad. Services include the preparation of tailor-made bids and proposals, free of charge, for all types of meetings and conferences, with details of suggested venues, PCOs, pre- and post-convention tours, menus and banquets, speakers and government department support. It has also negotiated discounted rates with its car rental affiliates for conference and exhibition visitors.

The GCB publishes complimentary information on Germany, which can be ordered via its Internet home page. The home page also provides a general survey of convention services and news from the meetings industry. The GCB also organizes 'Meetings Made in Germany', a trade show, which, from 2003, will be incorporated into 'IMEX', the new 'worldwide exhibition for incentive travel, meetings and events', to be held in Frankfurt.

Contact details are: German Convention Bureau, Münchener Strasse 48, D-60329 Frankfurt/Main, Germany (tel.: +49 69–2429300: fax: +49 69–24293026; email: info@gcb.de; website: www.gcb.de).

Hong Kong

Conference destination marketing for Hong Kong is undertaken by a specialist team within the Hong Kong Tourism Board (HKTB). The Board plays an impartial role in representing all tourism products and services, including conference venues, hotels, tour operators, PCOs/DMCs, and retailers.

HKTB's specialist convention and incentives team is head-quartered in Hong Kong, but also has three dedicated overseas teams based in Los Angeles, Sydney and London. The work of the teams is divided into two sections, one to cover incentive travel and corporate meetings, the other to research for association events and exhibitions. HKTB has a further 16 offices worldwide that can assist in the planning and promotion of events to be held in Hong Kong.

The specialist team offers impartial advice and practical assistance to conference organizers at every stage of planning their events, including:

1 production of bid documents;
2 identification of suitable venues and selection of accommodation;
3 coordination of inspections of conference facilities by decision makers;
4 sourcing reliable service suppliers such as airlines, PCOs and exhibition contractors;

5 suggestions for social, sightseeing or accompanying persons' programmes;
6 'Value Plus' – an added-value benefits package for all confirmed international association conventions and for exhibitions, which, depending on group size, can include welcome packs for delegates, a discount card, lion dance, or police band to open or close a convention;
7 ideas and contacts for gifts and convention materials suppliers;
8 promotions to delegates to maximize attendance, and participation in planning committees;
9 advising on customs and immigration procedures.

HKTB offers a wide range of promotional material, including 'Meeting Your Choice' video, 'Coming Conventions & Exhibitions' (details of confirmed events up to 2010), 'Venues' (a guide listing different types of venue with capacity details, etc.), 'Conventions and Exhibitions' leaflet (giving facts and figures of Hong Kong's selling points), CD-ROMs, presentation materials and shell posters.

Contact details are:

- Business Development Unit, Hong Kong Tourism Board, 9–11/F. Citicorp Centre, 18 Whitfield Road, North Point, Hong Kong (tel.: +852 2807–6543; fax: +852 2806–0303; website: www.DiscoverHongKong.com/eng/meetings).
- London office: Hong Kong Tourism Board, 6 Grafton Street, London W1S 4EQ, UK (tel.: +44 (0)207–533–7126; fax: +44 (0)207–533–7111; email: lonwwwo@hktourismboard.com).

Ireland ● ● ●

Tourism Ireland

Tourism marketing structures in Ireland have undergone major change, leading to the creation of 'Tourism Ireland' as a new organization marketing the island of Ireland overseas as a holiday destination in a new era.

Tourism Ireland was established under the framework of the Belfast Agreement of Good Friday 1998. As a company, its two goals are:

- to promote increased tourism to the island of Ireland;
- to support the industry in Northern Ireland to reach its potential.

Jointly funded by the two governments, South and North on a 2:1 ratio, Tourism Ireland has been fully operational since the beginning of 2002, when it launched an extensive programme to market the entire island overseas as a tourism destination.

In addition to the company's primary strategic destination marketing role, Tourism Ireland also undertakes regional/product marketing and promotional activities on behalf of Bord Failte (Irish Tourist Board) and the Northern Ireland Tourist Board through its 18 international market offices.

Product marketing includes conferences, meetings and incentive travel, necessitating close collaboration with the two existing bodies involved with MICE sector marketing, the Northern Ireland Conference Bureau and the Convention Bureau of Ireland, further details of which are given below.

Tourism Ireland may be contacted at:

- Tourism Ireland, 5th Floor, Bishop's Square, Redmond's Hill, Dublin 2, Ireland (tel.: +353 1 476 3400; fax: +353 1 476 3666; email: info@tourismireland.com).
- Tourism Ireland, Beresford House, Coleraine, BT52 1GE, Northern Ireland (tel.: +44 28 70 32 6632; fax: +44 28 70 32 6932; email: coleraine@tourismireland.tv).

Northern Ireland Conference Bureau

The Northern Ireland Conference Bureau (NICB) was established in February 1994. The Bureau is part of the Northern Ireland Tourist Board (NITB), the statutory organization responsible for encouraging and developing tourism in Northern Ireland. NITB, in turn, is responsible to the Department of Economic Development for Northern Ireland.

The NICB, as part of the national tourist board, is wholly funded by the Government, although the industry in Northern Ireland pays to participate in marketing activities, generating additional operating income. The Bureau has a small team, consisting of a Manager and administrative backup. With the establishment of Tourism Ireland, however, the Bureau has representation through 18 overseas market offices.

NICB's main role is to work with the conference and incentive industry in Northern Ireland to maximize the number of national and international conferences and incentive trips that can be attracted. In this regard, the Bureau works to coordinate a positive market awareness of Northern Ireland, through exhibitions, familiarization visits, PR, sales calls, workshops and direct marketing. In many cases, the Northern Ireland presence at international exhibitions is as part of a British Pavilion or an all-Ireland stand, with the choice being made as a result of buyers' perceptions of the destination. The Bureau has a marketing spend in excess of £100 000 per annum.

The Bureau continues to work with conference organizers and meeting and incentive planners once they have made a formal decision to meet in Northern Ireland, ensuring that they have the necessary information and contacts to run a successful event. The

Bureau advises organizers on the logistics of meeting in Northern Ireland and on the marketing of the destination to potential delegates.

Contact details are: Northern Ireland Conference Bureau, St Anne's Court, 59 North Street, Belfast BT1 1NB, Northern Ireland (tel.: +44 (0)28–90–315513; fax: +44 (0)28–90–315544; email: nicb@nitb.com ; website: www.northernirelandconference.com).

Convention Bureau of Ireland

The Convention Bureau of Ireland is a specialist unit in the Industry Marketing Services Department of Bord Failte. It focuses on the marketing of conferences and incentive travel in partnership with the trade in Ireland. A council made up of 18 industry representatives, and chaired by Bord Failte, oversees the marketing activities undertaken by Bord Failte and acts as an information exchange forum for trade specializing in these sectors.

The main marketing activities are:

- participation at overseas promotions such as IT&ME (Chicago) and EIBTM (Geneva), and coordinating Irish trade attendance;
- production of marketing material;
- organizing and supporting familiarization visits and site inspections by overseas incentive houses or conference organizers;
- supporting conference ambassadors in their efforts to secure conferences for Ireland (see below);
- development of new websites to assist organizers with their planning of conferences and meetings in Ireland. The sites contain an extensive database of available facilities.

Three-year strategic marketing plans are in place for the conference and incentive sectors with trade working groups for each to oversee implementation. A budget in excess of £1 million (Irish) (approximately 1.5 million euros) is allocated by Bord Failte to these product marketing campaigns.

Increased funding has enabled the 'Conference Ambassador' partnership to be revived. This programme is aimed at encouraging Irish members of international associations or employees of multinational companies to use their influence in attracting conferences and meetings to Ireland. It entails the following.

- A direct-mail piece to targeted top executives in Irish-based international companies and senior Irish executives in companies located in Britain and the USA. This mailing includes encouragement from the Minister for Tourism. Each mailing is followed by a telephone call and/or direct meeting.

- Presentations to leading Irish business associations to publicize the scheme, i.e. Chambers of Commerce, marketing associations, etc.
- Support to Conference Ambassadors includes help with organizing a national invitation and bid documents, support with site inspections, literature and promotional material, and garnering support from Government/State agencies where appropriate.

Contact details are: Convention Bureau of Ireland, Bord Failte, Baggot Street Bridge, Dublin 2, Ireland (tel.: +353 1–602–4322; fax: +353 1–602–4336; email: dmulligan@bordfailte.ie ; website: www.conference-ireland.ie).

In late 2002, plans were announced for Bord Failte to be merged with CERT, the Council for Education, Recruitment and Training in Tourism, to form a new National Tourism Development Authority which will be known as Failte Ireland. Its primary function will be issues concerning tourism development, environment, hotel and guesthouse registration, standards and training, but it will also be responsible for product and niche marketing (including business tourism), trade promotions, and domestic market tourism. The new Authority was expected to be in operation by April 2003.

Japan

Convention and incentive travel promotion is the responsibility of the Japan Convention Bureau (JCB), a specialist department of the Japan National Tourist Organisation (JNTO). The JCB was first established in 1965, as a joint initiative with local public entities and other interested parties, and was merged with JNTO the following year.

In 1994, the Japanese Diet (parliament) approved a special law called the 'International Convention Promotion Law'. JNTO has subsequently restructured its Japan Convention Bureau to establish a cooperative relationship with 42 government-designated 'International Convention Cities', which are keen to attract more international meetings and events.

The reorganized Japan Convention Bureau comprises two departments in JNTO's head office in Tokyo: International Marketing Department, and Promotion and Support Department, the latter being responsible for domestic marketing within Japan. Operating alongside these two departments are two overseas marketing offices, one in New York and the other in London. Each is staffed by three convention specialists. Additionally, a Convention Manager has been appointed from the directorial/managerial staff of JNTO's 14 overseas offices to create a worldwide marketing network to promote Japan as an international convention destination.

In 1995, Japan Congress and Convention Bureau (JCCB) was established with the aim of promoting Japan as a location for international conventions and developing the convention industries in Japan. JCCB is composed of convention cities, convention bureaux, convention-related industries, the Ministry of Transport and JNTO. JNTO provides the Secretariat office and JCB the staff for JCCB's operation. In 1996, three new destinations were added to the list of government-designated 'International Convention Cities', bringing the total number to 45. This list does not include Tokyo, even though Tokyo is one of Japan's leading international meeting destinations, partly because the city does not possess a convention bureau or specialist business tourism department but chiefly because the main aim of the Bureau's convention promotional activities is to achieve the decentralization of international meeting traffic.

Japan Convention Bureau is not a membership organization but its activities are partly funded by annual contributions from the 45 International Convention Cities. These are set contributions, at two levels, depending on the size of the cities concerned.

Marketing activities include market research and the publication of statistics, participation in convention industry trade shows, organizing sales missions to the USA and Europe, coordinating an annual study tour (familiarization visit), advertising, producing a detailed guide 'Convention Destination Japan', as well as newsletters and events calendars.

Contact details are:

- Japan Convention Bureau, 2–10–1, Yurakucho, Chiyoda-ku, Tokyo 100, Japan (tel.: +81 03–3216–2905; fax: +81 03–3216–1978; email: convention@jnto.go.jp ; website: www.jnto.go.jp).
- London office: Japan Convention Bureau, Heathcoat House, 20 Savile Row, London W1S 3PR, UK (tel.: +44 (0)207–439–3458; fax: +44 (0)207 734–4290; email: jcb@jnto.co.uk).

New Zealand

Following a restructuring in 2000, New Zealand Convention Association (NZCA) has as its members: Tourism New Zealand, nine convention bureaux and two international airlines. The wider conventions and incentives industry is represented on the Board of NZCA by four individual appointments: one each from the accommodation sector, major convention centres, destination management companies and professional conference organizers.

NZCA's Business Plan 2002–2006 states that its mission is 'to increase the economic value of convention and incentive business to industry stakeholders and the wider New Zealand economy'. This is to be achieved through nine key functions, described in the Plan as:

- to market New Zealand offshore, and in particular in Australia, as a convention and incentive (C&I) destination of choice;
- to develop, manage and enhance the value of New Zealand's C&I 'brands' and to brand New Zealand as a C&I destination;
- to ensure effective training and development of the C&I industry in order to deliver improving service delivery;
- to ensure core data, information and research is available to add value to industry stakeholders;
- to lead ongoing effective strategy development for the C&I industry;
- to be an effective advocate for the industry and on behalf of its key stakeholders;
- to address seasonal trends in the hotel and airline sectors with high yield visitors;
- to facilitate a cohesive approach to C&I development in conjunction with key stakeholders;
- to promote effective partnership between NZCA and convention bureau members to maximize benefits to the industry.

NZCA is funded through contributions from Tourism New Zealand, major airlines and regional convention bureaux. This funding base of 12 partners means that NZCA is reliant on the long-term commitment of its stakeholders.

NZCA fulfils a number of 'generic activities' (industry advocacy and media liaison, industry communication, Internet presence, brand management), 'base member activities' (industry training, research, meetings, domestic leads database, association/rest of the world marketing and sales support), and 'modular marketing activities' (Australian marketing and sales support, incentive marketing and sales support).

Contact details are: New Zealand Convention Association, PO Box 331 202, Takapuna, Auckland, New Zealand (tel.: +64 9–486–4128; fax: +64 9–486–4126; email: admin@nzconventions. co.nz ; website: www.conventionsnz.com).

Spain – Turespaña (Spain Tourism Board)

Turespaña is a central government-run body under the auspices of the Ministry of Economics. It does not, therefore, have a membership structure and its staff are mostly civil servants.

Meetings and Incentive Travel is one of the sectors or products on which Turespaña concentrates its resources (the others being Sun and Beach, Sports and Nature, and Cultural Tourism), although it has only had this involvement since 1995. Promotional activity is undertaken in conjunction with the 31 Spanish Tourist Offices overseas (20 in Europe, eight in America, one each in Japan, China and Singapore), which assist with the provision of local market research and intelligence. Each overseas office has a business travel specialist dedicated to Meetings and Incentive Travel.

Meetings and Incentive Travel sector promotional activities include organizing the participation of the Spanish public and private sectors in international exhibitions, organizing business workshops, and coordinating familiarization visits in partnership with local authorities, convention bureaux or regional governments. Publications include 'Spain Land of Congresses', a comprehensive guide giving full details of the main conference facilities and support services offered by individual cities. Turespaña has developed a major website offering full information on Spain and its tourism facilities: www.spain.info.

Contact details are: Turespaña, C/ José Lázaro Galdiano 6, 28036 Madrid, Spain (tel.: +34–91–343-35–00; fax: +34 91–343-34–46; email: info@tourspain.es).

United Kingdom

Within the UK, there are two national conference marketing organizations: the British Tourist Authority, operating primarily in overseas markets, and the British Association of Conference Destinations (see Chapter 8), operating principally in the domestic marketplace. Scotland, Wales and Northern Ireland also have their own national conference bureaux, subsumed within their National Tourist Boards, while the islands of Guernsey, Jersey and the Isle of Man also have independent conference marketing organizations. At the time of writing (September 2002), plans are well advanced to establish a new organization to market England as a tourism destination, although its specific responsibilities within the conference and business tourism sector remain to be defined.

British Tourist Authority

The British Tourist Authority (BTA), a government agency (or 'non-Departmental public body') responsible to the Department for Culture, Media and Sport, is the official, non-profit-making body charged with the promotion in overseas markets of Britain as a leisure and business tourism destination. It also has a general responsibility for advising the Government on tourism matters. In 2001–2002 BTA had a total operating budget of £63.4 million (£35.5 million of this being grant-in-aid from the Government, supplemented by support from industry partners to the value of

£15 million plus a further grant-in-aid from the Government to help combat the effects of the foot and mouth epidemic). It maintains a network of overseas offices in 27 markets.

Statistics from the Government's 'International Passenger Survey' show that, in 2001, for the first time, 'business tourism' overtook (by spend) 'holidays' as the primary purpose of visits to the UK, accounting for 33 per cent of the UK's tourism revenue. While a significant part of this is individual corporate travel (as defined in Chapter 1) and is non-discretionary, a growing proportion consists of group travel for conferences, exhibitions and incentives, the discretionary sector.

BTA has a dedicated Business Tourism Department at its headquarters in London, with a staff complement of seven: Head of Business Tourism, two Managers (with responsibility for specific sectors and the long haul and European markets) and four Marketing Executives. There are also a number of specialist Business Tourism personnel in key BTA overseas offices around the world. Overseas office staff report directly to their own office/regional managers, although of necessity there is close and regular collaboration with the Business Tourism Department in London.

The Business Tourism Department's activities include:

- encouraging international associations to hold their conferences in Britain;
- initiating or supporting research into the conference, incentive and exhibition sectors, and maintenance of appropriate databases;
- publishing promotional print and directories, as well as advisory materials (including market intelligence) and information for the British trade;
- coordination of workshops in Britain to which overseas buyers and decision-makers are invited providing an opportunity for one-to-one meetings with the UK business tourism trade;
- coordination of British participation in overseas missions, trade fairs, such as 'EIBTM' (Geneva) and 'IMEX' (Frankfurt), and presentations (participants include other UK national marketing organizations, namely Scottish Convention Bureau, Northern Ireland Conference Bureau and Wales Tourist Board Business Tourism Unit);
- coordinating press trips, familiarization trips and site inspections;
- ensuring maximum publicity for business tourism marketing opportunities offered by BTA's overseas offices;
- providing a business tourism destination PR service to targeted business tourism and professional media worldwide, both directly and through the BTA overseas offices;
- promoting and maintaining a specific business tourism website within the main BTA www.visitbritain.com site.

Contact details are: British Tourist Authority, Business Tourism Department, Thames Tower, Black's Road, London W6 9EL, UK (tel.: +44 (0)20–8563–3253; fax: +44 (0)20–8563–3257; email: businesstourism@bta.org.uk; website: www.visitbritain.com/businesstourism).

In November 2002 the UK Government announced plans for the British Tourist Authority to merge with the English Tourism Council to form a new body from April 2003. At the time of writing, the name of this new body was not known but it was anticipated that business tourism would figure prominently within its remit.

VisitScotland and Scottish Convention Bureau (SCB)

The remit of VisitScotland (the national tourist board for Scotland) is to attract leisure and business tourists to destinations in Scotland, to encourage the development of visitor facilities, and to coordinate tourism interests.

VisitScotland submits to Government (i.e. the Scottish Executive) an annual Business Plan, which details VisitScotland's targets and priorities. VisitScotland does substantial marketing of Scotland in the UK and overseas, and also works with the British Tourist Authority in overseas markets. In 2002–2003 VisitScotland's gross budget was £39 million, comprising £35 million grant-in-aid from the Scottish Executive and around £4 million income from other (mainly private sector) sources.

A New Strategy for Scottish Tourism, produced by the Scottish Executive in 2000, identified five priority areas for action: the need for effective use of IT, for better marketing, for higher standards of quality and service, for the development of the skills of those who work in the industry and a need to get the support structures right.

Scotland currently (2002) has 14 Area Tourist Boards covering the whole of Scotland. Working closely with Local Enterprise Companies, local authorities and VisitScotland/SCB, the Area Tourist Boards produce local area tourism strategies for their areas, which in many cases include convention and business tourism activities. In addition, some of the smaller Area Convention Bureaux do occasional joint sales activity, pooling resources to make spend more effective.

In 1991 VisitScotland established the Scottish Convention Bureau as its specialist business tourism division. Its aims are to promote Scotland as a prime destination for conferences, meetings and incentive travel, and to increase the economic benefit and development potential of this high-yield sector. Particular importance is placed on increasing value and economic benefit, and on geographical and seasonal spread.

A programme of targeted sales, marketing and research activities is undertaken in conjunction with local convention bureaux, Scotland's business tourism suppliers and the British Tourist Authority. This includes coordination of a Scotland stand at major trade exhibitions in the UK and overseas; inbound familiarization trips; organization of sales activity on territory (i.e. in overseas markets); website; production of appropriate print items; direct mail; e-marketing; and industry and business press/media work.

The Bureau also operates a business tourism enquiry service, passing specific enquiries on to local area convention bureaux and tourist boards, and coordinating their responses. The service handles around 2500 enquiries a year. The Bureau has nine staff (seven full-time, two job-sharers): Head of Sales and Marketing, Marketing Manager (job share), Sales Manager – Europe, Sales Manager – UK, Sales Manager – North America, Departmental Assistant, two Sales Coordinators, and a net budget in 2002–2003 of £1 010 000. In addition, SCB has two overseas agencies, in the USA and Germany, who act as sales agencies developing awareness of the Scottish product in these countries, undertaking sales calls and creating leads, and organizing sales activity. SCB also uses the services of a PR agency in the USA.

Contact details are: Scottish Convention Bureau, VisitScotland, 23 Ravelston Terrace, Edinburgh EH4 3T, UK (tel.: +44 (0)131–343–1608; fax: +44 (0)131–343–1844; email: conventionbureau@visitscotland.com; website: www.conventionscotland.com).

Wales Tourist Board Business Travel Unit

The Wales Tourist Board, which is responsible to the Assembly Government of Wales, set up a Business Travel Unit in the early 1990s with the aim of raising the profile of Wales as a destination for conferences, meetings, incentives and events.

The creation of the Business Travel Unit was the outcome of a research study, which revealed that business tourism was a seriously underexploited market segment in Wales. Two members of staff were appointed and an annual marketing budget of £200 000 allocated. The production of a Business Travel Planner followed by direct mail and insert campaigns led to the establishment of a Business Travel database. Over time the Business Travel Planner became two separate biennial publications: *Wales. Where the World Can Talk*, the conference and meetings planner (print run circa 18 000) and *Wales – The Incentive Destination* (print run 6000). The current database holds details on some 5000 buyers interested in holding events in Wales. The contacts are predominantly UK-based (85 per cent) with 15 per cent being overseas contacts.

The prime focus of marketing activity is centred on UK segments, largely due to resource constraints, although some work is done overseas in conjunction with the BTA, targeting the USA, Germany and France.

Marketing activities include:

- production of a conference planner and incentive guide;
- handling enquiries (250–500 per annum) and passing leads to local conference bureaux or to venues;
- maintenance of a database of around 5000 contacts;
- direct mailing of publications, newsletter and promotional offers to database plus rentable lists;
- a small amount of advertising in trade press and directories, both in the UK and USA;
- familiarization trips for buyers and press;
- attendance at some overseas trade exhibitions, workshops and sales missions with BTA and industry partners;
- management of two dedicated websites – www.meetings. visitwales.com and www.incentives.visitwales.com;
- liaison with a dedicated Marketing Agency and PR Agency in the UK;
- liaison with a US-based PR consultant.

In addition to the marketing activities listed, the Wales Tourist Board also supports the development of business tourism by:

- providing financial assistance to some of the local conference bureaux for joint marketing schemes;
- undertaking research into the business tourism sector and providing statistics;
- providing funding to upgrade hotels to business class standard.

In 2000, the Wales Tourist Board was called on by the National Assembly Government to investigate 'How Wales could achieve its Business Tourism Potential'. An independent study was conducted and reported back in June 2001 to a Steering Group comprising the WTB and 12 key Welsh industry suppliers.

The study recommended that the budget be increased to £500 000 per annum (currently guaranteed for three years), and that staffing levels be increased from two to five dedicated and full-time staff, headed up by a Director. The Business Travel Unit would become the Wales Convention Bureau, which would be a non-membership organization and would remain part of the Wales Tourist Board. The recommendations made in the study were accepted by the Steering Group. Currently (October 2002), the new entity is expected to be set up by April 2003.

Contact details are: Wales Tourist Board Business Travel Unit, Brunel House, 2 Fitzalan Road, Cardiff CF2 1UY, Wales (tel.: +44 (0)29–2049–9909; fax: +44 (0)29–2047–5321; email: business-tourism@tourism.wales.gov.uk; websites: www.meetings.visit wales.com and www.incentives.visitwales.com).

United States of America . . .

There is no national umbrella marketing organization in the USA responsible for promotion to the conference sector. Marketing activity is undertaken by individual cities/destinations, often working in partnership with their state tourism body. In other cases, the state tourism body will take the lead in promotions.

Conference venue marketing

It is very difficult for an individual conference venue to market itself effectively by operating on its own. Venues seeking to establish a market presence must contend with factors such as the scale of the competition (several thousand other venues in Britain alone), the substantial costs of marketing (both in human and financial resources) and the predisposition of buyers to buy location first.

It is for these reasons that most venues work in partnership with the destination in which they are located to generate awareness, and enquiries from potential clients. The venues build links with the appropriate destination marketing organization, be this a convention and visitor bureau or conference office, an area or regional tourist board, and/or a national tourism organization. Many venues are also members of marketing consortia (groupings of similar properties interested in the same types of clients), which give them a higher market profile and through which they engage in collaborative marketing activities. Consortia can also provide tangible business benefits, such as bulk purchasing discounts, networking, benchmarking and training. Belonging to a consortium can also give a venue credibility in the eyes of the buyer. Examples of major consortia operating in the conference industry include the following.

Hotel groups

Hotel groups, such as Hilton, Accor, Six Continents, Marriott, Starwood Hotels & Resorts, Moat House, Thistle, and Holiday Inn. These are not strictly consortia as they are groups of hotels under common ownership and management systems. Most, if not all, have central reservations and marketing departments, which undertake national and international marketing campaigns and which control the promotional activities of the individual properties to a greater or lesser degree. Even so, the majority of hotels within these chains are also allowed some discretion and budget to engage in their own marketing campaigns, for which the broad strategy and promotional materials are determined by head office. Over recent years, all of the large chains have developed their own branded conference product (see the next section in this chapter on the 'branding of hotel venues').

Best Western Hotels

Best Western Hotels is the world's largest global hotel brand, established for more than 50 years, with over 4000 independent hotels in membership worldwide. It is a non-profit making organization whose sole purpose is to enhance the success and profitability of its member hotels. It has reservations centres across the world with fully automated links to global distribution systems. Its recruitment brochure claims that 'Best Western brand markets to, and attracts, a bigger universe of customers than any single property on its own could ever hope to reach'. For the conference and meetings market, 'Best Western First Place' is the consortium's venue sourcing service with a national conference sales network. Best Western Hotels also offers joint marketing opportunities for its members, such as a presence at trade shows like EIBTM and International Confex. For more information, see the website: www.bestwestern.com.

Conference Centres of Excellence (CCE)

Conference Centres of Excellence is Britain's largest consortium of dedicated, specialist conference and training venues, with some 30 such venues in membership. It was formed in 1992, with objectives to:

- undertake joint marketing through pooling marketing resources;
- share PR activity designed to enhance the image of management centres in membership;
- investigate opportunities to market the Centres in mainland Europe;
- share information and expertise.

One of the main aims of CCE has been to promote and market the unique benefits of conference venues that offer first-class facilities and professional standards (making comparison with other venues that do not dedicate staff or facilities to the business conference, meeting or training sector). Members are required to meet certain minimum criteria, which include 'actively seeking to attract conference, meeting or training events as their main Monday to Friday source of business' and to 'embrace and maintain the *Hospitality Assured Meetings* accreditation'. Criteria are also laid down to cover the standard of conference rooms, bedrooms and other facilities provided. They are also expected to participate in the Consortium's booking referral system and to promote its Hotline 'One Call'. Would-be member venues are required to submit to inspection by the CCE's membership committee before being accepted into membership.

Whilst users of the CCE venues are guaranteed to receive excellent service in quality surroundings, the individual nature of the member properties offers contrasting atmospheres ranging from country houses in beautiful settings to purpose-built centres often attached to academia.

For further information, see the website: www.cceonline.co.uk (tel.: +44 (0)1306 886900).

Venuemasters

Venuemasters is the name of a consortium of academic venues in the UK, formed in 2001 following the merger of two former consortia, the British Universities Accommodation Consortium and Connect Venues. It now represents approximately 100 university and college venues throughout the UK. Marketing activities undertaken on behalf of its members include publication of a directory, organization of an annual exhibition and attendance at other trade shows, maintenance of a website and provision of a free venue-finding service. For further details, see the website: www.venuemasters.co.uk (tel.: +44 (0)114 249 3090).

Other examples of venue consortia include Historic Conference Centres of Europe (www.historic-centres.com) and Leading Hotels of the World (www.lhw.com).

For venues in the UK, there is a very useful guide to conference marketing published by the British Tourist Authority under the title of 'The Meetings & Conference Market – are you really in the business?'

The branding of hotel venues

In the early 1990s, Forte Hotels (now broken up and sold off among other hotel groups) pioneered a branded conference product when it launched 'Venue Guarantee' as a standard package available at conference hotels across the Forte Group. Since then most, if not all, the major hotel chains have introduced their own conference brand, examples being: 'Hilton Meetings' and 'Hilton Conventions' (Hilton), 'Meeting Edge' (Marriott), 'Conference Network' (Holiday Inn), and 'Rendezvous@Novotel' (Accor).

There are certain variations in each branded product, with some laying emphasis on high-specification, purpose-designed conference and meeting rooms, whereas others place the focus on bookability and the level of service. Overall, however, there is more common ground than distinctive features in these products, which are usually accompanied by a money-back guarantee if a hotel fails to deliver on any aspect of its quality-assured service. An example of such a guarantee is the Moat House Hotels' 'Seal of Assurance' shown in Figure 4.2.

SEAL OF ASSURANCE CONFERENCE GUARANTEE

"The Moat House Seal of Assurance" is your guarantee of satisfaction. It governs our enquiry, pricing, booking procedures and standards of service: everything from the provision of meals and facilities to the efficient administration of your account. Should we fail to deliver any service covered by our Seal of Assurance, we will delete the relevant charges from your bill.

Your Enquiry

1   Your enquiry, right from the start, will be looked after by professional dedicated Conference Managers.
2   Within two working days of contacting the hotel, you will receive a brochure, price details and proposal letter (where appropriate).
3   Our terms and conditions of business will always be included with our brochure and proposal letter.
4   You will always receive an invitation to visit the hotel, to view the facilities and discuss your requirements, at the first point of your enquiry.
5   We will always suggest conference rooms and package prices which are genuinely suitable for your particular event.

Pricing

1   You will not find any hidden extras. All prices - for packages and additional services - will be clearly presented, in plain English so they can be clearly understood.

Your Booking

1   We will confirm the full details of your booking, in letter or contract form, within three working days of a verbal booking being made.
2   At least three working days before your conference, we will contact you and check final details, changes and any amendments you may wish to make.
3   We will not depart from your confirmed details and timings unless this is agreed with you in advance.
4   Your billing arrangements and account details will be agreed when you confirm your booking. We will only make changes, or supplementary charges, on receipt of signed authorisation from your nominated signatories.

The Service

1   A senior member of our staff will look after the smooth running of your event every day. They will meet you when you arrive and check with you that all details and timings are as you want.
2   Your meals and refreshments will be served promptly at the times you have requested.
3   Your main conference room and syndicate rooms will be serviced and refreshed during all meal breaks.
4   Telephone messages and faxes will be given immediate attention and delivered promptly to your chosen system.
5   We will provide clear instructions on fire and safety procedures before your conference starts. If there are any planned fire drills or alarm tests during the conference, we will tell you about these in advance.

The Facilities

1   Your conference rooms will be correctly set up, in line with your specified requirements, at the agreed time before your conference is due to start. If you need to change anything at the last minute, we will do everything possible to do this for you.
2   Audio visual equipment will be fully tested and in good working order. If you would like, we will provide a demonstration of how the equipment works before your conference starts.
3   We will ensure that all heating, lighting and air conditioning/comfort cooling (where available) is working properly for you. We will also explain any controls to you before your conference starts.
4   The name of the event or your company, will be clearly displayed on the hotel's notice board, showing which conference rooms you will be in, unless of course, you prefer total privacy and have requested otherwise.

The Bill

1   Your bill will be sent out no later than five working days after the conference is over. It will clearly reflect your written quotation plus any extra charges which you have authorised.
2   Extra charges will be clearly itemised and will only be charged if you, or your nominated signatories, approved them.
3   If you have any queries, we will address these for you within five working days.

Your Money Back Guarantee - "The Moat House Seal of Assurance"

1   If we fail to deliver any service covered by this conference guarantee, we will remove the charges relating to those elements of your bill.

MOAT
HOUSE
HOTELS

Figure 4.2 The Moat House Hotels' seal of assurance.

The objective behind branding is to convey to the client that he can expect ethical practices, and quality service and facilities at the same high standards, no matter whether the hotel is in Belfast or Bombay, Jakarta or Buenos Aires. It is to reassure customers that, having staged a successful conference at one hotel within the group, they can expect a similar outcome by using other hotels in the group. Branding is about building customer loyalty and increasing business retention because customers will have the confidence to keep their conferences and meetings within that particular group. Their own success is assured by the branded service and product that those hotels guarantee.

This approach has many strengths and, as all major chains have adopted branding, it seems to justify in financial returns the substantial investments required in venue and staff development. For customers, it also has many attractions, yet it has one drawback: the very sameness of product can serve as a disincentive to its use. Conference organizers are constantly looking for somewhere new, somewhere a little different to make their event live long in the memory of their delegates. If delegates find that their surroundings and the type of service received are more or less identical at each conference, regardless of where it is being held, delegate perceptions of the event may not always be as favourable as the organizer would have wished.

In the author's experience, it is always important for an organizer to inspect a conference venue before booking because it is the quality of staff and their service standards that is always one of the most decisive factors in venue selection and reselection. No matter how strong the branding, and how good the staff training, the cloning of conference sales managers and banqueting coordinators has not yet been achieved (fortunately!). Individual personality and friendliness are often the crucial unique selling propositions (USPs), and these must be experienced at first hand.

Overseas marketing

The promotion of destinations to overseas markets is a huge subject that cannot be covered adequately in this book. The international marketplace is fiercely competitive and those organizations wishing to give themselves a realistic chance of success must take a long-term perspective, develop collaborative partnerships with other organizations (airlines, national tourist boards and other marketing consortia), identify substantial financial and human resources, and follow through a detailed marketing plan similar to that outlined earlier in this chapter.

Friel (1997) notes that:

> It is instructive to observe that the former Soviet states of Eastern Europe chose tourism as the engine of

economic recovery but the focus of their market positioning was not Russia but Moscow and St Petersburg; not
the Czech Republic but Prague; not Hungary but
Budapest.

He contends that it will be the city or 'urban region' that will be
the future unit of analysis and the vehicle through which
overseas markets will continue to be approached.

Bids to stage international association conventions are presented by cities, though positioned within a national framework.
Edinburgh, for example, is positioned within the context of
Scotland, and Helsinki is marketed under the umbrella of
Finland. It is not a viable option for individual venues to market
themselves overseas in isolation. It is even more important than
in the domestic marketplace for venues, which are looking to
attract overseas business, to work in partnership with their
destination or to be marketed as part of an international chain or
consortium.

No active steps into overseas markets should be taken without
widespread consultation with experienced practitioners, and the
preparation of a detailed and costed marketing plan.

Summary

- The importance of location in decisions over the selection of
  conference venues has led to the creation of destination
  marketing organizations, whose role is to promote the venues,
  facilities and attractions of a given area in order to generate
  increased conference business.
- A focus on the needs of customers should drive all marketing
  activity, which has to be planned through the specific application of marketing principles and strategy to the conference and
  business tourism sector.
- Destination marketing is undertaken by convention bureaux
  and conference offices/desks, which involve the public and
  private sectors in collaborative partnerships. The structures,
  funding and activities of such organizations vary from destination to destination, although two basic models are apparent.
- The activities of city or local area convention bureaux
  are complemented in many countries by national tourism
  organizations.
- Some conference venues join marketing consortia, which
  comprise venues with similar characteristics, in order to
  develop a stronger profile in the marketplace.
- Many hotel chains have invested substantial resources in the
  development of a branded conference product as a means of
  reassuring and retaining their customers.

Review and discussion questions

1 Undertake a 'SWOT' analysis of two conference destinations, summarizing the strengths, weaknesses, opportunities and threats for each. Use the analysis to propose the most suitable target markets for both destinations.

2 Research the work of two convention and visitor bureaux. Compare and contrast their structures, funding, and marketing activities, commenting on the strengths and weaknesses of each.

3 Compose a marketing plan for a modern, four-star conference hotel in your capital city. The hotel has six conference rooms, the largest seating up to 200 delegates, and two other rooms seating up to 100 each. It has 160 bedrooms and well-equipped leisure facilities. The hotel is privately owned. Three staff are involved in sales and marketing activities, and have a marketing budget of £10 000 (15 000 euros, US$15 000).

4 Undertake an in-depth appraisal of a venue marketing consortium. The appraisal should, ideally, include comments from venue members of the consortium on the value and benefits of membership.

5 Compare the branded conference products offered by two of the large hotel chains, noting both differences and similarities. To which kinds of conference organizers might these products appeal, and why?

Notes and references

Cooper, Chris; Fletcher, John; Gilbert, David and Wanhill, Stephen. *Tourism Principles and Practice*. Longman (1993).

De Chernatony, Leslie and McDonald, Malcolm. *Creating Powerful Brands*. Butterworth-Heinemann (second edition, 1998).

Doyle, P. Building successful brands: the strategic options. *Journal of Marketing Management* Vol. 5, no. 1 (1989).

Friel, Eddie. *Compete & Conquer*. A presentation to the BACD annual convention (1997).

Gartrell, Richard B. *Destination Marketing for Convention and Visitor Bureaus*. Published under the auspices of the International Association of Convention and Visitor Bureaus by Kendall/Hunt Publishing Company (second edition, 1994).

Gartrell, Richard B. Strategic partnerships for convention planning: the role of convention and visitor bureaus in convention management. *International Journal of Hospitality Management*, Vol. 10, no. 2 (1991).

Hankinson, G. *Journal of Brand Management* Vol. 9, no. 2 (November 2001).

Interbrand. *Brands – An International Review*. Mercury Books (1990).

Morgan, Roger; Pritchard, Annette; Pride, Roger. *Destination Branding*. Butterworth-Heinemann (2002).

Further reading

Guidelines and Suggestions for Destinations or Venues New to International Marketing in Business Tourism. Free factsheet published by the British Tourist Authority (2002).

Conference management – an organizer's perspective

The conference industry is based upon events of different kinds (including conventions, meetings, seminars, product launches and management retreats) and of different sizes and durations, requiring sophisticated planning and administration to ensure their success. Events are organized by people with varying degrees of knowledge and experience, many finding themselves responsible for organizing conferences without much, if any, formal training. This chapter provides a framework for those who take up the challenge, and summarizes the main processes involved in planning and staging an event. In particular it looks at:

- a general introduction to conference organizing;
- pre-conference planning and research;
- budgeting and financial management;
- sourcing and selecting a venue;
- negotiating with venues;
- programme planning;
- event marketing;
- conference management and production;
- event evaluation.

A general introduction to conference organizing

The organization of a conference requires a similar strategic approach to that needed for planning and managing most other events. Clear objectives should be set from the beginning, a budget has to be established, a venue must be sourced and delegates' accommodation and travel arrangements made, a programme has to be prepared and the conference managed for its duration. (Increasingly, health and safety, security, venue contracts and service guarantees are among a number of other aspects needing serious consideration, but there is not space to cover these adequately here.) Then, after the conference is over, final administrative details have to be completed and some evaluation of the conference should take place. While there are different factors to take into account when organizing a conference for 500 delegates rather than one for 50, the essential components are the same.

Similar steps are required for the organization of other events, such as sporting events, concerts, celebrations and rallies, whether these are of national or international significance like the football World Cup Finals or the Olympic Games, or of more localized importance, such as an antiques fair or agricultural show.

Organizing conferences is a high-pressure activity, not recommended for those of a nervous disposition. Yet, well handled, it can be tremendously exhilarating and rewarding. It goes without saying that excellent organizational skills are a must, as are attention to detail and a willingness to work long and often irregular hours, especially in the immediate build-up period and during the event itself.

Conferences need to be planned with the precision of a military operation. Indeed, it is not surprising that a number of those now working successfully as conference organizers have come from a military background. Cotterell (1994) suggests that:

> A conference for 200 people for two or three days is likely to take up to 250 hours or around six normal working weeks, even without counting the two or three 18-hour days which will be needed just prior to the event.

But, in addition to hard work and attention to detail, conferences need a creativity and flair to be brought to them that will make them memorable occasions. They should live long in the memories of delegates, not only because of the benefits accruing from what has been shared and learned during the formal programme, but also for the opportunities they provide for informal networking and doing business, as well as socializing.

In some cases, companies and organizations will already have systems in place when the event is, for example, an annual event that runs along similar lines year after year. In other cases, it will be an entirely new event for which no previous organizational history or tradition exists. As shown below, both scenarios have their advantages and disadvantages.

- The regularly-held conference may operate smoothly with just some fine tuning and updating to established systems and procedures. It might, however, be failing to achieve its real potential as a conference, having become staid and predictable, and it may be that a completely fresh approach would be beneficial. The challenge for a new organizer would be to revolutionize the organization of the conference without alienating too many of the staff or members (if it is a membership organization) associated with the previous systems.
- Where there is no previous event history, an organizer has the benefit of beginning with a clean sheet of paper. There are no set ways of doing things, no established contacts, no 'venues that we always use'. There is a freedom to bring something of his own identity to the event, to build up his own network of information and suppliers, and to ensure that the event management systems are put in place to his own design. But such freedom brings with it a responsibility that can appear daunting if the organizer has been thrust into the role of running a conference with minimal training and experience. This, regrettably, is still the position in which far too many conference organizers find themselves.

This chapter attempts, therefore, to sketch out a framework for the successful organizing of conferences. A number of books have been written already on this subject, and the chapter will make reference to some of these in summarizing the principles and steps needed to ensure that a conference is run effectively.

Pre-conference planning and research

The initial phase, of planning and research, is the one which lays the foundations for success. It is a crucial part of any event, and mistakes or oversights made at this stage can be difficult to remedy later on. It needs, therefore, to be approached thoroughly and systematically.

It is also important to establish, at the outset:

> the degree of autonomy that you, as the planner, are being given. Crucially, what degree of control do you have over the budget? A word of advice: Think strategically and claim as much authority as you think you can

get away with. A conference organizer who has to check back to a superior (or, worse still, a committee) on the times of tea or the biscuit selection is doomed to preside over chaos and remain forever a bean counter (Carey, 2000).

The initial planning phase is the time when the broad objectives for the conference must be set. These will vary from event to event. For example, the main objective for a meeting with a company's sales force may be to present new products, introduce a new incentive scheme, update them on sales performance and motivate them to reach higher targets, or inform them about a restructuring of sales territories. The annual conference of American rose-growing societies (non-existent, as far as is known!) may have as its main aim to exchange information on new varieties of roses or to demonstrate the effectiveness of the latest pesticides, as well as maximizing attendance and generating a profit. Fisher (1998) quotes the example of objectives set for a real FMCG (Fast Moving Consumer Goods) conference:

- to debate future strategy;
- to encourage delegates to get to know each other on a first-name basis;
- to agree the general direction of the Group;
- to have an enjoyable, memorable experience.

Objectives should be clear and measurable: for example, an objective for a sales conference which is simply 'to launch new product X' is hardly measurable, whereas 'to communicate the positioning, target audience, features, benefits and price structure of the new product X to all customer-facing staff' would be. However, it is also important not to have too many objectives, as this can lead to confusion on the part of delegates and speakers.

These broad objectives will need to be supplemented with detailed answers to questions about the 'who, what, when, where, why and how' (Maitland, 1996) of the conference.

Who?

Pre-event planning needs to consider who the delegates will be, how many should be invited, and how many are expected to attend (essential for budgeting purposes). Is it appropriate for delegates' partners to be invited? Are there likely to be any special guests, including media representatives? Will there be any overseas delegates and, if so, is there a need to provide interpretation and translation facilities?

It also refers to the speakers who may be involved, either for presentations to plenary sessions or as leaders for workshops or 'breakout' sessions. Are there outside speakers to be invited, and will they require a fee as well as travel expenses?

'Who?' should also include the organizing team, which may be just one person or a dedicated group of people, some of whom could include intermediary agencies as described in Chapter 2. When there is a team involved, not all of them will necessarily participate from the initial planning stage right through to post-event evaluation, but their degree of involvement is something that will need to be thought through early on. The more complex the event and the numbers involved in organizing it, the more the need for some form of critical path analysis, mapping out the sequence of events in a logical order and within a realistic time-frame.

This is also the time to consider whether the conference should be organized in-house (using an organization's own staff resources and expertise) or outsourced to a professional conference (or congress) organizer (PCO). A PCO can undertake all aspects of the management of an event (see Chapter 2 for a list of typical PCO services) or simply be contracted to manage certain elements. If the decision is taken to outsource to a PCO, it is normal to prepare an 'invitation to tender' document, which will need to include as much information as can be provided to enable those PCOs contacted to draw up a detailed and costed proposal for running the event. The 'invitation to tender' will cover the types of information shown later in this chapter under 'Sourcing and selecting a venue' (see pages 153 ff.), but should also describe:

- the target audience and how to reach them;
- the likely final attendance numbers;
- how speakers are identified (i.e. whether by invitation or through the submission of papers), and the number of speakers and/or abstracts (i.e. summaries of specialist research or current work projects with which they are involved);
- the number of foreign languages for print materials and sessions;
- the level and nature of sponsorship required;
- whether there is to be an exhibition running alongside the conference;
- the spending power of the participants;
- the past history of the event;
- an indication of how many PCO companies have been invited to tender.

Some of the above headings relate particularly to national and international association and scientific conventions, rather than to corporate sector conferences.

If it is decided to outsource the event to a PCO, care needs to be taken in the selection of the PCO. It is still the case in many countries that anyone can start operating as a PCO without the necessity of formal training, qualifications or previous experience (a further aspect of the immaturity of the industry referred to in Chapter 1). Choosing a PCO who is inexperienced or inefficient can obviously have disastrous consequences for the client, for the delegates and for the venue, whose reputation may be tarnished through no fault of its own. It is advisable to short-list for consideration only those PCOs who are members of their professional association and who have had to prove their capabilities in the process (and/or who can provide strong testimonials from other satisfied clients). Professional bodies, such as IAPCO and ABPCO (see Chapter 8), can give assurances for the professionalism of their members. Case study 5.1 gives an insight into how one British PCO approaches his work, and what he is aiming to achieve for his clients and for his own business.

What?

What kind of conference is being organized? Is it a corporate or association event? Is it a management retreat, training course or incentive event? A conference to update delegates on new developments in a scientific or medical field? A launch to dealers and trade media, or some other kind of event? Will delegates be listening and passive, or is there a high degree of participation, perhaps involving team-building or outdoor activities?

What kind of message is the conference designed to convey? The organizer may have little or no control over this, as it may be something determined by senior managers or an organization's 'conference committee', but it is imperative that he understands this clearly.

When?

Timing is another major consideration. All too often inadequate time is allowed to plan and prepare for a conference. The conference organizer may simply be given the conference dates and asked to ensure that it happens. He may have made little input to the decision, even though his perspective is vital. The corporate sector, in particular, is notorious for allowing insufficient 'lead time'. Perhaps this is a reflection on the work that still needs to be done to raise the status of conference and event organizers to one which is on a par with an organization's senior management team. In the final analysis, it is a company's reputation, not simply that of the conference organizer, which is in jeopardy if an event is poorly run.

Some flexibility on dates can also be helpful in securing the best possible rates from the chosen venue. The venue may be able to offer more favourable rates if the dates selected assist in its maximization of yield (see Chapter 6).

Timing also needs to take into consideration the likely diary commitments of delegates. Are there any other events happening at the same time, or around that time, which might have an impact on delegate numbers? Is the conference occurring in a busy work period, or during holidays, or in winter months and, if so, what impact might any of these factors have?

Where?

Location needs to be determined at an early stage, whether this is expressed in rather broad terms, such as a state/county or region of the country, or quite specifically, such as New York, Nottingham, or 'within a 20-mile radius of Paris'. When deciding the ideal location, easy access to a motorway may be desirable (unless the event requires a venue off the beaten track). If many delegates are to use the train, location near a main-line station will be necessary, unless comprehensive local transport arrangements can be provided.

When events have an international dimension, with delegates arriving by plane, it is usually important to select a venue within reasonable travelling time of an international airport (often stipulated as 'no more than one or two hours' travel' from the gateway airport). Many hours sitting in a long-haul jet followed by several hours in transit around the country where the conference is to be held is not a recipe for a successful start to what will doubtless be a prestige event.

Does the location need to be a particular kind of venue to accommodate the event? Is there scope to explore an unusual venue, possibly to link in with the theme of the conference?

The choice of location may be taken out of the organizer's hands. He may be told to hold the event in a particular destination or the conference may rotate around specific destinations/venues in a regular sequence. The organizer's role may simply be to draw up a short list of potential venues from which other people will make the final selection.

Why?

Maitland (1996) suggests that:

> The 'Why?' is almost certainly the most crucial question that needs to be asked at this stage. Don't ignore or underestimate it. You must be able to answer it well if you are going to proceed with your plans. Is 'because we always do it at this time of year' a good enough reason? It could be a huge waste of time and money if it is held for this reason alone. Are you staging it because it is the quickest and easiest way of putting across your important message to many people in a friendly and personal manner? That's a better motive. Consider carefully if a

conference is really necessary. Are there less time-consuming and costly ways to achieve the same goals – perhaps a sales report, a promotional brochure or a press release?

How?

The format and duration of a conference are also very important factors, which will have an effect on some of the preceding considerations. Events requiring lots of syndicate rooms, as well as a main auditorium, plus exhibition space and catering areas will have a much more restricted range of options than events needing just one room with theatre-style seating for 75 people. Duration will also impact on venue availability, rates charged, accommodation requirements and other factors. It may be appropriate to use videoconferencing technology or satellite conferencing, or to examine the benefits of webcasting (i.e. enabling delegates to attend 'virtually' via their computer screens as conference sessions are broadcast via the Internet) to increase attendance levels.

'How?' should also take into account the way in which an event fits into a company's overall marketing or training programme. Where a membership organization is involved, such as a professional association or a trade union, how does a conference contribute to its communication links with members, and facilitate links between the members themselves? Are there ways in which these could be improved?

Fisher (1998) provides many useful tips on other practical aspects of managing an event, which there is not space to cover in this book. He describes the invitation process, the reception of delegates, travel and logistical arrangements, making the best use of refreshment and lunch breaks, handling overnight accommodation, the correct treatment of VIPs, the effective management of conference catering (traditionally the most common cause of problems and of delegate dissatisfaction) and organizing a conference overseas.

A conference organizer must also undertake a risk assessment for his event and develop contingency plans for dealing with crises that might occur. Swarbrooke and Horner (2001) give examples of some of the commonest problems:

- keynote speakers who are unable to attend because of illness or travel problems;
- participants being seriously delayed or unable to attend at all due to transport difficulties or bad weather;
- overbooked hotels;
- fire alarms and bomb threats;
- failures of audiovisual equipment.

They contend, correctly, that:

> all these risks are foreseeable and the organizer should have in place contingency plans to implement if they arise – what we might term the 'what if' approach. This may involve having an alternative schedule in reserve, or a suitable additional set of audiovisual equipment available. It is important that everyone on the team knows about these contingency plans.

Risk assessment will also lead to taking out appropriate insurance cover for the event, and there are today a number of specialist event insurance providers operating at a global level.

Budgeting and financial management

Assembling a budget is crucial to the success of any event. Anticipated costs impose parameters or a framework when putting the budget together and these, combined with an organizer's previous experience and detailed quotes from potential suppliers, provide the building blocks on which the budget is constructed. Whether the conference is being organized for a corporate organization or for one in the 'not-for-profit' sector, financial management is equally important. There are, however, some key differences as follows:

- Within the corporate sector, the budget is set by the company. Budgets may be allocated per event or as an annual total budget that needs to be used effectively to finance a number of events. The budget is required to cover delegate expenses as well as the other costs associated with planning, promoting and staging the event.
- Within the not-for-profit sector (and with entrepreneurial conferences – see Chapter 2), conferences have to be income-generating with delegate fees being charged to defray costs. The events are designed to cover their own costs and perhaps make a profit, which, in some cases, is used as a start-up fund to pay for the initial promotion and planning of the next event.
- Within the government and public sectors, either of the above approaches may apply.

Even so, the same principles hold good for all types of organization: budgets must be drawn up to show projected income and expenditure, systems need to be in place to manage income and expenditure flows and, at the conclusion of the event, a balance sheet should be prepared to show actual income against expenditure. This balance sheet then forms the basis for planning the next event, particularly if it is one in a sequence of conferences taking place on a regular basis.

Income streams will vary according to the nature of the organization and the event. With corporate events, the income source will be the company itself, but there may also be scope for attracting sponsorship for certain elements. With associations and other organizations in the not-for-profit sector, income will come primarily from delegate fees, although there may also be substantial opportunities to offset the costs of the conference through sponsorship and by running an associated exhibition. Trade union, political party and medical conferences and conventions, for example, often have concurrent exhibitions, which attract exhibitors wishing to promote their products to delegates. Opportunities also exist to attract sponsorship, as typified by pharmaceutical companies sponsoring aspects of medical conferences.

Many destinations are prepared to host a civic reception or banquet for delegates, as a form of welcome and expression of gratitude that the event is being held in their town or city. Some convention and visitor bureaux (CVBs) offer interest-free loans, particularly for events with a lead time of several years: the event organizer may incur expenses, especially promotional costs, well before any income is received from delegate fees. Loans are designed to assist with cash flow but will have to be repaid once the event is over (and, if the conference has made a profit, the CVB may require a share of the profits).

Expenditure projections have to cover a whole host of items, but the main ones are usually:

- venue hire;
- catering costs;
- accommodation costs – delegates, partners, speakers/invited guests and organizers;
- speakers' expenses – travel costs, fees, subsistence and possibly presentation materials;
- delegate materials – written materials, CDs, badges and possibly gifts;
- social and partner programme costs – entertainment, transport, other venue hire, and food and beverage;
- conference production costs – audiovisual equipment and technical staff to stage-manage the event plus, when appropriate, set construction;
- promotional costs – leaflets and publicity material, press releases, possibly advertising and/or direct mail, and e-marketing;
- on-site staff (organizer) costs plus, in some cases, freelance event staff;
- miscellaneous costs – event insurance, security, couriers, interpreters, and many others, and taxes (both local taxes and tax on profits).

	Month			Month			Month		
	Estimated	Actual	Variance	Estimated	Actual	Variance	Estimated	Actual	Variance
A. Income									
Sponsors									
Delegates/partners									
Other									
Total income (A)									
B. Expenditure									
Venue									
Accommodation/									
Housing									
Speakers/partners									
Delegates/partners									
Publicity									
Outside assistance									
(e.g PCO/DMC)									
Rehearsals &									
production costs									
The programme									
Social programme									
Activities									
Other, incl. taxes									
and contingency									
Total expenditure (B)									
Net cashflow (A-B)									
Opening balance									
Closing balance									

Source: Maitland, I. (1996) (with some author's additions).

Table 5.1
Cash flow forecast form

Maitland provides a cash flow forecast form (see Table 5.1), which can be computerized (spreadsheet software handles this very easily) or in paper format. This is a recognized way of keeping an overview of what is happening with the finances for an event, and helps to flag up any potential problem areas at an early stage.

It is now also possible to download, from websites, workbooks and spreadsheets for tracking expenditure across a number of meetings/events. One such website is located at www.plansoft .com, and spreadsheets can be accessed and downloaded free of charge.

	Fixed costs	Likely percentage
1.	Production, staging and outside speakers	
2.	Invitation process, marketing, design	
3.	Conference rooms	
4.	Agency fees, initial recce	
5.	Signage	
6.	Security, car parking set-up	35%
7.	Cabaret, entertainment	
8.	Registration costs	
9.	Conference office costs, telephones, faxes	
10.	Wet weather back-up, if applicable	
	(Item 1 could be as much as 25% of total costs)	

	Variable costs (per delegate)	Likely percentage
1.	Meals, breaks	
2.	Drinks at meals, breaks	
3.	Accommodation (housing)	
4.	Travel	
5.	Delegate print	
6.	Table/room gifts	50%
7.	Porterage, car parking per delegate	
8.	Partner programme	
9.	Late bar drinks	
10.	Insurances, VAT (value added tax)	

	Contingency	Likely percentage
1.	10% to cover all contingencies for direct costs	15%
2.	Allowance for currency movements (if abroad)	
	Total budget	**100%**

Table 5.2
Budget allocations for a typical corporate conference

Fisher suggests an allocation of budget for a typical corporate conference, drawing a distinction between fixed costs and variable costs,which is reproduced in Table 5.2.

Case study 5.2 provides an example of a planning budget for an international medical association conference.

Sourcing and selecting a venue

There are many sources of information and advice to assist with choosing the venue most suited to a particular event. These include directories and brochures, websites and CD-ROMs/DVDs, trade exhibitions, trade press, and specialist agencies.

Directories and brochures

There are a number of annual directories available that provide a very useful reference source, some of which are international in their coverage, others national, and updated annually. Examples of international directories include:

- *Venue – The Worldwide Guide to Conference and Incentive Travel Facilities*, published by Haymarket Business Publications;
- *Worldwide Convention Centres Directory*, published by CAT Publications;
- *Official Meeting Facilities Guide*, published by Reed Travel Group;
- *Recommended Business Meeting Venues Guide*, as well as a series of Recommended Hotel Guides covering over 1200 privately owned and independently run hotels throughout the world – published by Johansens.

Most, if not all, international trade associations (see Chapter 8) produce member directories (also accessible in electronic format via their websites) detailing their memberships and the services available through the trade association, which may include a venue finding and enquiry referral service. From a client (i.e. meeting planner) perspective, membership of a trade association by a venue or convention bureau can give a greater assurance of accredited standards and quality service.

At a national level, directories or brochures are produced by trade associations (BACD's *British Conference Destinations Directory* has a well-established track record as a valuable reference guide), by national convention bureaux and tourist boards, by hotel chains, and by venue consortia of the kind listed in Chapter 4.

All venues produce some form of promotional brochure and conference organizers should keep up-to-date copies of such information for those venues they use on a regular basis. However, because of the number of available venues (between

4000 and 5000 in the British Isles alone), it would require a huge filing system to maintain a comprehensive set of brochures, many of which are designed in different shapes and sizes. It would also be a full-time occupation to keep these up-to-date.

A better use of limited filing and storage space would be to obtain a set of *destination guides*, produced by all conference destinations (CVBs) and mostly updated annually or biennially. These tend to be produced in A4/quarto format, and describe all of the venues in a destination as well as summarizing attractions, communications, support services and other features.

Websites and CD-ROMs/DVDs

Computer software packages, listing conference venues, have been in existence since the early 1990s, although it is fair to say that the early versions struggled to achieve widespread acceptance among conference organizers. Nowadays, websites and CD-ROMs/DVDs have replaced the more traditional software format. Two of the leading Internet-based venue finding and enquiry systems are: www.venuedirectory.com and www.plan-soft.com. Sites such as these allow browsers to enter their own venue search criteria online and details of venues that match are supplied to them within a matter of seconds. Browsers can then look at detailed information on the venues, including photos, and may also be able to undertake a 'virtual' tour of the venue. There is also the facility to send a specific enquiry ('request for proposal' or 'RFP') to venues short-listed. Similar information is available in CD-ROM (or DVD) format, with meeting planners receiving updated CD-ROMs several times a year.

Many of the directories and brochures referred to in the previous section above can also be accessed electronically through their respective websites.

For those conference organizers who prefer to source their own venues, rather than use an intermediary organization, websites and venue brochures/directories are a useful way of whittling down the options to a manageable shortlist. They do not, however, obviate the need to visit venues before making a final choice. Computer or printed images and text can help, but they do not replace the need to see a venue at first hand and meet the staff.

As Cotterell says, inspection visits:

> are important because there is much that cannot be ascertained from a brochure. The experienced organizer will travel to a venue the way most delegates will, to experience at first hand any problems with finding it or reaching it. Judgements will be made on the overall first impressions, the attitude of the staff, the quality, colours,

style and condition of furnishings, the ease of getting from one area to another, and so on. Many experienced organizers make a check-list of points they need to cover . . .. It is sometimes easier to attend one of the group inspection visits organized by hotels, tourist boards, convention bureaux, trade associations and some trade magazines. These give an opportunity, often over a weekend, to inspect a variety of venues within a location in the company of other organizers, an aspect that can be a most valuable opportunity to add to one's own personal network.

Trade exhibitions

There are a number of trade shows and exhibitions specifically designed for conference organizers and meeting planners, where the exhibitors include conference venues and destinations, conference service suppliers, intermediary agencies, transport companies and trade magazines. The advantage for conference organizers is that an exhibition enables them to make contact with potential suppliers, all under one roof – people it would be very expensive and time-consuming to contact individually away from the show. Exhibitions are a good way of updating information files, making personal contacts, finding out about new developments and facilities. Many exhibitions also have a seminar programme running alongside, covering topics of relevance to conference organizers in their everyday work.

Major industry exhibitions include the following.

1 *Incentive Travel & Meeting Executives Show* (normally referred to as IT&ME) – the largest of the trade expositions in North America (and part of the huge *Motivation Show*), held at McCormick Place in Chicago in September/October. Organized by Hall Erickson Inc. Further details: www.motivationshow.com.

2 *EIBTM* (European Incentive and Business Travel and Meetings Exhibition) – a truly international exhibition (see Chapter 1) held at Palexpo, Geneva, in May (but moving to Barcelona from December 2004) and organized by Reed Travel Exhibitions. Several thousand buyers are hosted to the show each year by the organizers, who provide complimentary flights and overnight hotel accommodation. Further details: www.eibtm.ch.

3 *IMEX* – a new exhibition to be held for the first time in 2003 (April) at Messe Frankfurt, Germany. The organizers plan to invite 2500 hosted buyers whose travel and accommodation will be paid for. *IMEX* will incorporate a German trade show, *Meetings Made In Germany*. Further information: www.imex-frankfurt.com.

4 *International Confex* – the largest of the British shows, which is held at Earls Court Exhibition Centre, London (usually late February/early March). Exhibitors are British and overseas companies and organizations. Organized by CMP Information Ltd. Further information: www.international-confex.com.

5 *Asia Incentives & Meetings Exhibition (AIME)* – held at the Melbourne Exhibition and Convention Centre, Australia in February (first staged in 1993). Organized by Reed Travel Exhibitions. Further details: www.aime.com.au.

6 *Incentive Travel & Conventions, Meetings Asia (IT&CMA)* – this show has been running since 1993, and was held at the IMPACT Convention Centre in Bangkok, Thailand in October 2002. It was held in Hong Kong from 1993 to 1996, and Malaysia from 1997 to 2001. It is organized by TTG Asia Media Pte Ltd. Further details: www.itcma.com.sg.

Trade press

Conference industry trade magazines are a valuable source of up-to-date news and feature coverage on conference venues and destinations, both national and international. As well as articles reviewing the facilities and attractions of specific areas, some magazines also include case studies of events which illustrate how other organizers have staged events in particular locations.

Readers of trade magazines need to bear in mind that all of the magazines depend for their survival on attracting advertising support from conference venues and destinations, a fact which can sometimes influence editorial content. Despite this caveat, trade magazines are an important source of information and provide a service which does not exist elsewhere. They also contain many other features, for example on trends and statistics and new legislation, which provide essential background for professional buyers.

A list of the main trade magazines is given in Appendix A.

Agencies

Various agencies provide specialist venue finding services. These include venue-finding agencies, professional conference organizers (PCOs), conference production companies, and destination management companies (DMCs) (see Chapter 2). Agency services are usually free to buyers (unless the agencies are also involved in the planning and organization of a conference), with commission being charged to the venues where business is placed. Some agencies have been criticized from time to time for recommending to their clients those venues that will pay them the highest levels of commission, rather than putting forward the venues that are best suited to clients' needs. Such a practice is, however, short-sighted, as a disappointed client is unlikely to make use of their services again.

Whichever source(s) of information organizers choose to use (one of the most popular sources, not listed above, is that of peer group recommendations, i.e. recommendations of venues by colleagues or by other conference organizers), they will need to have at their finger tips the answers to questions about their event that will be posed by venue staff or intermediary agencies, who will require information on:

- the nature of the conference/event and its key objectives;
- the duration of the event (including any build-up and break-down time for stage sets, exhibition stands, etc.);
- proposed dates (and any possible flexibility with these to secure the best deal);
- the number of delegates/partners/exhibitors/speakers;
- the preferred location(s);
- the type of venue sought and space/meeting room requirements, with room layouts;
- the technical and audiovisual equipment needed and whether a specialist conference production company is to be used;
- catering requirements, with any special arrangements (e.g. private dining, receptions, entertainment);
- accommodation (numbers, types of bedroom);
- social programme activities/requirements (where appropriate);
- the budget;
- the deadline for receipt of information and details of the decision-making process.

Venue inspection checklist

Once a short list of potentially suitable venues has been produced, the next step is to inspect these venues by visiting in person. When undertaking an inspection visit, it is useful to go armed with a check-list of questions, such as the following.

- Is there the correct combination of rooms available for plenary sessions, syndicate groups, catering, possibly an accompanying exhibition?
- Is there good access for disabled delegates? Is the venue equipped in other ways to cater for the many different disabilities that delegates (and speakers) may have?
- What style of seating will be needed? U-shape, boardroom, theatre-style, classroom, hollow-square and herringbone are just some of the options (see Figure 5.1). For the purposes of calculations, a room which seats 100 delegates theatre-style will seat 50 classroom-style, 25 hollow-square/boardroom/U-shape, and about 75 for dinner/lunch at round tables/top table with sprigs.

- Do the meeting rooms have natural light? If so, can the room be blacked out satisfactorily?
- How noisy is the heating and air conditioning system?
- If the event is residential, how many bedrooms will be available at the venue, and how many of these are single/double/twin bedrooms? Is it important for all delegates to sleep under the same roof, or can they be accommodated in different hotels and be transported to the conference venue?
- Does the venue have leisure facilities and, if so, are they available to delegates free of charge?
- What are the options for social activities in the vicinity, if there is time in the conference programme for these?
- Does the venue have a dedicated conference coordinator (or team) who can assist with the detailed planning and arrangements?
- Are there other venue staff with whom you will be working and, if so, when will you be able to meet them? At what stage will the sales manager – usually the conference organizer's initial point of contact – pass on the booking details to colleagues, who then become the main points of reference?
- Are there in-house technical staff to operate audiovisual equipment? If so, is there an additional charge for using their services? If there are no such staff on site, what arrangements does the venue have with independent audiovisual companies, and what do they charge? What audiovisual equipment is needed during the event (normally this can be decided quite close to the event, unless the requirements are specialized or the event is a large one requiring substantial equipment and sophisticated production)?
- Can the venue offer any transport assistance for delegates travelling by public transport (e.g. collecting them by minibus from the airport or railway station)? How much car parking space does the venue have?
- Is there a high turnover of staff in the venue, which might create problems in the build-up? Does the venue team give the impression of being experienced, professional and easy-to-work-with?

Carey (1997) provides a series of check-lists for conference organizers. An example of one of these, a 'meeting room checklist', is given in Figure 5.2.

Negotiating with venues

Once a short list of suitable venues has been produced and inspection visits made, the process of negotiating a final rate or package with the preferred venue takes place. Conference organizers should be aware of a venue's need to maximize yield from its bookings (as described in Chapter 6) but, nonetheless,

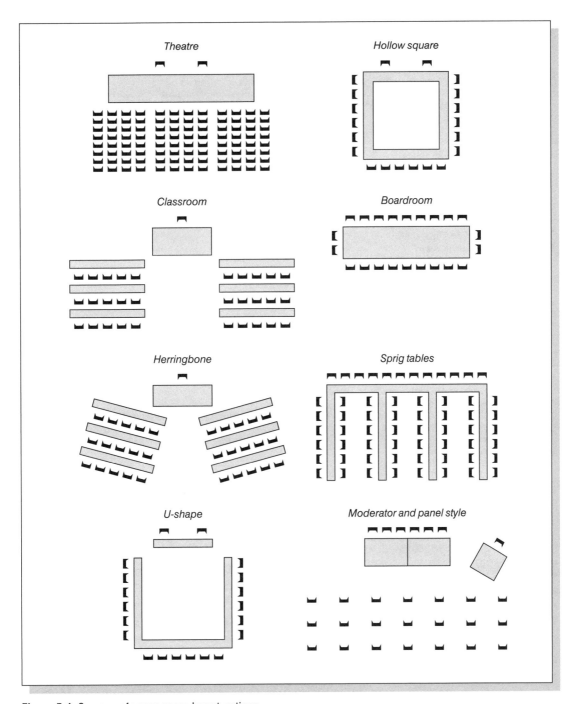

Figure 5.1 Some conference room layout options.

To attend a site inspection without a check-list is a recipe for extra work, as vital questions will remain unasked and important features remain uninspected. Every conference brings its own demands but if you investigate the following you will be halfway there.

A. Location
- Independent access[1]
- Freight access[1]
- Easy to find? (well signed?)
- Proximity to:[2]
  - Main entrance and car park
  - Meal areas and kitchens
  - Fresh air
  - Lifts
  - Toilets and cloakrooms
  - Telephones
  - Break-out rooms
- Disabled access

B. Fixtures
- Decor
- Wall and floor materials[3]
- Pillars/obstructions
- Room shape and partitions[4]
- Location of doors
- Where doors lead to[5]
- Fire exits[6]
- Natural light/views

- Chandeliers and mirrors[7]
- Stage area and access to it
- Registration area
- Light switches or regulators
- Power and telephone points[8]
- Temperature controls (location)[9]
- Blackout curtains
- Acoustics
- Ceiling height[10]

C. Non-fixtures
- Chairs (comfort factor)
- Tables (size and coverings)
- Table furniture[11]
- Signage

D. General
- Cleanliness
- Overall comfort
- Capacity
- Ambience
- Pre-function space
- Smell

Notes:
1. Direct on to concourse, foyer or street.
2. Explore for yourself.
3. Should be sound absorbent, not bright and not 'busy'.
4. Are partitions really soundproof?
5. Beware doors that open on to kitchens or garbage areas.
6. Are they blocked or locked?
7. Chandeliers can impede projection. Mirrors toss light from projectors and lecterns indiscriminately around a room.
8. You may need lots for PCs, modems and fax machines.
9. Are they in the room?
10. High enough for maximum screen height.
11. What is provided? e.g. Water, cordials, note pads, mints.

Did you hear about the organizer who checked the dimensions of the access doors with the venue (over the phone) and computed that the car would fit through them? Sadly, he was unaware until the day of the launch that the room he had booked wasn't on the ground floor!

Figure 5.2 Meeting room check-list. (*Source*: Carey (1997) *Crisis or Conference?*)

there is almost always scope to negotiate on a venue's published delegate rates.

Carey suggests that:

> As a professional conference organizer, you are in a powerful position to negotiate a good deal with your chosen venue and it can be tempting to bully the management into ridiculously low room, food and beverage rates. This may make you feel good and impress

your Finance Director but it will almost certainly jeopardize the vital relationship between you and the venue. As a rule, it is better to pay a reasonable rate for facilities and accommodation and then negotiate added value and service.

In short, good negotiation is about creating a win–win situation for both the event organizer and the venue, but also about building relationships and partnerships, and doing business with people who want to do business with you.

Some flexibility on the part of the organizer can assist in the negotiation process, particularly if this can help to make a booking even more attractive in the eyes of the venue. The following points should also be borne in mind:

- Only negotiate with venue staff who have the authority to make decisions.
- Underline and sell the stature and value of your event to the venue.
- It is a good sign if the venue asks lots of questions about your event. Give them as much information as possible *before* discussing rates.
- Be prepared by doing your homework on the venue's 'rack' (i.e. published) rates and having a copy of the venue's brochure on file before discussing a deal. Establish what the venue's tariffs are for other types of business.
- Give the venue manager an indication of your budget (unless it is higher than their published rates!).
- If you can offer some flexibility on dates/timings, you are likely to get a better deal, bearing in mind that venues are seeking back-to-back bookings. If the event is to be held midweek, rates charged are likely to be higher than at weekends. Significant reductions can be achieved by holding an event at least partially over a weekend when occupancy levels, especially for hotels, are generally lower.
- The scope for negotiation will also depend on the time of year (autumn and spring are the peak seasons for conferences, and so the busiest for the venues), the number of delegates, nature of the organization (lower rates may be available for not-for-profit organizations).
- Published rates do not cover the same package from venue to venue. It is, therefore, important to examine what the rates do actually include. The provision of audiovisual equipment is one of the areas where wide variations can exist.
- While most venues (and certainly almost all hotels) promote a delegate package (expressed either as a non-residential or eight-hour or day delegate rate, *or* as a residential or 24-hour delegate rate), it is also possible to ask for room hire and catering charges separately, and sometimes these may be cheaper than an integrated package.

Cotterell puts forward a number of strategies to be used by conference buyers in the negotiation process, including:

- prepare – for example, know the prices charged by the venue to other clients (*if possible*), and know the prices charged by similar venues in the area;
- be nice, but gain respect;
- don't lie;
- be flexible;
- never reveal deadlines;
- name drop;
- hint at other business to be placed;
- be patient;
- disclaim responsibility (for the final decision);
- don't underestimate the sellers.

Programme planning

It is of prime importance that the conference programme matches the overall objectives. The content, style and pace of the programme will, of course, vary from event to event. There is now a stronger business orientation to most conferences, plus a noticeable trend for even larger conferences to be more participatory, inviting delegate contributions to plenary presentations and, particularly, through a greater use of syndicate sessions. There is also a requirement for programmes to cater for different delegate needs: this may be less of a concern for corporate conferences where delegates' levels of experience and expertise can be checked and controlled, but a challenge for association conferences where delegates are self-selecting to a much greater extent and will have disparate levels of experience.

Research undertaken by McGill University (USA) over a 10-year period has consistently shown that, for scientific international association conferences, programme content is the single most important determining factor in increasing delegate attendance (reported in *The PCO*, the newsletter of the International Association of Professional Congress Organizers, Autumn 2002). The research shows that 48 per cent gave the programme as the key reason for attending, followed by 26 per cent giving destination, 16 per cent stating that they always attend and 10 per cent other reasons.

The choice of speakers, and leaders of syndicate or workshop sessions, is crucial to the success of any event. In some cases, decisions about speakers may be imposed upon the organizer by senior managers or a conference committee. Where this is the case, the organizer's role is to ensure that speakers are properly briefed about the aims for the conference as well as for their own presentation, and that all of the technical and environmental factors (room layout, audiovisual facilities, introductory speeches) are carefully planned to create a successful 'performance'.

When the organizer has to source speakers himself, imagination and recommendation should be uppermost in his mind, probably in equal proportions. It is often stimulating for delegates to listen to a speaker with new ideas or controversial views, and a rousing opening session that generates discussion and debate may be just the spark needed to ensure a lively and productive conference. But few organizers will be willing to put their own reputations on the line by inviting relatively unknown speakers to the platform, unless they come recommended by others. Colleagues are clearly an important source of such speaker recommendations. Other sources can include trade associations, editors of trade magazines, university or college departments, speaker bureaux and professional conference organizers.

Some conferences are strictly business events with little or no free time. Others, particularly in the association sector, combine a business programme with a social programme. The social itinerary is another area where an organizer has an opportunity to display his creativity and really make the conference memorable. The social programme should allow delegates to mix informally and network (for many this is often the most worthwhile part of the event), but also to experience something of the destination in which the conference is being staged. It may be possible for social activities to extend, in a lighthearted way, the theme of the conference. Invaluable assistance in the design of social programmes is available from the local convention bureau or conference office, as well as from PCOs and, especially, DMCs. Examples of social events at BACD conferences in recent years have included:

- a tour of the Whisky Heritage Centre in Edinburgh followed by dinner, concluding with a late-evening guided tour of the narrow streets around Edinburgh Castle by a 'ghost' (Adam Lyal, deceased) – a truly haunting experience!
- a banquet in the splendour of Cardiff Castle featuring Welsh dancers and a male voice choir;
- a Caribbean evening in Leicester, with delegates in Caribbean costume being entertained by steel bands and cabaret;
- a torchlit drinks reception in the Roman baths in Bath, followed by a banquet in the Pump Room;
- a formal whisky tasting, under instruction, at Glamis Castle near Dundee, followed by a tour of the Castle and a sumptuous banquet;
- a boat trip to the island of Sark (from a conference in Guernsey) with rides by horse-drawn carriage and bicycle (there are no cars on Sark), followed by dinner.

Each of these gave the event a unique character, and made it an enjoyable and memorable experience.

Event marketing

Marketing is an essential part of the event management process. There is little point in devoting a great deal of time and resources to the organization of a conference, if few people bother to attend. The marketing should begin at the earliest possible stage, even if this only entails publicizing brief details of the event so that potential delegates have reserved the date in their diary.

Event marketing is not just about maximizing delegate numbers. It also creates a positive attitude towards the event for everyone concerned with it (speakers, delegates, venue and suppliers, trade media, etc.) and helps to raise its profile, both within its own industry sector but also within the conference sector.

Clearly the greater the budget for marketing, the more that can be done, but much can still be achieved without a huge promotional 'pot'. The following are some ideas that can be used or adapted to meet the needs of any organization.

- Ensure that the printed brochure/leaflet used to promote the event, containing the conference programme, is of the highest standard affordable. This sets the tone for the event and, if well done, goes a long way to creating interest in, and positive expectations from, the conference. It should contain:
  - an introduction (possibly in the form of an invitation/ welcome from the organization's Chief Executive or Chair);
  - the conference programme (in as much detail as is confirmed at this stage – a final programme can be circulated nearer the event to registered delegates);
  - short biographies of speakers and contributors;
  - upbeat information on the venue (and destination) being used, ideally with some photographs;
  - details of any event sponsors;
  - a booking form (either as part of the leaflet or as a separate insert).
- If the conference has been held previously, favourable quotations from delegates should be included in the promotional material and programme brochure. Peer-group quotes are one of the most effective ways of generating interest in a conference.
- A PR strategy should be prepared for the event. This will include the issue of press releases to help create awareness of the conference and raise its profile as an event 'not-to-be-missed'. As well as giving key facts and figures about the conference, the releases should contain details of new or controversial issues, and topics to be discussed at the conference, quotes from the organizers and keynote speaker(s) (where appropriate), and set out briefly what the conference is intended to achieve.

- Direct marketing, including e-marketing, is one of the main marketing tools to be used, especially with association and entrepreneurial conferences, but is dependent on access to a good-quality database of potential invitees.
- Maximize use of the world-wide web by developing a site for the event and/or incorporating full event details in other websites. The website may offer online registration facilities, including payment over the web, but the site must be secure and all data encrypted.
- Advertising may also be appropriate when promoting an entrepreneurial type of event, and sometimes when marketing to the association sector where delegates can choose whether or not to attend. Advertising should normally be used to complement other press and PR activity, rather than being used in isolation.

Conference management and production

The general management of a conference requires, in Carey's words, 'common sense, forethought, meticulous planning and attention to detail, team work and sometimes crisis management'. Much of the administration can be enhanced by the use of event management software packages, which are designed to handle delegate registrations and correspondence, itinerary planning, accommodation arrangements, abstract management, speaker liaison, exhibition management, invoicing, report production, delegate evaluations and other aspects. Increasingly such products are also available as web-based tools, which allow online registrations and other real-time applications.

Examples of such software packages and web-based services include the following.

- 'Events Pro' and 'Events Interactive' produced by the Australian company Amlink. Further details from www. amlink.com.au.
- 'Visual Impact System VI' from UK company Event Management Systems. Further details from www.event managementsystems.co.uk.
- 'Meeting Management Solutions', referred to earlier in this chapter, and produced by US company Plansoft. Further details from www.plansoft.com.
- 'Conform' delegate management software, complemented by a complete online solution, produced by the UK company Eventbookings.com. Further details from www. eventbookings.com.
- There are many other products on the market to be viewed at websites such as: www.meetingsnet.com, www.seeuthere.com, www.cvent.com, www.peopleware.com, and www.gomem bers.com/california/meetingtrak.htm.

There is a very useful free e-newsletter detailing the latest developments in technology and web applications for meetings, hospitality and travel industry professionals, circulated every two months and compiled by Corbin Ball. It is entitled 'Corbin's Techtalk Newsletter' – anyone wishing to be added to the circulation list should email him at: corbin@corbinball.com.

It is useful to provide delegates, either in advance or at the registration desk, with a printed itinerary detailing the timing and location of individual sessions, which is particularly important when there are a number of sessions running concurrently. When this is the case, delegates will normally have been asked to preselect the sessions of most interest to them. It is worth producing a reminder list of these sessions for them, perhaps with a list of the other delegates who have chosen the same sessions. Delegate badges can now have a microchip inserted to track whether delegates are attending the correct conference sessions or which stands they have visited in a major exhibition.

It should be remembered that a conference is an event that needs to be stage-managed and requires a very professional approach to its production and presentation on the day. Through familiarity with television programmes and other broadcast media, delegates now expect the same high standards of presentation in their working environments. Poorly produced slides or overheads, problems with projectors or microphones, ill-prepared chairmen, intrusive air conditioning and uncomfortable seating are just some of the all-too-frequently voiced criticisms of conferences and all are less and less acceptable. What is more, all can and should be avoided with proper planning.

While the message is, of course, more important than the medium used to convey it, the message may get lost or misinterpreted if not presented in a way which holds delegates' attention. For this reason, the appropriate use of audiovisual technology should be discussed with speakers, who will usually have their own ideas about how best to make their presentations. If something more than just an overhead projector and flipchart, or data projector and computer, are to be used, an organizer should look at employing a specialist conference production company. The services of such companies are not cheap, but their costs can be built into the budget and will minimize the risk of embarrassing crises, as well as reassuring speakers that their presentations will not be plagued by technical hitches.

Wherever possible, speakers should participate in rehearsals, both to familiarize themselves with the room and technical equipment to be used, and also to run through the sequence of introductions and cues to be used with the session chairman.

Technology is now on the market that allows an entire conference to be recorded on video, audio and in text format, translated into any language and placed on a single CD to be played back on a computer by the delegate (or, of course, sold to those who were unable to attend the conference, both to extend the conference audience and to generate additional income streams for the organizers). Some products contain a complete 'virtual' environment, allowing delegates to walk between lecture theatres and meeting rooms as if present at the conference.

Event evaluation

Once the conference is over, an evaluation of the event needs to take place as soon as possible. Ideally, delegates should complete assessments for each session as soon as it ends or shortly afterwards. Delegate itineraries can include evaluation questionnaires (a sample from a BACD conference is shown at Figure 5.3) for each session, as well as an overall evaluation sheet for completion at the end of the conference. Feedback from delegates is crucial in assessing the success of the conference. It is also very important as a means of gathering ideas for future events. It may be appropriate for delegate questionnaires to be completed anonymously to encourage honest comments, and some form of incentive can also increase the number of responses.

In some cases, of course, a fully objective appraisal of the conference will not be possible until months later, as the outcomes of the event are translated into improved sales, enhanced performances, a more effective sharing of information, or whatever objectives were set in the first place.

The organizer will also want to evaluate how, from his perspective, the conference was managed and to what extent it met the set objectives. Ideas for improving those aspects that did not work well should emerge, and the more successful elements can be developed further in the future.

An appraisal should also take place with the venue. In the author's experience, this is an area where many venues lose marks. Discussions with the client after the event seem to be the exception, whereas they should be the norm. Even when an event appears to have run smoothly, there will always be scope for further improvement. Venues should take the initiative in following up with clients to assess all aspects of their performance. Unfortunately, relatively few seem to bother.

Finally, it is worthwhile preparing a post-conference/convention report: a detailed summary of every aspect of the event, from total attendance to room usage to food and beverage functions and more. It will take time to prepare such an in-depth document, but the rewards are worth the effort. It is both an invaluable reference tool for planning next year's conference (it is much easier reading through a detailed four-page or five-page summary document than having to work through bulky files), and a powerful negotiating tool, since it contains accurate figures

BACD AGM & SPRING CONVENTION

CONVENTION SESSION 1 - EVALUATION SHEET

Session Title:

Session Date:

Presenter:

The following is a general questionnaire, some statements may not be applicable to this session. If so, please omit.

Please indicate the extent to which you agree or disagree with the following statements regarding this session. (4=strongly agree, 1= strongly disagree; circle one number only.)

	Strongly Agree			Strongly Disagree
The speaker demonstrated knowledge of the subject	4	3	2	1
The speaker was effective in communicating the subject matter	4	3	2	1
The subject matter was of relevance and interest	4	3	2	1
The visual aids/handouts formed a useful part of the presentation	4	3	2	1
The question and answer session was of benefit	4	3	2	1
I learnt new skills/gained new insight and understanding	4	3	2	1

My overall impression of the session was:

_____

_____

_____

_____

Additional Comments:

_____

_____

_____

_____

Figure 5.3 Evaluation questionnaire.

from the conference, including details of all revenue spent at the conference venue. A good example of such a summary document can be found on the website www.mpoint.com/guides.

Summary

- The planning of a conference involves steps that are similar to those involved in the staging of many other events. It demands a logical approach and great attention to detail on the part of an organizer, but also affords scope for creativity and imagination.
- At the outset, clear objectives for the conference should be set and as much information collected as possible about the participants, programme, timing, location and format. Financial aspects are another important part of the planning process: budgets need to be drawn up and, where appropriate, cashflow forecasts prepared.
- The selection of a suitable venue is crucial to the success of any event, and time and resources should be allocated to ensuring that the right choice is made. Various forms of assistance in venue finding are available, including directories, brochures, computer software, exhibitions, magazines and specialist agencies. Once a short list of the most suitable venues has been completed, inspection visits are made and negotiations take place between organizers and venues to determine an agreed package.
- Planning the detail of the conference programme should always take account of the objectives set for the event from the start. The choice of speakers is a critical factor in delegate perceptions of the event. Social programmes present an ideal opportunity for organizers to bring something distinctive and memorable to an event.
- Marketing the conference needs to begin at the earliest possible moment, ideally at the previous year's event when it is part of a regular sequence. Various promotional tools are available, designed to increase the profile of the conference as well as to maximize delegate numbers.
- No conference ends with the closing session. Organizers should spend time evaluating the event through feedback from delegates and other interested parties. Ideas for improving future events will emerge from this evaluation process.

Review and discussion questions

1 From the perspective of an event organizer, compare and contrast the various information sources (directories, brochures, computer software, magazine features, Internet

sites) for a chosen conference destination. Evaluate the strengths and weaknesses of each source.

2 Reread the section on 'Negotiating with venues' together with the sections on 'Yield management' and 'Negotiating with clients' from Chapter 6. Describe the characteristics of a 'win–win' negotiation that both organizer and venue would consider a success.

3 You have 12 months to plan a new medical association conference for 300 delegates (plus partners). There is no previous event history. Produce a schedule that details the actions and decisions required on a month-by-month basis in the planning and staging of the conference. The schedule should include budget and cashflow forecasts. The conference committee has given you an initial promotional budget of £3000 and asked you to make a profit of £5000, which can be used as a start-up fund for the following year's conference.

4 A venue charges £30 per delegate as a non-residential or day delegate rate, to include room hire, lunch, and morning and afternoon teas/coffees. Alternatively, these may be bought as separate items at a cost of £600 for room hire, £16 per person for lunch, and £2 for each tea/coffee consumed. Calculate the best way of buying for 40, 70, 100 and 150 delegates.

Notes and references

Carey, Tony. *Crisis or Conference?* The Industrial Society (1997).

Carey, Tony. Planning the planning. *Meeting Planner* (Winter 2000 issue, Volume 4 Number 16).

Cotterell, Peter. *Conferences – An Organiser's Guide.* Hodder & Stoughton (1994).

Fisher, John G. *How to Run a Successful Conference.* Kogan Page (1998).

Maitland, Iain. *How to Organize a Conference.* Gower Publishing Limited (1996).

Swarbrooke, John and Horner, Susan. *Business Travel and Tourism.* Butterworth-Heinemann (2001).

Further reading

Polivka, Edward G., editor. *Professional Meeting Management.* Professional Convention Management Association (fourth edition) (2002). (www.pcma.org, click on resources, click on marketplace, view PMM4).

Carey, Tony, editor. *Professional Meeting Management – A European Handbook.* Published on behalf of the MPI Foundation.

Seekings, D. and Farrer, J. *How to Organise Successful Conferences and Meetings.* Kogan Page (1999).

Bowdin, G.A.J.; McDonnell, I.; Allen, J. and O'Toole, W. *Events Management*. Butterworth-Heinemann (2001).

Torrence, Sara R. *How to Run Scientific and Technical Meetings*. Van Nostrand Reinhold International (1996).

Lippincott, Cheryl. *Meetings: Do's, Don'ts and Donuts: The Complete Handbook for Successful Meetings*. Lighthouse Point Press (1994).

Allen, Judy. *The Business of Event Planning*. John Wiley & Sons (2002).

IAPCO documents:
- *How to Choose the Right PCO*
- *First Steps in the Preparation of an International Meeting*
- *First Steps for a Medical Meeting*
- *Guidelines for Co-operation between the International Association, the National Organising Committee and the PCO*
- *Guidelines for the International Scientific Programme Committee*
- *Guidelines on Poster Presentations*
- *Sponsorship Prospectus*
- *Housing Guidelines.*

CHAPTER 6

Conference management – a venue perspective

Organizing a successful conference is dependent upon many interlinking factors, not the least of which is effective communications and teamwork between the conference organizer and the conference venue. Chapter 5 has looked at the management of the event from the standpoint of the organizer, whether this is the 'end user' or 'buyer' (corporation, association, public body, etc.) who has ownership of the event, or a PCO or intermediary organization acting on behalf of the end user. This chapter explores conference management from the perspective of the venue or 'supplier', and describes the team approach within a venue, and between venue and client, to deliver successful events.

The chapter looks at:

- client-focused product innovations;
- professional inspection visits and showrounds;
- yield management and 'REVPAR';
- negotiating with clients;
- venue case studies.

Client-focused product innovations

In the aftermath of September 11th, venues found themselves with strong competition for fewer events. As always, it was those properties that 'put themselves in their clients' shoes that won the business'. This is not simply a question of providing discounted rates. Clients want more than anything for their suppliers to deliver services to the promised standards.

Some practical examples of the outworking of such a client-focused approach are given later in this chapter as seen through the eyes of several venues. Many venues are also investing heavily in their physical 'product' (e.g. bedrooms, meeting rooms, technology) to give them a competitive edge and to underline their customer orientation. One practical example of this is Le Meridien's Cumberland Hotel in central London, launching its first 60 'Art & Tech' rooms as part of a £72 million refit and described in an article entitled 'Bed and Broadband' in *Business Travel World* magazine (June 2002). The 'Art & Tech' rooms aim to capitalize on two emerging trends for the hotel world in the 21st century: boutique-style design and the use of high technology to enhance the guest experience. The new rooms have: 42-inch plasma televisions providing interactive services, including fast Internet connections and movies on demand; safes large enough to take laptops as well as provide battery recharging connections, and electronically controlled beds to elevate guests' legs and torsos. In the article, John Ryan, Le Meridien's senior vice president of worldwide sales, explained their philosophy as follows:

> Over the past 15 years hotels have tended to invest in technology that was primarily geared to hotel operations rather than guests, such as electric door locks, computerized operations and yield management systems. In the 21st century we need to turn this around and focus on what the customer wants from new technology, especially as the hotel guests of today already have modern technology in their homes and offices. We need to look, therefore, at such things as better entertainment services and improved communication tools.

The same *Business Travel World* article reported that Marriott Hotels had unveiled new conference technology in many of its UK hotels, including the latest webcasting facilities and high-speed net access, video conferencing for meetings at different hotels, and email kiosks and Internet cafes for delegates to use during meeting breaks. Hyatt Hotels has introduced a computerized billing system for conference groups, providing a summary and detailed support information including room charges, functions, convention services, audiovisual and other charges. This system is designed to overcome the frustrations of meeting planners who found it time-consuming and frustrating to reconcile separate bills.

The International Convention Centre, Birmingham (England) has produced an interactive CD containing video clips, animated three-dimensional plans and images of the Centre, which, once a booking is made and the customer is given a password, changes to a planning tool. It then provides order forms, check-lists, high-resolution images for literature, and a searchable directory of hotels, restaurants, nightlife and attractions in the area.

For some years now, debates have been raging over the impact of electronic communications media and whether virtual conferences (by linked telephone, video or Internet) will take over from the real thing. Campbell (2000) contends that

> the weight of argument and evidence suggests that precisely because technology is invading our lives, then so is there an increased requirement for human contact and inter-personal chemistry. In other words, touchy-feely events will always matter, and perhaps even more so. Some suggest that motivational and morale-boosting get-togethers will, in fact, grow in importance, for precisely the reason that technology exacerbates the sense of working in isolation.

In his article, Campbell outlines other ways in which venues are seeking to meet the needs of the 'inner delegate'. He comments that:

> leisure clubs with swimming pools have always been rated highly by many organizers, but these too have been overtaken by progress. Today's increasingly essential facility is a spa, offering a full range of look-good and feel-good options. Facials are no longer just for women, nor massages just for men. Pampering delegates in strawberry-flavoured wraps with honey-infused oils against a background of soothing meditative music for the inner soul is no longer a freakish idea, but part of the esteem-enhancing, equilibrium-guaranteeing process of preparing top executives for the conference fray. Consequently, venues have to be up to speed with their holistic lifestyle features. Against this background of body awareness it is hardly surprising that more organizers are requesting a higher proportion of no smoking bedrooms for their guests, with 60 per cent no longer being unusual.

Campbell also waxes lyrical on conference seating:

> curiously, a seat is no longer a seat. Instead, it's a figure-contoured, posture-supporting, attention-assisting investment in delegate involvement. They are moulded to the delegate in a bid to keep him or her awake and alert. Old-fashioned banqueting chairs no longer pass the test, nor, for that matter, the minimalist and stylish scrap of aluminium and leather. Today's organizers want a 'smart' chair that reduces delegate snoozing!

To conclude this section, it is interesting to note the results of Riley's survey of those hotel features that are considered to be the most important by (a) meeting planners and (b) hotel managers in determining the selection of such venues for meetings and conferences. Table 6.1 compares the opinions of both in answer to the question: which are the attributes of a hotel that are most significant in determining its suitability for the meetings market?

Meeting planners' opinions, in descending order of importance	Hotel managers' opinions, in descending order of importance
High quality of food	Helpful staff
Cleanliness of hotel	High quality of food
Experienced conference manager to deal with	Cleanliness of hotel
Comfortable seating in conference room	Comfortable seating in conference room
Good sound insulation in conference room	Experienced conference manager to deal with
Complete blackout available in conference room	Availability of basic audiovisual equipment
Hotel able to accommodate all delegates in-house	Good acoustics in conference room
Helpful staff	Hotel experienced and specialized in conferences
Efficient check-in and check-out procedures	Efficient check-in and check-out procedures
Good acoustics in conference room	Hotel able to accommodate all delegates in-house
Air-conditioned conference room	Good road links
Hotel experienced and specialized in conferences	Good sound insulation in conference room
Availability of syndicate rooms	Good parking facilities
Competitive room rates	Purpose-built conference room

Table 6.1
Attributes of a hotel considered to be most significant in determining its suitability for the meetings market

Professional inspection visits and showrounds

One of the most important parts of the sales and marketing process is the opportunity to show a potential client the benefits of a venue through a personal showround or inspection. In the author's experience, this is often an activity in which venues fail to do justice to themselves because it is conducted by inexperienced, untrained and ill-informed staff, who fail to sell the benefits of their venue and to convince the customer that his event will be successful if held there. The guidelines below set out how such visits should be handled by the venue to maximize the chances of winning the business. They draw heavily (as does the later section on 'Negotiating with clients') on venue training courses run by Peter Rand, one of the most respected trainers in the UK conference industry (email: PeterRand@peter-rand-group.co.uk – initial capitals must be used as shown).

The showround provides an opportunity to:

- build a rapport with the client that demonstrates an understanding of his needs;
- develop his confidence in the venue team;
- address detail, recognize and use confidence signals, remembering that clients cannot sample the actual service before an event.

Careful preparation and planning are vital. When the appointment is being made, the following should be covered:

- decide on the appropriate level of hospitality to be offered and whether this should involve an overnight stay;
- check that the right staff and the correct facilities will be available on the proposed visit date;
- ensure the client's correct contact details are held, including mobile phone number for emergency contact, and numbers of people visiting;
- clarify the client's travel arrangements (e.g. arrival time, time available to spend at the venue, method of transport being used).

A written acknowledgement of the appointment and arrangements should be sent (if necessary by fax or email), with reassurances of meeting any specific interests or concerns (e.g. availability of the chef) and enclosing full venue location details.

Before the visit takes place, internal communications within the venue should determine the appropriate venue personnel (numbers, job role, specialist knowledge) to meet the client. Full details of the client should be circulated, including the reason for the visit. Agreement will be needed on the appropriate layout for the conference rooms (subject to other commitments). And, finally, the person overseeing the showround should check that he has the authority and knowledge to cover any potential areas of negotiation, has got the necessary venue and destination product knowledge to hand, and has prepared a photo file of the venue (especially if the conference room(s) are not available or are set up for a different kind of event).

On the day of the visit, the 'welcome' from the venue's reception staff must show that the client is expected. Appropriate introductions should be made, refreshments offered and the agenda for the visit reconfirmed. The venue representative(s) will need to:

- discuss the enquiry in a logical way (chronologically);
- clarify the client's needs, objectives and priorities for the event;
- show an interest in the client's organization, products/services and future development;
- use open questions, listen carefully to replies and check understanding, where necessary;
- give the client a site plan of the venue, showing its general layout and indicating the route of the showround;
- show those parts of the venue relevant to the client;
- highlight the venue's benefits based on the client's needs (rather than just listing the 'features' of the venue);
- introduce and involve appropriate personnel;
- if appropriate, show the grounds and/or leisure facilities, and kitchens;
- throughout the visit, invite questions, check understanding, make notes, indicate locations on the floor plan as they relate to different aspects of the client's event, and look/listen for buying signals.

At the conclusion of the visit, it is important to find a quiet corner with the client to summarize the event, check and overcome any concerns, clarify the next step(s), and agree a time for the next contact. The 'close' should include a reaffirmation of interest in staging the client's event. After the visit, there should be a written follow-up with the client, and the venue's sales follow-up system should be updated. In due course, feedback on the visit to the venue staff should be given.

Yield management and 'REVPAR'

The 1990s saw the adoption of the theory and practice of yield management by conference venues, especially hotels. The application of yield management is seen most importantly towards the end of the marketing process, at the time when a customer (conference organizer) is negotiating a booking with his chosen or shortlisted venue.

Yield management aims to 'maximize revenue by adjusting prices to suit market demand' (Huyton and Peters, 1997). It:

> emphasizes high rates on high demand days and high occupancy when demand is low. The focus of yield management is to maximize revenue every day, not for seasons or periods. It places the needs of the customer secondary to those of the hotel.

Huyton and Peters suggest that:

> for many years prospective hotel guests have become used to bargaining for their room rates or at least expecting that a room, at the rate they normally pay, will be available. Hotels have been seen by their customers as simply providers of rooms and beds. The idea that they are organized establishments, whose sole purpose is to make money for the owners, appears not to be a part of hotel guests' thinking. For as many years as this attitude has been expressed by customers, the hotel industry has permitted it by acceding to guests' needs, wants and whims. The idea seems to have been that we should be grateful for who we can get to come and stay. Yield management has turned this aspect of hotel operation on its head. What the system now tells the customer is that there are certain rooms set aside at certain price categories and, once they are full, you will have to pay more.

Yield management principles apply not just to the sale of bedrooms. Hartley and Rand (1997) explain that:

> For a venue having conference, function and/or exhibition space, yield management systems, designed to increase the overall profitability of the venue, must include consideration of many factors beyond room inventory and room pricing. While the yield-related information needed to handle a bedroom booking can be assessed relatively quickly, conference function and exhibition space can be sold and used in many different ways and for many different purposes – combinations of which will produce significantly varying profit potential. Ultimately, yield will be determined by how you sell the total facilities available.

Hartley and Rand outline a 'conference capacity strategy', which a venue's sales team should develop in order to maximize yield from conference business. The strategy looks at business mix, market strength and competitive edge, profitability, lead times and refused business. They expound the factors and techniques involved in allocating capacity to particular enquiries, and give practical tips on how to secure the business. They contend that:

> Price, and the way the pricing issue is managed by the venue, are components of the 'package' that the venue constructs at this stage of the enquiry. The overall relevance and quality of the package will be determining factors in winning or losing the business.

They strongly discourage the frequently used terminology of '8-hour', '24-hour' or 'day delegate rates', preferring to use 'residential' and 'non-residential rates' as more appropriate terminology. They put forward what they describe as a:

> Radical but still potentially flexible approach: the 'up to' tariff where the maximum rate is quoted as the published rate but it is still apparent that a reduced tariff may be

	Target (potential) (week)	Actual realized (week)
Accommodation		
Number of bedrooms		
(allocated to conference sector)	400 rooms	325 rooms
Accommodation rate	£70	£65
Conference space		
(capacity of 850* sq. mtrs)		
*inc. private dining facilities		
Revenue per sq. m	£93	£75

Conference sector bedroom yield

$$\frac{\text{Rooms sold}}{\text{Rooms available for sale}} \times \frac{\text{Average rate of rooms sold}}{\text{Average rate potential}} = \frac{325}{400} \times \frac{65}{70} = \frac{21\,125}{28\,000} = 75\%$$

Conference space – revenue earned

$$\frac{\text{Revenue per sq. m realized} \times 850}{\text{Potential revenue per sq. m} \times 850} = \frac{£75 \times 850}{£93 \times 850} = \frac{63\,750}{79\,050} = 81\%$$

Conference sector capacity yield

$$\frac{\text{Accommodation revenue realized} + \text{Conference space revenue realized}}{\text{Accommodation revenue potential} + \text{Conference space revenue potential}} \times 100$$

$$\frac{21\,125 + 63\,750}{28\,000 + 79\,050} \times 100 = \frac{84\,875}{107\,050} \times 100 = 79\%$$

Figure 6.1 Measurement of conference capacity yield in a venue over one week. (*Source:* Yeoman and Ingold (1997) *Yield Management – Strategies for the Service Industries*)

available, dependent on the overall attractiveness of the booking to the venue.

Figure 6.1 (taken from Hartley and Rand, 1997) illustrates the measurement of conference capacity yield in a venue over a period of one week, showing the potential and realized figures.

Revenue per available room (REVPAR) is increasingly used as the definitive measure of a hotel's performance, replacing or complementing the measurement of occupancy and average rate. (This information on REVPAR is taken from an article written by Pamela Carvell of Pampas Training (email: pampasmark@aol .com) and is reproduced with her permission.) And yet, too often, too few people in a hotel fully understand the significance of this measurement. Similarly, too many people think that REVPAR and yield are the same measurement. Many hotels that claim to practise yield management are simply measuring REVPAR on a daily basis and staff are incapable of explaining to a guest why different rates are charged on different days for the same room.

Yield management and revenue management (as opposed to REVPAR) are one and the same thing. Essentially, they are an approach to increasing profit by responding to what we know about the past, what we know about the present and what we think will happen in the future. In other words, we are trying to sell the right room at the right time, at the right price to the right person. You could say that this is nothing new but, on the other hand, many hotels are focused on occupancy or average rate and make most decisions on a very short-term basis. Yield management is a systematic approach to simultaneously optimizing both average rate and occupancy, the ultimate aim being 100 per cent yield, i.e. 100 per cent occupancy at rack rate (the published rate).

Yield is derived from the basic economic theory of supply and demand. In times of high demand, high prices can be charged. Conversely, when demand is low, prices will be lowered. Also, when supply is limited, prices rise and when there is an oversupply, prices drop. We are trying to match supply and demand by establishing a customer's willingness to pay a certain price.

Yield management only really operates in hotels and airlines by virtue of the following:

- capacity is relatively fixed;
- demand is derived from distinct market segments;
- inventory (bedroom and meeting room stock) is perishable (see below);
- the product is often sold well in advance of consumption;
- demand fluctuates significantly.

Whilst airlines started using yield management in the 1970s, hotels have only really been using it in a disciplined way since the mid-1990s. The common factor in both industries is that, if a seat or bedroom is empty on one flight/night, it cannot be sold twice the next day to make up lost revenues (it is thus a 'perishable' product). This is unlike most other industries whereby sales shortfalls today can be made up at some time in the future. Also, other industries can increase and decrease manufacturing output to match fluctuations in demand, but a hotel cannot increase or decrease its number of bedrooms or meeting rooms to match demand.

Yield is measured as a percentage, being the actual room revenue as a percentage of total room revenue (see Figure 6.1). The closer it is to 100, the better the yield is, but a typical hotel will achieve around 60 per cent yield. A yield measurement enables comparisons between hotels of different standards and in different countries.

REVPAR is a monetary amount and is calculated by dividing the total room revenue by the total number of rooms. The psychological disadvantage of both these measurements is that they will be lower than the traditional measurements of occupancy and average rate. But, they are a truer reflection of a business's performance.

Yield management is about forecasting, discounting, managing inventories, overbooking, evaluating group (including conference) enquiries, redirecting demand and logical rational pricing. Essentially the key to successful yield management is the ability to differentiate customers who are prepared to pay high prices from those who are prepared to change their travel plans to secure low prices or make a commitment well in advance to secure the low price.

Negotiating with clients

The principles and practice of yield management provide the backcloth against which sales activity takes place, one key element of which is negotiating with the venue's conference clients. Some aspects of negotiating have already been touched on (see section on 'Professional inspection visits and show-rounds' above). However, there are a number of other factors that a venue will need to consider as part of this negotiation process, all of which link with the objectives of maximizing occupancy and yield, and help in determining whether a venue wants the piece of business and, if so, at what rate. Such factors include:

- decisions on the correct business mix for the venue (identifying the most appropriate conference market segments (see Chapter 2) as well as other types of business if, for example, the venue is a hotel also seeking individual business travellers, leisure tourists, coach groups, etc.);

- dates – accepting business that allows the venue to maximize bookings on 365 days a year, including factors such as whether the event is weekday or weekend or a combination of the two;
- timings of a meeting or conference – if, for example, the event does not start until the afternoon or evening, is there an opportunity to sell the meeting room(s) to another client for the first part of this day?
- duration and seasonality;
- numbers of delegates, bedroom occupancy, and overall value of the piece of business;
- numbers of meeting rooms required, and implications this might have for other potential business that might have to be refused;
- future opportunities for business from this client.

Before commencing negotiations, it is also important for the venue sales manager to prepare fully through an understanding of the market:

- knowing the main sources of business for the venue;
- understanding market segmentation and the different types of conference clients with different types of events, objectives, budgets – what is the market position of the client?
- keeping abreast of the current state of the conference market (strengths and weaknesses, trends) and of the general economy (local/national and, increasingly, international);
- being aware of the venue's principal competitors;
- being fully informed of major events in the locality (sporting, cultural, business), which will have an impact on demand for bedrooms and possibly function rooms.

The venue needs to decide, prior to negotiation, what the ideal outcome would be, but also what a realistic outcome would be and, finally, what its fallback position should be.

Once negotiations start, it is important to establish at an early stage:

- what are the important criteria (i.e. critical factors in determining how successful an event has been) for the client;
- what alternatives are available (both other venues being considered, but also alternative dates and formats for the event to allow maximum flexibility);
- whether the buyer/organizer has any concessions to offer and, if so, what he might be expecting in return;
- what concessions the venue can bring to the negotiating table that will cost little but be perceived as valuable by the client.

Venue case studies

This section of the chapter elaborates on points made in previous sections: it looks at the ways in which four different types of venue are structured and operated to enable them to compete effectively in winning and retaining conference business through the delivery of successful events. It examines a national hotel chain venue, an international hotel chain venue, a purpose-built convention centre and a residential conference centre. While these are all UK venues, it is suggested that the principles and systems they have adopted are relevant (and indeed are practised) on a worldwide basis.

Case study 6.1

The Majestic Hotel, Harrogate

The Majestic Hotel is one of 14 mainly four-star and five-star hotels that make up the Paramount Group of Hotels (www.par amount-hotels.co.uk). It is an impressive 19th-century building in the centre of Harrogate, set in 12 acres of landscaped gardens. The town of Harrogate, in Yorkshire, is one of the leading conference destinations in the UK, with the Harrogate International Centre (purpose-built conference and exhibition centre) located just a short walk from The Majestic Hotel. The information below has been provided by the Resident Manager and the Events Manager of the hotel.

From the very outset, the hotel and its representatives must make an impression – the first point of contact for most organizers is with an Event Manager whose role is to extract as much information from the potential client as possible. This is not simply a process of 'order taking' but a balance of questioning techniques, probing and finding out not only the detail but also the purpose of the whole event. By listening and asking open-ended questions in a logical order, the basic details can be obtained in terms of dates, numbers, layout, accommodation and catering requirements. This should then be followed by some secondary questioning to establish the nature of the event, what the client's priorities are and what they expect to achieve from the event. You need to know, for example:

- who will be attending, as this will give you some indication of the seniority of delegates (and could possibly offer the chance to upsell);
- how they will be travelling to the event – is car parking a priority?
- how formal are the dinners – will they need toastmasters, entertainment and could you upsell a menu?

Once this has all been noted, it is up to the Event Manager to sell the property to the client – you now know what they need, what is important to them, and you take each of their requirements in turn and turn the relevant feature that the hotel can offer into a benefit to the potential client. For example:

- if delegates are travelling by car, sell them the benefit of free car parking spaces;
- if team building is important, sell them the fact that the whole event (meetings, dinners, entertainment, accommodation, etc.) can all be housed under one roof and guests will all stay together;
- if they have heavy equipment, sell them the ease of street level access;
- if professional service is a priority, sell them the 'one event, one contact' approach;
- if it is a training meeting, sell them the benefit of large airy rooms with natural daylight, which is more conducive to this style of meeting and keeps delegates alert.

This list is by no means exhaustive but, whatever you offer, you must always remember the 'what's in it for me' syndrome.

Having done all this, you will now have built up a rapport with the organizer, and you should have made them feel as if your venue was built for them and that their event is the most important piece of business you have on your books. However, if they have an idea or a plan that you don't think will work or can be done better for their benefit, tell them, be honest and don't promise what you know you can't deliver. There is often a workable alternative, which the organizer may not have thought about. For example:

> The organizer is holding a meeting for 300 delegates for whom timings are a priority and he has requested a buffet lunch. What he hasn't thought about is the time it will take for all delegates to queue and, once at the buffet point, to decide what they want to eat from the selection on offer. Remember, timings are important to the organizer, so suggest that they have a seated lunch instead with a set meal. This way, the benefit to the conference Chair is that all delegates are served at the same time with no queueing and the conference reconvenes on time. The benefit to the venue is a happy organizer, better portion control, less waste and a better food gross profit.

Getting as much information from the organizer prior to the event is one of the key factors to a successful event, crossing the Ts and dotting the Is, confirming all conversations in writing, listening to the client and actioning every point no matter how small. It is often the little things and last-minute changes that, if left unactioned, cause untold stress to organizers and can ruin an event. There should never be any surprises for the client: if they have to sign a contract, explain to them in advance the implications; agree numbers before issuing the contract and make sure they know what they are signing for. In so doing, you again will build up trust and a feeling on the client's part that they are not going to be exploited. The client will also have a clear understanding of what they will be expected to pay should they reduce their numbers in any way. This reduces the possibility of any ill feeling should the worst scenario occur. There is nothing worse for an operations team who have to work with a client during an event where there has been mistrust, aggravation and a lack of understanding in the days and weeks beforehand.

The next key factor to the smooth running of any event is the transferring of information from the sales office to the operations team. Remember that, up to now, the organizer trusts the Event Manager only but is possibly unlikely to have met any of the people who are responsible for the success of the event on the day. The priority is to limit the number of people who are responsible for the success of the event on the day and who the organizer has to deal with. Arrange a meeting between the Event Manager, Organizer and Operations Manager so that all the details of the event can be handed over in an open, honest and professional manner. In this way, trust will continue and the client will have the assurance that he is still in safe hands. Always remember that, although you will know the layout of the venue inside out and may have organized hundreds of events, your client may not so make it easy for them.

Any changes the organizer now needs to make should be made with his new contact, the Operations Manager. The Operations Manager will be solely responsible for ensuring any changes actually happen and will keep a control of the day's events. How will he do this? A regular morning meeting is held when all the details and any last-minute changes for each event for that day are discussed with a member of every department. Each Line Manager will then relay these changes to their departments who, in turn, will action any salient points but, at all times, the organizer only has to speak to one person.

The checking and double checking that were done prior to arrival by the Event Manager are now continued by the Operations Manager throughout the event. He will constantly liaise with the Organizer and then feed the changes and comments back to the Line Manager. And so the process continues until the end of the event, constantly evaluating what has just occurred and planning what is about to, seeing what has worked and what hasn't, and what can be improved upon during the event.

This all culminates in a review meeting with the organizer prior to his departure, a possible run-through of the account and, hopefully, a rebooking. Within three days, further contact is made by the original Event Manager to collect any other feedback regarding the event. All comments, good and bad, are then relayed back to the Operations Team on a daily and weekly basis, so that improvements are made where appropriate and positive feedback is rewarded.

The Westin Turnberry Resort, Ayrshire

The Westin Turnberry Resort is part of the Westin brand within the international Starwood Hotels and Resorts chain (www.westin.com/turnberry). A five-star resort hotel complete with a globally renowned golf course, The Westin Turnberry (Figure 6.2) is located on the Ayrshire coast of south-west Scotland, enjoying stunning views across to the Isle of Arran.

The following information was provided by the hotel's Sales Director.

Figure 6.2
The Westin Turnberry Hotel.

The Venue Team/the responsibility chain for an event

There are various potential communication/booking chains that can be associated with an event. The enquiries can be marketing-generated and transmitted directly to the Resort Events team who will prepare the proposal, and send it directly to the client, copying either the Turnberry-specific or Starwood Sales Manager responsible for that account or geographical area.

Alternatively, the sales function, either Turnberry-specific (see organization chart (Figure 6.3)) or Starwood Worldwide, will secure the enquiry directly from the client/agency. In this instance, the sales function will prepare and follow up the proposal to the point of provisional booking.

The follow-up process is a combination of the in-house Events Team and the sales force. The external sales function will become more involved if further price/package negotiation is required.

Once written confirmation from the client for the event has been received, the Events Team will finalize the contracting process (only if further negotiations on deposit/terms and conditions are required will the Account Manager remain involved). When the signed contract is received, the Events Team will develop the detail of the event with a focus on upselling until the event orders are complete. At this stage, the event orders are distributed to the appropriate operational departments who will feed back any questions. Once the client arrives on the property, the Events Team will act as the liaison/coordination with all operational departments.

Client relationship

The ideal client relationship is where the client clearly communicates his specific requirements and can highlight any problems or opportunities from experience of the same event in another venue. It is also highly beneficial for the client to be introduced to, and develop a relationship with, some of the key players who will deliver their event such as the Banqueting Manager, Executive Chef, Golf Director, Outdoor Activities Manager, etc. We try, wherever possible, for large events to arrange a pre-convention meeting on the day before or the day of arrival. At this stage, we can present to the client a detailed understanding of his event by all of the team involved. At this pre-convention meeting ('pre-con'), we can also better understand the finer details, such as VIP arrivals, individual room amenities, time/pressure points, etc.

We have had some good examples of where either a third-party event organizer or inexperienced client has, through poor communication, impacted our ability to deliver an event to a five-star standard. We emphasize to all our clients the important role that they play in the success of their event. With a very large event or series of small events, we can demonstrate better ability to deliver where the client has played an excellent communication role in the build-up to the event.

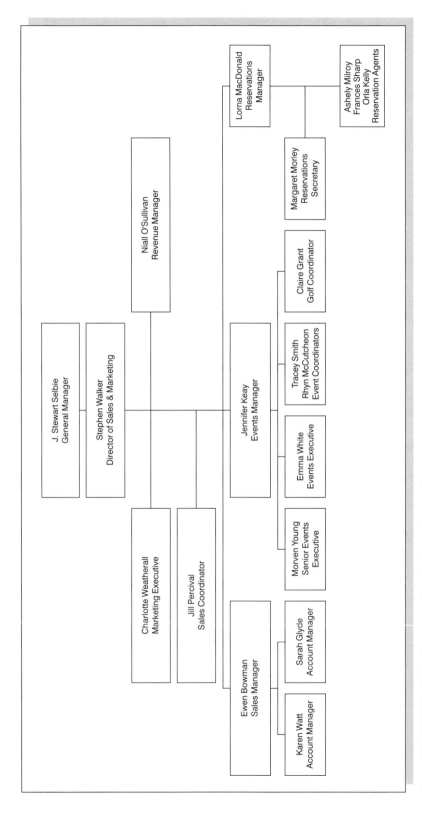

Figure 6.3 [**9]The Westin Turnberry Resort: sales and marketing.

Client advice

We have an excellent in-house service for social programmes, guided tours, audiovisual, etc. However, we also have a range of specialist suppliers we recommend for clients with a particularly detailed requirement.

Health and safety

Our Resort Security/Health and Safety department will liaise directly with our clients on any questions about legislative requirements the organizer may have.

Training of the Conference Department

We value all members of our Events Team as being an extension to our sales force. All of the team enjoy extensive training in professional sales skills, negotiation skills to an advanced stage, presentation skills and the financial/profit aspect of group business. An Events Executive with us for three years may enjoy an investment of up to £12 000 in their training in this period. This training is available to all Events Teams within Starwood.

The sales process in a resort property like Turnberry, with such diverse products as spa treatments, golf, fishing, fine dining, etc., requires a broad skill set and certain maturity as we seldom service two events that are identical.

Case study 6.3

The International Convention Centre, Birmingham

The International Convention Centre (ICC), Birmingham, is part of the NEC Group of venues (www.necgroup.co.uk), which also includes the National Exhibition Centre, the NEC Arena, the National Indoor Arena, and Symphony Hall (see also Chapter 3). The ICC opened in 1991 and is the UK's largest purpose-built convention centre. It handles approximately 350 conferences a year, 150 stand-alone banquets and 200 concerts (Symphony Hall is one hall within the ICC complex). The NEC Group directly employs 1000 full-time staff.

The ICC, Birmingham differs from many comparable venues across Europe, which outsource most of their services (catering, cleaning, security, even some PR) and just have a core management team. In Birmingham, all of these functions (except for cleaning) are managed internally. Operations are guided by a very detailed 'Operations Manual' (introduced in 2000), which sets out, for each department, fully documented objectives and processes for each part of an event, from initial client enquiry through the staging of the event and post-event evaluation.

Once an event has been contracted, an internal meeting is held involving the following:

- The Event Manager – responsible for the logistics of the event from a venue viewpoint, and will become the primary client contact and the client's conduit to other venue department managers/teams. The Event Manager manages the event on the day, and oversees timings, room layouts and any additional requests (e.g. flowers, logos). He is also responsible for all of the technical aspects of the event (e.g. from the floor plans for an exhibition to advising a speaker on how best to preview his presentation). This includes compliance with health and safety regulations, Internet access, and rigging.
- The Catering Manager – deals with everything from 'crisps to caviar'! He also looks for innovative solutions to food and beverage issues for the client.
- The Security Manager – oversees stewarding, traffic management for exhibitions, the security of the building (closed circuit television in operation 7×24), and graphics and signage.
- A representative from the graphics team (signage and promotional material).
- Sales Account Manager – responsible for winning the business in the first place, building customer relationships and managing the 'bottom line' financial aspects (including oversight of invoicing).

Following this internal meeting, the Sales Account Manager will convene an initial planning meeting of all the above with the client (who, by this stage, will also have received the CD-ROM described earlier in this chapter). This initial meeting (typically held two years ahead of a national event and anything from two to seven years ahead of an international conference) will discuss any areas of concern the client may have, look at innovative features for the conference, clarify overall objectives and arrangements for the event – a written agenda is prepared. Depending on the client and the event, several such planning meetings can take place before the event itself. A comprehensive event-planning schedule is then issued and sent to the client in advance of the conference.

Once the event has taken place, a comprehensive evaluation questionnaire is sent to the client, whatever the size of event.

The ICC Director has an event planning team with eight staff. Conference sales are part of an NEC Group-wide Conference Sales function, with 13 staff, generating annual sales of approximately £12 million. The NEC Group also provides Group Operational Services, covering security, technical/engineering and cleaning.

Case study 6.4

Cranfield Management Development Centre

Cranfield Management Development Centre is a member of the Conference Centres of Excellence Consortium described in Chapter 4. It is situated in Bedfordshire close to the M1 motorway and the new town of Milton Keynes. It is a residential conference centre offering 18 conference rooms, 41 purpose-built syndicate rooms (for up to eight people) and 186 study bedrooms. It is an integral part of Cranfield School of Management.

Cranfield adheres to the quality service standards briefly outlined in Chapter 4 (see also www.cceonline.co.uk and www.cranfield.ac.uk/som/cmdc). Other systems and practices are summarized below.

- Sales leads and enquiries are generated through a planned sales and marketing activity schedule which covers a 12-month period.
- These are followed up either by the Business Development Manager or the Meetings & Events team and converted into provisional bookings, or released.
- Once a provisional booking is confirmed, a Meeting Planner is allocated. The Meeting Planner is responsible for confirming all the details to the client, including the provision of 'joining instructions'. Nearer the date of the event, the Meeting Planner will liaise with the client to confirm finer details, e.g. times of breaks, room layout, number of syndicate rooms, whether or not private dining is required, special dietary requirements, etc.
- Prior to the commencement of the conference, meeting or training course, the Meeting Planner prepares name badges and cards for each delegate, and a delegate list to go with the fire drill (for the conference leader or trainer). Another list is put up outside the meeting room so that messages received for delegates can be sent to the correct room. The Meeting Planner also prepares signage for the meeting room, syndicate room and restaurant, and ensures the provision of any specialist equipment.
- On the day of arrival, the Meeting Planner will liaise with the conference leader or trainer to ensure that arrangements are as required, and will perform a 'meet and greet' service to the delegates. Where required, the Meeting Planner will also give the housekeeping talk at the beginning of the conference/course, covering fire evacuation procedure, smoking policy, security, information on break times, etc.
- After the event, the Meeting Planner will contact the client to check for any additional feedback (delegates having been issued with feedback forms at the end of their conference/course).

Summary

Venues must continuously invest in their physical product to maintain a competitive edge. They must also adopt a customer focus in their sales and marketing strategies and in their service delivery, while aiming to maximize return on investment through their approach to, inter alia, yield management and client negotiations.

Discussion questions

1 'Investments in a venue's physical product (meeting rooms, audiovisual technology, furniture and décor, bedrooms, etc.) can compensate for any failings in service delivery by the venue's operational team'. Discuss, and debate and illustrate with specific examples.
2 Compare and contrast the approaches of The Majestic Hotel and the Westin Turnberry Resort to winning and retaining conference business. Look at their websites and identify the key conference market segments for each hotel.

Notes and references

Campbell, David. 'Market-driven venues adapt to meetings needs'. An article in *Catering Magazine*, Issue 15 (December 2000), Croner CCH Group Ltd.

Carvell, Pamela. 'Managing yield to increase profits', www.pampastraining.co.uk/ezines/managingyield.htm.

Hartley, Jerry and Rand, Peter. Conference sector capacity management. In Ian Yeoman and Anthony Ingold, editors. *Yield Management Strategies for Service Industries*. Cassell (1997).

Huyton, Jeremy R. and Peters, Sarah D. Application of yield management to the hotel industry. In Ian Yeoman and Anthony Ingold, editors. *Yield Management: Strategies for the Service Industries.* Cassell (1997).

Riley, M. *International Journal of Contemporary Hospitality Research.* Cited in TTI (2000) The Mice Industry, Travel and Tourism Intelligence.

Riley, M. and Perogiannis, N. The influence of hotel attributes on the selection of a conference venue, *International Journal of Contemporary Hospitality Management*, Vol 2. (1990).

Further reading

McCabe, Vivienne; Poole, Barry; Weeks, Paul and Leiper, Neil. *The Business and Management of Conventions*. Wiley (2000).

Shone, Anton. *The Business of Conferences*. Butterworth-Heinemann (1998).

Prerequisites for a conference hotel. An advisory paper prepared by the International Association of Professional Congress Organizers (IAPCO).

CHAPTER 7

A people industry

Introduction

The conference industry depends for its success and future profitability on attracting people with the highest-quality interpersonal and organizational skills. Such skills are equally important to both the buying and supply sides of the industry. Education and training opportunities specific to the conference sector are now emerging. Stimulating and rewarding careers can be enjoyed, although clear entry routes and progression paths do not yet exist in most countries. This chapter examines:

- the importance of people skills;
- education and training opportunities;
- development of occupational standards for the meetings industry;
- careers in the conference industry;
- salary levels;
- career profiles of leading industry figures.

The importance of people skills

The conference industry is, by definition, about people. The word 'confer' implies a discussion or meeting involving two or more people. It follows, therefore, that those wishing to make their career in the industry need to be 'people' people. They need to have very good interpersonal skills and enjoy mixing with a very wide range of people. Diplomacy, flexibility, tact, patience, friendliness, approachability, a sense of humour and being a 'team player' are just some of the skills needed for success. A variety of other skills is also required depending upon the actual position occupied.

The following job vacancy descriptions are based on actual advertisements and are quoted to highlight the types of skills needed for different posts:

Conference Administrator: Small, high-profile conference company seeks an administrator to organize prestigious events. Computer-literate, well-organized, meticulously accurate team player required. Competitive salary according to experience.

Conference and Publicity Coordinator: Are you a graduate with experience of organizing major high-profile conferences and publicity events? Do you have proven knowledge of media and public relations? Have you at least two years' experience of project management and budgetary control? If you fit this description, you could be responsible for the planning, marketing and coordination of events, an Annual Conference and Exhibition and public relations for (a professional medical association). You will lead a small dynamic team and, in addition to the stated skills, will be able to prioritize and juggle tasks, and will have excellent oral, written, presentation, negotiation and decision-making skills. The post is likely to attract candidates who are computer literate, are ambitious, have established media contacts and enjoy UK travel.

Event Coordinator (with a conference centre): Acting as principal contact between the Centre and the client, developing, organizing and managing events to ensure client requirements are carried out to the highest standard with the main objective of securing repeat and increased business. It is essential that the successful applicant has proven experience of organizing events where the focus is on high-quality customer care/service, possesses excellent communication skills together with the ability to produce detailed and accurate documentation. Applicants must be team players who are organized, thorough, able to work in a pressurized environment and possess a high level of motivation. This is a role for a dedicated and highly committed individual.

Conference Organizers: An international company, based in London, seeks two people to join its training and seminars office. We produce high-level seminars for ministers and senior officials of foreign governments. Skills required: an analytical mind, ability to work under pressure, attention to detail, experience of seminars or courses, interest in world affairs, knowledge of languages (especially Spanish, Russian, French), excellent written skills and ability to deal with senior people.

Head of Convention Bureau: ... Convention Bureau seeks conference/meetings/exhibitions/incentive industry professional to drive the marketing and selling of this international city as a business destination, working closely with – and providing benefit for – the range of hotels, venues and professional service suppliers in this market. Candidates will need 3–5 years' experience in at least one of these specialist sectors and will, ideally, have a wide network of UK and overseas contacts. A blend of marketing and sales skills will impress, but the prime requirement is the personal confidence to build positive and productive relationships with both prospective clients and the destination's suppliers.

Trainee Conference Producers: Is business research your forte? Are you ambitious, entrepreneurial, analytical and quick to grasp new and complex topics? If a career producing and devising influential, international, high-level business conferences is your aim, you'll need a good degree/Ph.D. in Science/Geography/Surveying/Law, proven business experience (minimum one year) and financial acumen. European languages desirable.

Senior Manager – Convention Bureau: Due to a promotion, we have a vacancy in one of our key posts for a talented individual who will be a commercially oriented team player who understands the need for a high level of operational support to sustain a division within a highly competitive conference marketing and sales environment. Reporting to the Director for the successful coordination and implementation of a target-led marketing and sales programme, including production of print, development of operational systems, coordination of research, membership recruitment and the motivation and management of a sales and operational team of 8 people. Highly developed leadership, communications and excellent organizational skills plus computer literacy and a full appreciation of the conference industry are pre-requisites for this position.

A number of skills and personal characteristics recur in this small selection of advertisements. Some also reappear later in the chapter, identified by leading conference industry figures as important requirements when they outline their own career profiles. The industry is broad enough to accommodate people with various working backgrounds and educational qualifications, but the common thread is the ability to build productive relationships with a wide variety of people (colleagues, clients and customers, suppliers, the media, and others) and to enjoy doing so.

Research has consistently shown that, where conference organizers and meeting planners have problems with venues, it is not, for the most part, with the facilities and equipment but with staff service, specifically a lack of professionalism and friendliness. As the physical attributes of conference venues become more standardized and of a generally acceptable level, it is likely to be the quality of the staff which will differentiate one from another. This point was expressed very lucidly in a report published in the UK by the Department of National Heritage (DNH – now Department for Culture, Media and Sport) in 1996. Entitled 'Tourism: Competing with the Best – People Working in Tourism and Hospitality', the report said that:

> The quality of personal service is perhaps more important to tourism and hospitality than to any other industry. Consumers who buy one of this industry's products will often have made a significant financial investment, but also an emotional investment and an investment of time. Of course the *physical* product – the facilities of the holiday village, the distinctiveness of the tourist attraction, the appointments of the hotel, the quality of the restaurant's food – is very important to them. But during the period customers are in the establishment, they will have many interactions with *people*: some indirect, with the management and chefs and cleaners; and many direct, with the front-line staff. The quality of those interactions is an integral part of the experience and has the potential to delight or disappoint the consumer. We do not believe that this potential is there to the same extent in any other employing sector.

The DNH report rightly claims that:

> Excellent service at a competitive price can only be provided by competent, well-managed and well-motivated people. This means recruiting the right people in the first place, equipping them with the skills they need, managing staff well to create motivation, job satisfaction, and high productivity.

The report analyses some of the tourism industry's short-comings in respect of these objectives, specifically:

> The threat of a self-perpetuating vicious circle that is harmful to profitability and competitiveness. In some parts of the industry a number of characteristics reinforce each other: recruitment difficulties, shortages of skilled and qualified staff, relatively low pay, high staff turnover and a relatively unattractive image as an employing sector.

The report then gives examples of good practice, and makes some proposals for future improvements to overall standards, through better dissemination of good practice, a greater understanding of customer needs and improving quality, improving the image of the industry and improving the supply of skills to the industry.

The conference sector of the tourism and hospitality industry is not immune from these criticisms. While they apply specifically to the supply side of the industry, it is undoubtedly the case that there is also scope to improve the training and professionalism of those on the buying side of the industry. Perhaps there is a need for a 'Code of Practice' for buyers, in the same way that conference venues now offer quality-assured branded products delivered with customer guarantees. In the author's experience, familiar failings on the part of buyers include the following.

- Ludicrously short lead times for planning events and booking venues and services.
- 'No shows' or last-minute cancellations from buyer familiarization trips, when flights have been paid for and hotel rooms booked.
- A failure to evaluate events. Research regularly shows that around one-third of organizers do not obtain delegate feedback and evaluate the effectiveness of their meetings.
- A failure to provide fully comprehensive technical and organizational specifications.
- A tendency to assume too much about a venue's capabilities and responsibilities.

- Failing to inform bureaux and agencies that have provided them with a venue-finding service of bookings made, and then complaining when they get follow-up calls.

The conference industry is a wonderful, dynamic, seductive industry but one which still fails to command the recognition it deserves. For it to achieve its full potential and be appreciated as a major benefactor to national economies, both sides of the industry must embrace and maintain the same high standards of integrity and professionalism. The status of the conference organizer must be raised to that of a real profession, of equal standing with solicitors, accountants, sales or production managers.

There is a need to invest in education and training programmes for buyers (a few are now available and others are coming on stream, but there is still a long way to go), to develop career structures so that experience and expertise are retained within the meetings industry, to enhance college and university courses so as to give appropriate coverage to conference and business tourism, and to provide recognized qualifications in line with other professions.

Buyers and suppliers are interdependent, neither can succeed without the other. Effective collaboration and partnerships should be born of respect for the skills and knowledge of each other, built on mutual trust and confidence.

To translate such needs and aspirations into reality will depend to a great extent upon developments to education and training programmes. As described in earlier chapters of this book, the profession is certainly more established as a true profession in the USA than in most, if not all, other countries and high-quality education programmes are in place. There must be scope to tailor and develop further such programmes so that they are relevant to other cultures and educational systems, as well as for individual countries to initiate their own.

The next section looks at the opportunities for education and training currently available within the conference industry, some of which are appropriate to those looking to make a career in the industry, others are for those already employed within it.

Education and training opportunities

This section will look first at the provision of opportunities at an international level. It will then focus on the current situation in the UK as an example of one country's response to perceived education and training needs. It is the author's impression that educational provision in the UK is at least on a par with that in other European countries and may be more advanced than many, but as yet no research exists that fully documents the range of meetings industry education on a European or global scale.

International courses and qualifications

IAPCO courses . . .

The International Association of Professional Congress Organisers (IAPCO) runs courses at several levels through its Institute for Congress Management Training. The best known is the annual IAPCO Seminar on Professional Congress Organisation, popularly known as the Wolfsberg Seminar, first staged in 1975. This is a week-long seminar held in Switzerland in late January and provides a comprehensive training programme for executives involved in conference organization, international conference destination promotion or ancillary services. Topics covered include: introduction to the industry, marketing a PCO company, congress promotion, meeting programmes, on-site management, finance, communications, technology, security, contracts, sponsorship and exhibitions, cooperation with hotels, and more. Attendance at the Seminar can earn points towards the 'Certificate in Meetings Management' (see below) of Meeting Professionals International (MPI) and continuing education units in the programme of the Professional Convention Management Association (PCMA) (see below). IAPCO also runs advanced management courses.

Full details of all IAPCO courses are available from: IAPCO Secretariat, 42 Canham Road, London W3 7SR, UK (tel.: +44–20–8749 6171; fax: +44–20–8740–0241; email: info@iapco.org; website: www.iapco.org).

'Certification in Meetings Management' Programme . . .

The Certification in Meetings Management (CMM) has been developed by Meeting Professionals International (MPI) and is the first university co-developed global professional qualification for meeting professionals. It represents a major step towards encouraging and recognizing professionalism in meeting and conference management. The CMM focuses on strategic issues and executive decision-making. Once accepted on to the CMM programme and registered for a course, participants are required to complete four components:

(a) pre-residency (or pre-residential): preparatory reading and assignments, including a 'virtual' assignment requiring a number of participants to 'meet' through technology;

(b) residency (residential): a four-day full immersion course, with sessions covering strategic thinking and acting, strategic negotiation, strategic marketing, strategic management, strategic leadership, organizational culture and technology;

(c) examination: composed of essay questions requiring participants to apply what has been learned to their own organization/situation;

(d) post-residency (post-residential) business project: requires participants to produce a business plan based on what they have learned during the programme.

An MPI Task Force developed the structure, content and format of the CMM, and the academic framework was compiled by the Institut de Management Hôtelier International in Paris. After thorough study and market analysis, MPI decided in 1998 that the CMM programme should be adapted for meeting professionals worldwide and moved beyond the tactical to the strategic, advanced level, covering topics as outlined above.

While the core curriculum taught in the CMM varies only slightly from programme to programme, the curriculum is adjusted to take account of different cultures and industry realities in the country or continent in which the programme is being offered. MPI strives to ensure an appropriate balance of faculty members (teaching staff) from the geographic culture, while still offering global input from tutors from outside that culture. Some attendees have found it beneficial to attend a course outside their own region in order to broaden their perspectives, and build their skills in global meeting planning.

The CMM qualification does not affect the status of the Certified Meeting Professional (CMP) designation (CMP is a largely North American designation currently). In fact, the CMM is structured to complement, rather than compete with, the CMP designation: the former is more strategic in approach, the latter more tactical. Meeting professionals can apply for the CMP designation if they have:

- at least three years of meeting management experience;
- current employment in meeting management;
- responsibility and accountability for the successful completion of meetings.

The CMM is open to anyone working in the conference industry, such as:

Planners (buyers)	*Suppliers*
Corporate planners (full- or part-time)	Hotels and conference centres
Association planners	Staff of convention bureaux
Professional conference organizers	Audiovisual/production companies
	Airlines
	Destination management companies, etc.

Further details on the CMM are available from:

- MPI International Headquarters, 4455 LBJ Freeway, Suite 1200, Dallas, Texas 75244, USA (tel.: +1(972) 702–3000; fax: +1 (972) 702–3070; email: education@mpiweb.org; website: www.mpiweb.org).
- MPI European Office, 22 Route de Grundhof, L-6315 Beaufort, Grand Duchy of Luxembourg (tel.: +352 2687–6141; fax: +352 2687–6343; email: dscaillet@mpiweb.org).

Further details on the CMP are available from: Convention Industry Council, 8201 Greensboro Drive, Suite 300, McLean, Virginia 22102, USA (tel.: +1 (703) 610–9030; fax: +1 (703) 610–9005; www.clc-online.org or www.conventionindustry.org).

Certified Destination Management Executive programme

The Certified Destination Management Executive (CDME) programme has been developed by the International Association of Convention and Visitor Bureaus (IACVB), and is relevant to those working in the convention and visitor bureau (CVB) and destination management/marketing side of the conference and tourism industry.

Recognized by the CVB industry as the highest educational achievement, the CDME programme is delivered under the auspices of the World Tourism Management Centre at The University of Calgary, Canada, in collaboration with Purdue University (Indiana) and IACVB. It is an advanced educational programme designed for experienced CVB executives who are looking for senior-level professional development courses as well as an industry designation.

The main goal of the CDME programme is to prepare senior executives and managers of destination management organizations for increasing change and competition. The focus of the CDME is on vision, leadership, productivity and implementing business strategies. Demonstrating the value of a destination team and improving personal performance through effective organizational and industry leadership are the expected outcomes. Those completing the programme successfully are entitled to use the CDME designation.

The course has three core modules:

- strategic issues in destination management;
- destination marketing planning;
- destination leadership.

Participants also choose from a variety of elective modules, including:

- destination information and research;
- international tourism and convention marketing;
- destination financial management;
- rural and small community destination management;
- destination community relations planning;
- sustainable destination development and marketing;
- human resources in destination management;
- festivals and events tourism;
- communications and technology in destination management;
- resort destination management;
- destination promotion planning;
- wine destination marketing and management;
- gaming and destination management;
- visitor servicing in destination management;
- convention/tradeshow marketing and sales management;
- destination partnership development;
- destination product development.

Further details on the CDME programme are available from: Professional Development Coordinator, IACVB, 2025 M Street, NW, Suite 500, Washington, DC 20036, USA (tel.: +1 (202) 296–7888; fax: +1 (202) 296–7889; website: www.iacvb.org).

EFCT Summer School

The European Federation of Conference Towns (EFCT) has been running an annual Summer School since 1987, held in a different country each year (normally end of August/early September) over 3–4 days. The programme aims to give an overview of the conference industry, emphasizing the role of convention bureaux and conference centres, but also catering for related hotel, airline and PCO/DMC personnel. Topics at the 2002 Summer School (held in Stockholm) included: competing in the global marketplace, market research, conference technology, marketing a destination, who is king in marketing a congress centre?, using the Internet as a source of information and marketing tool, site inspection and familiarization trips, a client perspective on destination selection, successful bidding, the role of the PCO and Core PCO, exhibitions, and working with the press.

Further details are available from: EFCT, BP 182, 1040 Brussels, Belgium (tel.: +32 2–732–6954; fax: +32 2–735–4840; email: secretariat@efct.com; website: www.efct.com).

Professional Convention Management Association Education Foundation

The Professional Convention Management Association (PCMA) Education Foundation is designed to 'enhance the credibility and reputation of the Professional Convention Management Association by securing funding and developing, producing, and delivering education, training, research products and services for the meetings industry'. Established in 1985, the Foundation supports educational programmes to improve professionalism and to provide a university-level meeting management curriculum. Educational programmes are provided for meeting managers, hotels, convention and visitor bureaux, and others in the meetings industry.

At the time of writing (October 2002), PCMA was in the process of developing distance learning programmes. It has already launched 'Self-Study Programs', which can be taken at an individual's own pace. These include:

1 'Preparation for the Certified Meeting Professional (CMP) Exam' – a ten-lesson course available in both print and electronic formats; and
2 'Introduction to Small Meetings' – designed to help the new meeting planner who does not plan meetings as his primary job function. The course focuses on meetings with fewer than 300 attendees.

In addition to the CMP designation, other well-established designations (especially in the USA) include:

- CAE: Certified Association Executive – awarded by the American Society of Association Executives 'as the highest honour of professional achievement in association management';
- CEM: Certified in Exposition Management – a designation adopted by the International Association for Exposition Management in 1975.

Further information: PCMA, 2301 South Lake Shore Drive, Suite 1001, Chicago, IL 60616–1419, USA (tel.: +1 (312) 423–7262; fax: +1 (312) 423–7222; website: www.pcma.org/education/foundation).

UK University and College Courses

As will be made clear later in this chapter in the section on careers, it is *not* essential for those looking to make a career in the conference industry to have pursued a particular educational course, although certain courses can provide skills and knowledge that are readily applicable to the industry. For those wishing to study a course that is directly relevant to a future career, the best options are probably hotel and catering courses and, particularly, courses involving tourism and tourism management. Several hundred colleges and universities across the UK now offer full-time courses in travel, tourism and leisure, at a variety of levels.

Until very recently, conference and business tourism did not feature strongly on any of these courses. This is now changing as an increasing number of educational institutions offer 'conference management' and 'event management' modules as part of tourism and hotel and catering courses. However, it seems that many modules have been designed for those expecting to work on the supply side of the industry, as conference or event coordinators in venues, for example. Until the mid-1990s, there had been relatively little provision for people looking to find employment as conference organizers or in a conference agency.

Leeds Metropolitan University

In part to address this need, Leeds Metropolitan University launched a new degree course in Events Management in 1996. Available for study as a four-year sandwich course, three-year full-time course, or on a part-time basis for those in employment (as well as a one-year top-up degree for students who have gained a Higher National Diploma in a related discipline or have relevant experience). The areas studied include conference and meeting planning, convention and trade show organization, concert and event planning, security and law, and contracts and tendering. To underpin these essential areas, there is further academic study exploring financial management within the event industry, strategic management and strategic human resource management. The principles of marketing are also studied in depth. There is an industry placement (unless students have substantial previous work experience in the events field) in Year 2 lasting 48 weeks, which provides a learning experience for students to develop their skills while working in the event industry.

The University also now offers an HND Events Management course of three years' duration.

Further details are available from: The Course Administrator, The School of Tourism and Hospitality Management, Faculty of Cultural and Education Studies, Leeds Metropolitan University, Calverley Street, Leeds LS1 3HE, UK (tel.: +44 (0)113–283–3447; fax: +44 (0)113–283–3111; email: events@lmu.ac.uk; website: www.worldofevents.net).

City of Westminster College

There is also a course specific to the conference industry, an HNC in Business – Conference and Event Management, designed by the Association of British Professional Conference Organisers (ABPCO) in partnership with the University of Westminster and City of Westminster College, London. This two-year part-time course aims to equip students with:

- an understanding of the practical and theoretical applications of conference and event management;

- an awareness of the general principles within which conferences are managed;
- an awareness of the legal and financial implications in the context of conferences and events.

The first semester of the course focuses on helping students to understand the main principles of organizing a conference or event, and covers the practical skills necessary to become a competent Professional Conference Organizer (PCO). The second semester is dedicated to giving students an opportunity to apply their new-found knowledge, using a case study format, and requires them to combine the demanding aspects of organizing a conference with the skills necessary to promote their own organization.

Further details of the course are available from Caroline Roney, ABPCO Education and Training Coordinator, Congress House, 65 West Drive, Cheam, Surrey SM2 7NB, UK (tel.: +44 (0)20–8661–0877; fax: +44 (0)20–8661–9036; email: info@conforg .com); or Joy Gardner (tel.: +44 (0)20–8291–3053; email: cho@netlineuk.net).

Fife College

Fife College is now running a two-year HND in Events Management, the first year forming an HNC in Events Coordination. The College also offers, by distance learning methods, courses that can lead to a National/Scottish Vocational Qualification (N/SVQ) in Events, up to and including Level III, for those working in the events industry.

Further details are available from Fife College of Further and Higher Education, St. Brycedale Avenue, Kirkcaldy, Fife KY1 1EX, UK (tel.: +44 (0)1592 268591 ext. 2721; fax: +44 (0)1592 640225; email: b-neilson@mail.fife.ac.uk).

Sheffield Hallam University

Sheffield Hallam University offers an MSc in European Conference Management on both a full-time and part-time basis. The University has partnerships with leading universities in Spain, Italy and Germany. Entry requirements include an honours degree or recognized equivalent qualification, as well as ability in a foreign language (especially Spanish, Italian or German). In the 2002–2003 academic year, the University also introduced an undergraduate course (BSc) in International Hospitality Management with Conferences and Events.

Further details are available from Tourism Management, School of Leisure and Food Management, Sheffield Hallam University, City Campus, Howard Street, Sheffield S1 1WB, UK (tel.: +44 (0)114 225 3976; fax: +44 (0)114 225 3343; email: j.swarbrooke@shu.ac.uk).

Thames Valley University • • •

The Thames Valley University (Ealing campus in London) launched BA/Dip.H.E. courses in Event Management in 2002–2003. For further details, see the website: www.tvu.ac.uk/courses.

New College Nottingham • • •

New College Nottingham launched, in September 2001, a Foundation Degree in Events and Facilities Management. The course is two years' full-time (but may be completed over a longer period) and gives progression to an honours degree. It is aimed at people who want to follow a management career in the events industry.

Further details are available from Course Leader, New College Nottingham, Adams Building, Stoney Street, Lace Market, Nottingham, NG1 1LJ, UK (tel.: +44 (0)115 910 4504; fax: +44 (0)115 910 4501; email: a.willis@ncn.ac.uk; website: www.ncn.ac.uk).

Development of occupational standards for the meetings industry

At the time of writing, Meeting Professionals International's European Council was actively engaged in the creation of a set of occupational standards for the European meetings industry, which would lead to the development of a European Union-wide professional qualification for conference organizers and meeting planners. The initiative would examine a set of standards established in Canada, which identified 13 core functions (e.g. financial management, venue selection, programme design, risk management) that have to be performed by meeting coordinators and meeting managers. Each of these functions is then broken down into tasks requiring specific skills.

The benefits expected to accrue from the establishment of such standards and qualifications would include:

- enhanced quality of meetings in Europe, including more valuable information exchange, better life-long learning experiences, more focused training;
- a guaranteed quality of services contracted from one country to another;
- a stimulus to the development of the industry into a truly recognized profession;
- the provision of development opportunities for low-skilled young people that can lead to a recognized career and a clear path for professional development.

It was anticipated that the development of the set of occupational standards should be complete in 2003.

Further details are available from:

- MPI European Office, 22 Route de Grundhof, L-6315 Beaufort, Grand Duchy of Luxembourg (tel.: +352 2687–6141; fax: +352 2687–6343; email: dscaillet@mpiweb.org; website: www.mpiweb.org.
- MPI Canadian Office, 329 March Road, Suite 232 Box 11, Kanata, Ontario K2K 2E1, Canada (tel.: +1 (613) 271–8901; fax: +1 (613) 599–7027).

In the UK, work has been under way since 1993 to establish nationally-recognized qualifications based on competence at work. The results are National and Scottish Vocational Qualifications (N/SVQs) specifically designed for the events industry and awarded by the City and Guilds of London Institute.

These N/SVQs are for almost everyone in the events industry, particularly those who are involved in:

- organizing events;
- working at event venues;
- exhibiting;
- supplying goods and services for events.

There are Events N/SVQs at Levels 2, 3 and 4 for practitioners, senior practitioners, supervisors and managers. The N/SVQs provide different qualification routes for:

- event organizers;
- venue providers;
- exhibitors;
- suppliers.

The efforts to establish N/SVQs have been spearheaded by the Events Sector Industry Training Organization (ESITO). ESITO is also an accredited assessment centre for the Events N/SVQs.

Such activity will be overseen by a newly created Sector Skills Council (SSC) covering Hospitality, Leisure, Travel and Tourism, which will have 'events' within its remit. The SSC will have money to support industry training, and to represent the industry's interests in areas such as qualifications and standards.

Further information on UK Events N/SVQs is available from ESITO, Riverside House, High Street, Huntingdon, Cambridgeshire PE29 3SG, UK (fax: +44 (0)1480–412863).

ESITO is also one of a number of European bodies (the others being the Institute for Vocational Training – Portugal; The Prague Congress Centre – Czech Republic; the German Trade Fair

Association, AUMA; and the Travel, Tourism and Events National Training Organization – UK), which together applied successfully in 2002 for part funding from the European Commission Leonardo Programme in order to develop a programme and support materials for international event organizers. The aims of this project were summarized as:

- to identify the skills, knowledge and understanding required of events organizers in an international context;
- to agree common learning objectives for international event organizers;
- to develop an agreed common learning programme and flexible learning support material, and to train trainers in how to use them;
- to develop common testing mechanisms to measure progress toward achievement of the agreed common learning objectives;
- to evaluate the effectiveness of the materials;
- to disseminate the details of the project, the support materials and the final results.

The project is not intended to compete in any way with programmes set up by national bodies within individual European countries.

Careers in the conference industry

Unlike many other professions, the conference industry does not yet have clear entry routes or easily identified career progression paths. It is one of the facets that illustrate its relative immaturity as an industry. This lack of structure may be somewhat frustrating and confusing for those, both within and outside the industry, who have set their sights on reaching a particular career goal but are uncertain about how best to get there. At the same time, however, this lack of precedent and structure can encourage a greater fluidity and freedom of movement between jobs. There is often no set requirement to progress in a particular way, or to have obtained specific qualifications before being able to move on.

Many of those now working in the industry have come to it as a second or third career. This is not surprising in view of the need to be at ease in dealing with a wide range of people, or in coping with a last-minute crisis in the build-up to a high-profile conference – situations that require a reasonable maturity and some experience of life.

Previous experience in hotel and catering, sales and marketing, business administration, secretarial work, financial management, local government administration, training, travel and transport, or leisure and tourism could be advantageous, depending upon the position being considered. But many other backgrounds and disciplines can also give very relevant skills and knowledge, provided that these are combined with a natural affinity for working with people.

For those looking to find employment straight from university or college, vacancies do arise in conference agencies (e.g. administrative posts, assisting in venue finding, computer work) and in conference venues (as assistant conference and banqueting coordinators, or in venue sales and marketing). It can be possible for new graduates to obtain posts in conference offices and convention bureaux, although, more often, 1–2 years' previous experience in sales and marketing or local government administration is desirable.

Relatively few conference organizers, especially within the corporate sector, are full-time conference organizers and meeting planners. They are first and foremost secretaries/PAs, marketing assistants/managers, training managers, or public relations executives, who find themselves asked to organize events on behalf of their department or company. Their role in conference organizing may, of course, develop if they prove to have the right talents and enthusiasm, and if this meets the company's own development needs.

Other openings arise, from time to time, in conference industry trade associations and, for those with an interest in publishing, in the industry's trade magazines (either in advertising sales or, for those with some journalistic background, as part of the editorial team).

Before beginning a career within conferencing, it is probably helpful to know whether one's interest is primarily in the buying or supply side of the industry, although it is quite possible at a later stage to switch from one side to the other, and an understanding of how both buyers and suppliers operate is obviously important and beneficial. It is a moot point whether intermediary agencies are best described as buyers or suppliers. Their activities certainly revolve around venue finding and event management, but they do this by providing a service to their clients, the actual buyers.

It should be stressed that most companies and organizations operating within the conference industry are small, employing limited numbers of people. This is true of most corporate and association event departments, convention bureaux, conference venues, agencies and trade associations. They cannot offer multiple career opportunities and endless possibilities for progression. But their smallness does often ensure that there is a great variety of work with considerable responsibility and lots of scope to display initiative. It does also mean that it is possible, quite quickly, to get to know many of the players in the industry, building friendships and networks of colleagues nationally and, indeed, across the world.

Salary levels

Perusal of vacancies in trade magazines or on websites is one good way to obtain information on salary or compensation levels for different types of positions within the industry. Another useful indicator are regular surveys undertaken by recruitment agencies and trade associations. The figures quoted below are taken from two such surveys carried out in 2002.

1 Specialist UK events sector recruitment consultancy, ESP Recruitment, in conjunction with research company Vivid Interface emailed a questionnaire to the 31 000 readers of *Event* magazine in Spring 2002, generating almost 2000 responses (in a ratio of 68 per cent from women, 32 per cent from men, clearly reflecting the prominent role that women play in the

Sector	Job title	Lowest salary	Highest salary	Average
1. Head of events				
Corporate	Head of events	£40 000	£90 000	£69 950
Production	Production director	£15 000	£53 000	£42 000
Venue	Head of events	£38 000	£40 000	£39 000
Exhibition services	General manager	£35 000	£60 000	£45 000
Commercial conferences	Head of logistics	£28 000	£45 000	£35 000
Exhibitions	Group operations manager	£25 710	£70 000	£43 576
Event management company	Account director	£28 000	£40 000	£34 750
Charity	Head of events	£35 000	£45 000	£37 000
2. Event manager				
Corporate	Event manager	£15 450	£50 000	£29 954
Production	Production manager	£19 500	£30 000	£28 000
Venue	Event manager	£20 000	£26 500	£25 000
Exhibition services	Project manager	£25 000	£35 000	£28 000
Commercial conferences	Conference manager	£20 000	£45 000	£27 644
Exhibitions	Operations manager	£16 000	£30 500	£24 181
Event management company	Account manager	£15 000	£63 000	£25 330
Charity	Event manager	£16 200	£36 000	£24 611
3. Event executive				
Corporate	Event executive	£20 000	£27 000	£24 622
Event management company	Account executive	£13 500	£24 000	£21 200
Commercial conferences	Conference coordinator	£19 000	£25 000	£21 333
Exhibitions	Operations executive	£19 000	£25 500	£21 200
Charity	Event executive	£18 000	£24 000	£21 000

Source: ESP Recruitment (reproduced with permission).

Table 7.1
UK Events Sector Salary Survey 2002 – ESP Recruitment

21st century conference industry). The responses form the basis of the survey findings, and this was the third year that the survey was undertaken. A small sample of the findings is reproduced in Table 7.1.

Complimentary copies of the full survey findings are available from ESP Recruitment by email only (contact: info@esprecruitment.co.uk). Survey results are normally available in September each year.

2 *MPI Salary Survey 2002* – Meeting Professionals International (MPI) carries out a biennial Salary Survey among its planner members. The 2002 Survey is based on replies from some 1500 meeting planners, mainly from the USA, but including some responses from its 'international' membership. The Survey provides a detailed breakdown by location, job title, educational level, experience and type of organization. A few of the key findings are listed below.

- The average US planner earned $60714 dollars in 2002, an increase from $54613 in 2000.
- The average salary for planners located outside North America was $62028 in 2002. This ranged from an average of $67478 for planners working for corporations to $53256 to those working for an association or society, and to just $40000 for those employed by an association management company.
- The average salary for all respondents, including those from Canada and the rest of the world, was $59447.

Other findings were as follows.

- 57 per cent of planners had a high level of job satisfaction, 38 per cent a moderate level, and only 5 per cent a low level.
- Only 29 per cent of respondents spent 100 per cent of their time working on meeting management. A further 31 per cent spent between 75 and 99 per cent of their time, and 19 per cent spent less than 50 per cent of their time in this way.
- Perhaps not surprisingly, 60 per cent of respondents felt that their salary/compensation package did not adequately reflect their responsibilities and their contribution to their employer.
- 30 per cent of respondents had achieved the Certified Meeting Professional (CMP) designation, 1 per cent the Certification in Meeting Management (CMM) and 68 per cent neither of these.

Further details are available from MPI International Headquarters, 4455 LBJ Freeway, Suite 1200, Dallas, Texas 75244, USA (tel.: +1 (972) 702–3000; fax: +1 (972) 702–3070; website: www.mpiweb.org).

Career profiles of leading industry figures

The last section of this chapter contains a series of career profiles written by well-known personalities within the international conference industry. They each describe their current jobs and those aspects of their work that they find rewarding and fulfilling. Some also outline the parts of their work that they find less enjoyable, and previous career experiences, including education and training, are touched on. It is hoped that these profiles will be instructive and maybe inspirational, encouraging some of the readers of this book to want to follow in their footsteps and forge their own careers in the infinitely varied and endlessly stimulating conference industry. Their specific experience, in the order in which they appear, is as a PCO, convention and visitor bureau chief executive, convention centre sales director, exhibition director, and managing editor of a conference and incentive industry trade magazine.

Sarah Storie-Pugh, Managing Director, Concorde Services Limited, UK

Armed with little more than a secretarial qualification, I started my career in politics, working at the Houses of Parliament in political research and as PA to the Secretary of the Shadow Cabinet. It was there that I went through the painful but (little did I know then for my future career) invaluable art of minute

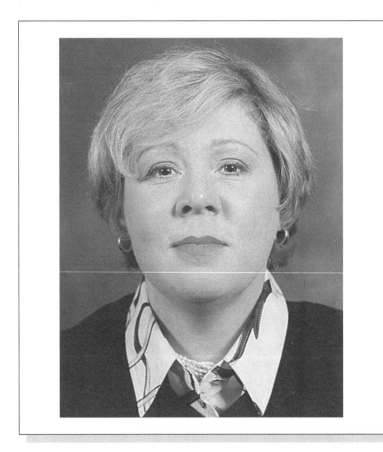

Figure 7.1
Sarah Storie-Pugh.

taking and interpreting what was actually meant as well as said. It stood me in good stead. Four years of working with politicians, ministers and leaders made me realize that I wanted to be instrumental in organization, not just a witness to it.

I therefore left the heady and sheltered world of politics and went to see what else there was out in the big wide world. I had no plans and no ideas as to which direction I wished to go, so attended hundreds of interviews seeking that mysterious challenge. After a while I was offered a job as PA to the Organizer of the Farnborough Airshow and, within six months, my first Show took place. I was hooked, and made a simple decision: this was what I was going to do for the rest of my life. And, 25 years later, I am still doing it.

My first break into the world of conventions came when I was lucky enough to be offered an apprenticeship by Conference Services Limited. At that time they were the leading professional conference organizing company, certainly in the UK and probably in the world. They trained me in all aspects of international association meeting management and gave me a very solid grounding for future growth.

It was also where I had my first management love affair! Every now and again, an event comes along with which you fall in love, and you devote everything to it. The World Petroleum Congress in 1983 was such an event. I loved it and it became a personal milestone. But, after such a passionate organizational love affair, I felt the need for change. So, when the opportunity arose to join Sarah Frost-Wellings' exhibition company, Concorde Services, to integrate the conference organization element, I jumped at it.

Our vision was to place equal emphasis on exhibition and conference management in the association market, joining them and making the two elements work together as a cohesive whole. This is now commonplace, but Concorde was the first company to promote the concept and, for many years, we created a niche market for ourselves. The company continued to grow as did, inevitably, my experience. This led to my close involvement with both IAPCO and ABPCO, and the honour of becoming, in due course, President of both.

After seven enormously successful years, 1989 saw another milestone that gave rise to a change of direction. Due to the retirement of my partner through ill health, I had to make a decision: stand still and take stock, or move forward and grow. At the end of the day, the decision was easy. Concorde grew but not without the help of a lot of people on the way. Friends, colleagues and clients all helped to nurture that growth and ensure the success of the company.

As I've grown older, I've realized the worth of other people and the value of their friendship and wisdom. I've laughed and cried, but mostly I've stood proud knowing that everyone in this industry busts a gut to get the event right on the day. I don't believe there is anyone in this industry – competitor or colleague, friend or foe – who, when the chips are down, will not come to your aid to ensure the success of an event. There is no other industry where there is such common purpose and camaraderie.

So, what are the requirements for a successful organizer? It's not just about being an organized person, although that helps. It's a passion. It's an all-embracing, totally engulfing love affair with events. And that love affair is fed by the desire for excellence: to be better, go further, make each event more successful than the last. It is a passion for detail to the nth degree. One of my favourite sayings is 'if you are going round in circles, perhaps you are cutting corners'. You cannot cut corners in this business; you rule the corners and measure them until they are perfect.

You need vision for this passion, this passion for excellence. You need to see everything in your own mind and then be able to communicate that vision to others: to your client, so that they can see the vision as well; to your staff and team-mates, so that they can bring it to fruition; and to your suppliers so they can produce it. And your love affair will prove infectious: the more you enthuse about what you are doing, the more everyone will go the extra mile with you. I strongly believe that if you do not have this passion for events, then don't bother to try – 'I like travel, I like being in a "people" industry, I am a good organizer' is not enough if you want to be the best.

But even with this passion, has it all been a quarter century of laughs and an easy ride? Not at all. Like any affair, there have been many tears along the way, both mine and my staff's. Tears are generally brought on by stress, tiredness and, perhaps, the straw that broke the camel's back that day. It might have been the rain pouring in through the marquee, or the coach getting stuck in traffic, or the plane being diverted, or the speaker providing the wrong presentation to the technician, or the session going on too long and the food being spoilt, or the briefcases not being delivered – sound familiar?

But, in contrast, there is that wonderful feeling when everything goes just right. The sort of feeling that gives you goose pimples, that makes you laugh out loud with the sheer joy of success: when the crowd comes pouring through the doors, when the first note of the band starts, when the first firework explodes in the night sky, when a client says 'that was the best conference ever, and I've been to many of them' – then it's all worthwhile. My passion remains!

Advice? Well I would say, never be too proud to seek help, or too arrogant to believe that you do not need it, or too tired to be unable to finish the job to the standard you know is right, or too frustrated not to be able to laugh at the situation and at yourself, or to fail to find time to communicate effectively with those around you. But most of all, never be too complacent to realize that you are in the best job in the world. Go for it; love your job, love your life. I do.

Gary Grimmer, Chief Executive Officer, Melbourne Convention & Visitors Bureau

It seems that most people you run into fell into their careers by chance and luck. But, often people do make their own luck.

I was a PR guy, who had moved to Boston, Massachusetts, in 1981 in search of fame and fortune. The travel industry appealed to me – it seemed glamorous and fun – getting paid to help other people have a good time travelling and maybe doing some travel myself. I figured that the best possible PR job in Boston would be doing PR *for* Boston, and it seemed that the best place to do that would be at the convention and visitors bureau (CVB). However, I guessed that, even if the bureau had a job opening, they wouldn't likely hire a guy with a southern accent (Charleston, South Carolina) to do PR for Boston. After a couple of months, I still hadn't gotten around to approaching the bureau.

Then I learned that the CVB actually had a PR job opening. I thought 'it couldn't hurt' to drop off my resume, and a couple of days later I got called in for an interview. Long story short, I got the job, and started happily working for my mentor, then the President of the Boston bureau, Bob Cumings. One day, about four months later, Bob told me that he had just seen my resume for the first time, that he had found it at the bottom of a big stack

Figure 7.2
Gary Grimmer.

of papers. He had lots of stacks of papers like that. It turned out that when he called me for an interview he had never seen my resume. Rather, he had seen a 'looking for work' notice that I had written for a trade publication. I almost didn't submit that little classified ad but, at the time, I thought 'it couldn't hurt.' If I hadn't put it in, I wouldn't be in the industry today.

It has been a pretty wild ride for the past 21 years. After Boston, I was CEO of the Albuquerque, New Mexico, bureau. And, after that, Portland, Oregon. I used to say that after Portland, I wanted to move into the international arena, and run a bureau outside of North America, preferably in Australia. In 1993, I had the privilege of being elected Chairman of the International Association of Convention & Visitor Bureaus (IACVB). In the same year, I raised my hand for my dream job, and was hired as the CEO of the Melbourne, Australia, bureau. Ironically, when this American moved to Melbourne, it was the first time that the Chairman of IACVB hailed from a bureau outside of North America. So, I guess it's a bit like going from marketing Boston with a Southern accent, to marketing Melbourne with a Yank accent . . . a lot of good people have been pretty accommodating to me along the way.

Yes, luck has a lot to do with it. But, my philosophy is that there's a lot to be said for knowing what you want to do. As they say, you are much more likely to get there, if you have a clear vision of where you would like to go.

For the past 12 years, I've had this quote stuck to the wall next to my desk. The quote is by W.H. Murray, leader of the Scottish Himalayan Expedition in 1951. In it he references a Goethe couplet – 'Whatever you can do, or dream you can, begin it. Boldness has genius, power, and magic to it'. In many instances over the years, it has become clear to me that Goethe has really got it right there.

I don't suppose that there could be an industry that is more fun than the conference industry to work in. Most of what is great about life is the people you get to know, and this industry seems to be filled with really good, interesting, intelligent people. And, they're all having fun! Hopefully, we are all also making a difference in people's lives and in the success of the communities that we live in.

On that last point, I thought that I might just slip a commercial message into the middle of this. Think of it as a subliminal cut. Did I mention that Melbourne is probably the finest business events destination in the world? We call it a 'purpose-built convention city'. I don't really have the space here to explain why, but, Melbourne is one of the coolest cities in the world. Don't just take my word for it, come check it out – you'll agree.

Now, Tony Rogers said that I have to present a balanced account. He said that I should make references to the difficulties and frustrations that I experience. OK. Did I mention politics? CVBs are usually private, not-for-profit corporations, but they rely heavily on government funding. Our problem is that public officials tend to have a difficult time understanding our business. It is frustrating for marketing people like us to have to spend a lot of time educating government policy people. Then, once we've done it, another election comes along and we have to start all over again.

The 'political' challenge is part of an overall greater challenge, which is that most bureaux are operating on very limited resources. When you believe in what you do, and you know you could make a much bigger impact with additional resources, it can be very frustrating not to have the funds you need to get the job done. That is a universal bureau frustration. But, the flip side is that we are very good at getting a lot done on limited resources. We're poor, but we're sharp!

Finally, there is an issue over inadequate research in our industry. As I was writing this, I had a consultant call me asking about certain types of data on the meetings industry in Australia. I had to tell him that it simply didn't exist. This is an issue that affects us globally and daily, it's one of the windmills I've tilted at for the past 21 years. I'm currently serving as Chairman of DOME (Data on Meetings and Events), an international foundation that is kind of headquartered in cyberspace, but incorporated in Washington, DC. We're trying to fix the research issue. Stay tuned.

So, how am I doing on my path to fame and fortune? Famous enough, I guess, to be featured in this book, but the fortune is still eluding me! I'm getting to the point where having fun, feeling fulfilled and having good friends is more important anyway. And, yes, there's been lots of good travel.

Jenny Salsbury, Director, Conferences, Scottish Exhibition and Conference Centre, Glasgow

This industry is a hidden and a very understated revenue earner. Like most people working in conferences, I discovered it pretty much by accident, loved it, got addicted and here I am 20 years later still loving it. My family, however, are still none the wiser and have a slight mumble about what I do when talking to their friends!

The reality of our role in selling convention centres is that we are really little more than grown-up space sales people – and some of us feel slightly less grown up than others. I have specialized somewhat in the field of association conferences, in particular, the international congresses, which are really fascinating to negotiate for but not for those who want the constant fix of a sale. There is a need to be an exceptionally good listener, to have a good memory to make the links that all go together to

Figure 7.3
Jenny Salsbury.

build the case and to remember who you've met before, plus having a talent for spotting an opportunity where the particular person you are with can see a link with your 'product' and also a gain towards their own goals, thus producing the ideal 'win–win' situation. The rest is common sense.

Other people actually put the event on and it's really up to us to spark the imagination and act as a kind of catalyst putting together the elements. In order to do this, I have always felt it necessary to understand what the organization is trying to achieve – hurrah for my bright idea to do a shorthand and typing course, as when I started out, I could just get the client talking and take down exactly what they said, since I could always figure it out later on!

It is surprising to me that so many organizers have not yet realized the revenue potential from their exhibition alongside their regular conference and still talk in terms of charity work done by not-for-profit organizations. The more sponsorship of an event can be encouraged, the more erudite aims and worthy causes can be achieved. Thankfully most of the main organizers today have realized this potential and are working really well with growing their conferences – it's great to work with them as you can then see ways in which your venue services can assist with an even bigger, better show or smarter, smoother presenta-tions. The older style secretary-general has pretty much retired by now but they do still pop up, usually as a fam trip luvvy.

People in convention centres do have a huge range of experience in many different types of events, and it is surprising that organizers are sometimes hesitant to trawl through the mental files to help their own event, transferring their experience from a totally different venue they have used before. Gaining this experience as a sales person can be a long and very frustrating road – try asking an operations person how many people can be fed in a certain room. The response depends on a seemingly endless list of factors that will cover the worst-case scenario in terms of health and safety issues. Sales people are always, therefore, talking second hand. The important thing is to take a situation or a perceived problem and work together to sort out how it can be managed, and have an open mind ready to consider all approaches. The solutions are not always about spending more money and are usually about the design of 'traffic flow' of people through an event.

There will, however, be certain battles a venue salesperson is not going to win, and knowing when to walk away from a situation, put a different face on to the particular case and move on is key to minimizing stress levels. My training in the industry has really come from on-the-job experience working in a convention bureau, where I was in an overseas office selling a high-value destination. We had to talk big whilst being quite small; the fact that I was selling my home town and I loved it was a huge help. I would spend hours researching and finding out details for people – and this was before the web, electronic databases and PCs on the desktop. There are really many things I would have liked to have learnt from some kind of study but there really were no courses beyond the one run every year by IAPCO (see earlier in this chapter for details), which I persuaded my boss in 1987 would be an exceptionally good investment for the company to send me on. I am continuously learning from the network of friends in the industry who all have a like-minded approach.

I also learnt from attending seminars alongside trade exhibitions and from endless discussions at the bar at the end of the day. The gatherings at convention industry trade associations are always great fun and one of the best I used to attend was the annual conference of the EFCT. Just what Hong Kong had to do with the European Conference Towns was totally beside the point: I was being introduced by Geoffrey Smith who had been taken on as a consultant to a complete novice.

Having done ten years at the Hong Kong Tourist Association, I felt it was time to move and wanted to take the next step in developing a lead rather than passing it on once it got interesting. The problem was I had the best job in the industry and it took me quite a while to find something that matched up. Eventually, I moved into sales in the Hong Kong Convention & Exhibition Centre.

Moving from a bureau to a venue is a culture shock and the relationship between the two disciplines is traditionally fraught with potential dispute not to say angst. I am a great believer in trying my utmost to keep a happy balance but it is hard to explain to a salesperson who has just won a contract that it was a team effort and also hard to explain to a local authority-funded organization that needs to justify its return to the community that the venue (i.e. the commercial world) played a part in winning.

The clients I love are the ones who have really become friends and with whom we develop new ways of doing things. Moving into the SECC in Glasgow, Scotland, in 1996 opened me up to the way the British conference industry works, and I have to say it is very satisfying working with repeat clients where we see annual conferences come back and how they have moved into new technology, etc. I do think Britain is way ahead of other countries in the field of presentation technology. International PCOs, too, bring more of their clients back to us, and I love the openness with which we talk/negotiate where they know we have to make something to continue the level of service and, where we are given enough space with this, to pull out all the stops to deliver a great event to the client.

Sometimes I think I would like a different job, one where you could spend more time with the family and know when you could book holidays and not be too tired to travel for short breaks with pals. But then something exciting comes along and I just get my teeth into the next presentation – hope we can convince them!

Ray Bloom, Chairman of IMEX, the Worldwide Exhibition for Incentive Travel, Meetings and Events (Frankfurt)

I suppose you could say that I fell into this industry by chance. My early career certainly gave me no indication that I would fall in love with the world of Incentive Travel and Meetings.

I left school at 17 to enter the family motor business. We were Volkswagen–Audi dealers and little did I realize that being the recipient of Incentive Travel Rewards and International Product Launches would be of such benefit later on! Having sold the business (giving me my first taste of the negotiating table), we entered the world of two-star hotels. With only 150 rooms between the two hotels, we found that our main business came from the residential meetings sector.

At this rather more naïve stage of my career, I felt that my learning curve was extremely steep, and looked forward to the day when I would be able to sit back with experience and 'level off'. Over the years I've begun to understand that it is at the point of 'levelling off' that you may as well stop. It is at this point that innovation ceases to exist and business can become stale. The mistakes never stop, but what I have learnt is how to use these

Figure 7.4
Ray Bloom.

mistakes to drive my various ventures forward, and how to accept when I've made one and change my course accordingly.

So how did I eventually get into the business? A childhood friend of mine, Ian Allchild, was the sales manager of an Incentive Marketing Exhibition held at the Metropole Exhibition Halls in Brighton; our home town. He was one of our hotels' best customers, booking numerous room allocations for exhibitors. One day in 1983, we just got talking and decided to join up and launch an Incentive Show at the Barbican in London. It started as an 1800 square metre show and ended up six years later as a 10 000 square metre show held at Olympia. Trials and tribulations were of course involved, but my overriding memory of the period was one of great satisfaction and delight at finally having found 'my' industry. It is, of course, the people that make it – you will hear that a lot over these few pages – that's because it is true. This industry is all about partnerships and relationships and making friends around the world. What could be better than that?

Ian and I launched EIBTM in 1986. As I said earlier, the learning curve never stops and, after a while, you begin to thrive on it. Launching an Incentive Travel Show was another steep one! We selected Geneva for a number of reasons – a great geographical location, together with the fact that my mother-in-law was there to feed and look after me were great incentives! The development of such an ambitious project proved to me the importance of inner conviction and positive attitude – values passed on to me through my family businesses. It really is true that, as long as you work hard enough to find it, the appropriate solution will manifest itself.

This was proved with the development of the now well-known 'Hosted Buyer Programme'. About seven months before the first show, having invested heavily in database and teleresearch to pinpoint decision makers in key European markets, I was a little uneasy about where exactly our buyers would come from and how many there would be. This was not a mistake I was willing to make. I decided to 'Host or Fail'. We got in touch with trade publications from around the world and invited them to bring groups of top buyers to the show – hosted and paid for by us. Some would say it was an expensive gamble, I would say that it is one that paid off. Sometimes in business you may feel that you are playing a roulette wheel, but calculated risks are usually worth it.

As I said earlier, relationships are paramount in this business. We established close partnerships with major international associations by ensuring that the relationship was always mutually beneficial – not always financially – but invariably supportive of each other's aims. These partnerships have now been proved to have stood the test of time and, once again, I am proud to be working closely with such prestigious and important associations as SITE, MPI, ICCA, IACVB, AACVB, AIPC, IAPCO, etc. Additionally, we worked hard to develop relationships with strong Swiss institutions, from the National Airline (SwissAir) to City Government. It was with our partners' support that we made our show a success.

Now I am entering a new 'phase' – a whole new learning curve in fact. Having dabbled in a completely different industry (the espresso bar market), I am now firmly back where I belong, having launched IMEX (The Worldwide Exhibition for Incentive Travel, Meetings and Events) in Frankfurt, Germany. Using my experience (at last!), using my prior steep curves and jumping on another in order to innovate and create a new show for a new era. When I re-entered the industry a couple of years ago, I did so with a fresh perspective, one which only a few years' break can give; and saw that innovation and creativity were once more needed in our market place. My new exhibition will combine a huge hosted buyer programme with a major outbound market – the only exhibition in the industry to do so. Additionally, our 'new vision' will ensure that our youth program, performance improvement pavilion, environmental initiatives, use of new technology and continued partnerships with international associations will create a global meetings and incentive travel exhibition 'for the industry, by the industry'. This is our mission and we are working hard to make the vision a reality.

There are no right or wrong ways to develop a career nor develop a business, although it's important to keep a few things in mind. First, have the courage of your convictions and take responsibility for the mistakes as well as the successes. Second, remember to try to keep a positive and balanced attitude towards your work and career. Third, remember always that goodwill takes years to cultivate and grow, but can be lost in a minute of thoughtlessness; and finally be assured that the incentive travel and meetings market is one of the most welcoming, gracious and sociable industries to work in. Enjoy it.

Martin Lewis, Managing Editor, *Meetings & Incentive Travel* magazine

Diversity of activities, products and services. That's what has made this industry fascinating for me.

After all, how do you produce a magazine to interest as eclectic a group of people as a personnel manager for a tyre company, a brand manager for a confectionery company, the chairman of a computer company, a hotelier, an audiovisual producer, a travel agent, an after-dinner speaker, the secretary of the National Union of Teachers, a professional conference organizer . . . need I go on?

It's more like producing a consumer magazine than trade publishing – the only common denominator is that all our readers are involved in the events business as a part of their lives. Some are involved for every working minute of their professional lives in organizing meetings or incentive travel programmes, product launches, training programmes and the like. Others do it as just a small part of a wider professional brief – personnel management, marketing and association managers, for example, are the part-time professionals. But all need to know how, where,

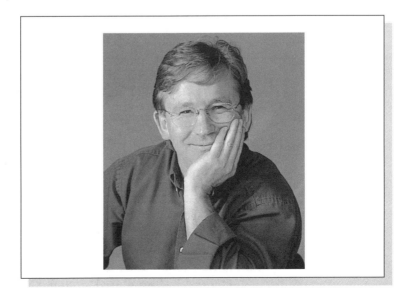

Figure 7.5
Martin Lewis.

when and why they should do things to be efficient and successful.

That's our brief – to produce a magazine to interest men and women, from chairman to secretary, from full-timer to part-timer, from corporate man to association woman. It's an interesting challenge and one that I often think can only result in degrees of failure. After all, *any* subject can alienate *part* of the target audience, so we start from that position. My aim has always been modest: to persuade readers there is at least *one* item in the magazine that will interest, inform and/or entertain them. If they happen to find more than one, we have reduced the degree of failure still further.

If the diverse nature of the readership is the challenge, it is the diverse nature of the business that is the reward. When I left newspapers where I had worked as a reporter and subeditor on news and sport for the apparently lush and cushier pastures of travel trade newspapers, I was initially attracted by the travel opportunities but then bored by the mind-numbing sameness of it all.

When I then joined a magazine called *Conference & Exhibitions* 22 years ago, it was because I was out of work and needed a job rather than out of any sense of professional calling. I joined my old mate Rob Spalding and, having done so, immediately wondered what on earth I was doing up this particular career cul-de-sac. But gradually the conference business wooed me and won me over. Yes, I liked the people and, yes, I liked the business – the idea of a business dedicated to better communication between people appealed to my naive and romantic view of a worthwhile industry. But the real reason I have stayed in it is because of the diversity – and it is constantly changing and totally international.

Even I, with the attention span of a two-year-old and the concentration level of a squirrel, cannot be bored in this business.

In *Meetings & Incentive Travel* we cover venues and destinations at home and abroad, technical equipment from simultaneous interpretation to back-screen projection, marketing methods from exhibitions to the Internet, event management methods from sponsorship funding to event software, staff movement from agencies to hotels, case histories of actual events from a BT roadshow to the Hong Kong handover ceremony, price surveys of hotels and conference centres, legal requirements at home and abroad, government policy at home and overseas, and the trading results of the leading agencies.

We also organize an exhibition once a year called the 'Meetings & Incentive Travel Show'.

We talk to tourist offices, airline people, conference producers, video designers, graphic artists, hoteliers, travel agents, interpreters, motivators, trainers, corporate entertainers, after-dinner speakers – the list is endless. We meet people of every nationality and every cultural background. How could I be bored?

It is interesting to see how many others stay in the business and how many of those who leave, then return and are delighted to be back. Rob Spalding once called it a 'global village hall' and the phrase has stayed with me. The meetings and incentive travel business is bigger and more international than ever, but still it is a tight community of old friends.

It has meant we have published things that some of my friends (I mean contacts) haven't liked and some of them are no longer friends. But, on the whole, a fairly 'shoot-from-the-hip' editorial style has won more friends than it has lost.

My first-ever editor told me on my first day's work as a reporter: 'Martin, don't get too close to your contacts'. I didn't understand the advice then, but I do now and he was right. Unfortunately, in this business I have not been able to follow his words. I'm afraid it just isn't possible. The meetings and incentive travel business is just too social, just too darned friendly and just too much fun.

Summary

- Excellent interpersonal skills are essential to anyone looking to make a career in the conference industry. A range of other qualities will also be needed, including organizational ability, computer literacy, a facility for working well under pressure, and oral and written communication skills.
- As the quality of the physical conference product (venues, equipment, infrastructure) reaches a generally acceptable standard, it will be the quality of service delivered by the industry's employees that will distinguish one venue or destination from another.
- The conference industry and the education sector have been slow to develop appropriate education and training opportunities for the industry's current workforce and for potential new entrants. This situation is now changing as educational institutions and professional associations begin to develop full-time, part-time and short course programmes.
- There is a lack of professional qualifications specific to the conference industry, although initiatives are under way to address this need, both at national and international levels.
- The industry is broad enough to welcome into its ranks people from diverse employment backgrounds and disciplines. The lack of clear career structures and progression routes can be confusing and frustrating, but also stimulates greater fluidity and freedom of movement between jobs.
- The conference industry offers a rich diversity of employment opportunities. Few people will become millionaires, but the rewards in terms of job satisfaction, fun, creativity and building friendships around the world are rich indeed.

Review and discussion questions

1 Reread the job advertisements and career profiles in this chapter, and use these to write a 'person specification' for three vacancies which are about to be advertised: (i) a conference organizer (with a company or association); (ii) a conference sales manager (with a venue); and (iii) a destination marketer (working for a conference desk or convention bureau).

2 The hotel sector has a reputation for high staff turnover, with insufficiently trained staff and limited career opportunities. To what extent is this an accurate description of the hotel sector in your country? What measures should be taken to change perceptions of the sector and ensure that it really does attract, and retain, the highest calibre of personnel?

3 What image does the conference industry have among the general public? Design a questionnaire, and carry out a survey among friends, family and colleagues to establish their understanding of what the industry is like, whether it is important and why, their experience of attending conferences, and to clarify their overall impressions of the industry. Use the findings to make recommendations for changes that could lead to greater recognition for the industry and for the people it employs.

4 The Department of National Heritage report quoted in this chapter says that: 'The quality of personal service is perhaps more important to tourism and hospitality than to any other industry.. . . The quality of interactions (with industry employees) is an integral part of the experience and has the potential to delight or disappoint the consumer. We do not believe that this potential is there to the same extent in any other employing sector.' Compare tourism and hospitality with another service industry and give reasons why you would agree or disagree with the DNH report.

Notes and references

A Quality Assurance Scheme for Conference Venues: Exploratory Research, research undertaken by Travel and Tourism Research on behalf of the Scottish Tourist Board, English Tourist Board, Northern Ireland Tourist Board and Wales Tourist Board (1997).

The Meeting Professional's 2002 Salary Survey. Meeting Professionals International (2002).

Tourism: Competing with the Best, No. 3. *People Working in Tourism and Hospitality*. Department of National Heritage (now Department for Culture, Media and Sport) (1996).

Leading industry organizations

Introduction

The conference industry has been described, or more accurately criticized, as being 'fragmented', because of its multiplicity of representative bodies and organizational structures. Even those working full-time within the industry are frequently confused by the bewildering array of abbreviations and acronyms in use. Within the British Isles alone, widely differing public and private sector structures for the 'management' of the industry are to be found, whether at national, regional or local level. At an international level, an ever-growing number of professional associations and industry forums, almost all established since 1950, seek to raise industry standards, increase recognition for the economic importance of conference tourism, and develop a clear vision for the evolution of the industry into the 21st century. This chapter attempts to identify the key players and explain their current roles. It looks at:

- the activities of international organizations and associations;
- the roles of selected national trade associations;
- an assessment of the conference industry's fragmentation.

The activities of international organizations and associations

American Society of Association Executives

Although not directly a conference industry trade association, the American Society of Association Executives (ASAE) is, nonetheless, a very important body for the international convention industry because of the scale of convention activity undertaken by its members. ASAE was founded in 1920 as the American Trade Association Executives, with 67 charter members. Today it has over 23 500 members worldwide who manage approximately 10 000 trade associations, individual membership societies, professional organizations and not-for-profit associations, which, between them, serve more than 287 million people and companies. Over 40% of its members are chief executive officers.

ASAE has as its core purpose to 'advance the value of voluntary associations to society and to support the professionalism of the individuals who lead them'. ASAE services to its membership include two annual conventions, publications, educational programmes (with a professional certification programme known as 'Certified Association Executive' – see Chapter 7), an information clearing house on association management and representational activities.

Contact details: American Society of Association Executives, 1575 I Street, NW, Washington, DC 20005, USA (tel.: +1 (202) 626–2855; fax: +1 (202) 408–9633; email: intlsec@asaenet.org; website: www.asaenet.org).

ASAE has a sister organization in Europe, the *European Society of Association Executives* (ESAE), whose Secretariat is based at: 840 Melton Road, Thurmaston, Leicester, LE4 8BN, UK (tel.: +44 (0)116–264–0095; fax: +44 (0)116–264–0141; email: esae@associa tionhq.org.uk; website: www.esae.org).

Asian Association of Convention and Visitor Bureaus

Established in 1983, the Asian Association of Convention and Visitor Bureaus (AACVB) is a regional association of ten leading national conference destinations in Asia. Its full members are: China, Hong Kong, Indonesia, Japan, Korea, Macau, Malaysia, the Philippines, Singapore and Thailand. It has six membership categories, representing a diverse range of entities including national tourist organizations, city convention bureaux, convention centres, destination management companies and industry publications.

AACVB aims to realize the full potential of Asia as a destination for meetings, incentives, conventions and exhibitions. Its activities include joint marketing and promotions in key target markets, education programmes, research and information exchange, international networking and affiliation.

Contact details: AACVB Secretariat, c/o Macau Government Tourist Office, 2/F Tourist Activities and Conference Centre, Rua Luís Gonzaga Gomes, Macau (tel.: +853 798–4156; fax: +853 703–213; email: secretariat@aacvb.org; website: www.aacvb.org).

Association Internationale des Palais de Congrès (AIPC)

The Association Internationale des Palais de Congrès (AIPC) (International Association of Congress Centres) was founded in 1958 as a professional association for senior convention/conference centre executives. It now has 124 members in almost 50 countries worldwide.

AIPC's mission is to 'encourage and recognize excellence in facility management'. This means developing the tools members need to achieve excellence and make them more readily available. This includes such things as targeted and relevant research, up-to-date industry statistics, educational programmes and clear measures with which members can chart their accomplishments.

At the same time, it means having effective ways to recognize excellence and ensure that all the benefits it confers are available to those who make the grade. To do this, AIPC maintains programmes such as its 'Apex Award' for the best congress centre of the year and promotes the quality commitment implied in AIPC membership. AIPC plans to create even broader exposure by promoting members' commitments as a 'Quality Brand' that can be recognized throughout the industry.

For the meeting planner, AIPC provides a 'guarantee of outstanding meeting facilities, high quality technical equipment, modern and caring management and careful attention to detail'.

AIPC publishes a quarterly Newsletter and also takes stands at leading industry exhibitions. It holds an annual conference, which is staged in a different country each year. AIPC maintains close contact with other international conference industry associations and also contributes to the wider development of the industry as a founder member of the Joint Meetings Industry Council. It is also a member of the World Council for Venue Management (WCVM).

Contact details: AIPC Secretariat Office, 55 Rue de l'Amazone, 1060 Brussels, Belgium (tel.: +32 2–534–59–53; fax: +32 2–534–63–38; email: secretariat@aipc.org; website: www.aipc.org).

Association Internationale des Villes Francophones de Congrès

The purpose of the Association Internationale des Villes Francophones de Congrès (AIVFC) is to bring together professionals from the conference world of all French-speaking countries into an association so that they can take part in commercial and technical exchanges in their own language. AIVFC also promotes the use of the French language during international conferences, more specifically through the use of simultaneous translation.

Contact details: Association Internationale des Villes Francophones de Congrès, Palais des Congrès, 8–10 rue de la Chancellerie, F-7800 Versailles, France (tel.: +33–1–30–97–89–00; fax: +33–1–30–21–15–82).

Confederation of Latin American Congress Organizing Entities and Related Activities (COCAL)

Established in 1985, COCAL is a civil, not-for-profit body of Latin American Professional Conference Organizers specializing in congresses and events. The Confederation aims to unite the efforts of the region's countries to improve the performance of the Latin American meetings industry. Fifteen associations, one per country, are members: Argentina, Brazil, Chile, Colombia, Costa Rica, Cuba, Dominican Republic, Ecuador, Mexico, Panama, Paraguay, Peru, Uruguay, Venezuela, with Spain as an associate member.

Contact details: Confederation of Latin American Congress Organizing Entities and Related Activities (tel.: +54–11–4342–3216; fax: +54–11–4331–0223; email: mlentino@congresosint. com.ar; website: www.cocalnet.org).

Convention Industry Council

The Convention Industry Council (CIC) (previously known as the Convention Liaison Council) comprises 30 organizations representing the convention, meeting and exhibition industry, and travel and tourism generally. It is an American organization, although some of its members (such as MPI and IACVB) are international in nature. CIC's purpose is to provide a forum for the industry to work collectively to exchange information, recommend solutions to industry problems, develop programmes to serve the industry and its publics, and create an awareness of the economic dimensions of the industry.

This is achieved principally by the following:

- providing an open forum for identifying trends and problem-solving;
- administering the Certified Meeting Professional (CMP) programme (see Chapter 7);
- publishing *The Convention Industry Council Manual (with Glossary)* and other reference and research information;
- spearheading the APEX (Accepted Practices Exchange – see Chapter 1) initiative, developing accepted practices for the industry in order to improve;

- recognizing industry leadership through the CIC's Hall of Leaders;
- maintaining the CIC website;
- monitoring legislation and establishing positions on public issues.

Contact details: Convention Industry Council, 8201 Greensboro Drive, Suite 300, McLean, Virginia 22102, USA (tel.: +1 (703) 610–9030; fax: +1 (703) 610–9005; website: www.conventionindustry.org).

European Federation of Conference Towns

In 1964, a few far-seeing people met in Brussels to establish the European Federation of Conference Towns (EFCT). Their main ambition was for EFCT to be a focal point for the youthful European conference industry; although many things have changed, this remains a key objective. A second prime aim was to provide advice and assistance for conference organizers to identify suitable destinations and venues for their events.

EFCT now has over 100 member destinations in 30 countries. It has assumed a major role in seeking to persuade the European Union of the vital economic importance of conference and business tourism. Its Liaison Office in Brussels has built good working links with the staff of appropriate European Union Directorates, and is active in scrutinizing new legislation and providing guidance on all aspects of the industry.

EFCT is one of the founder members of the Joint Meetings Industry Council (JMIC) and of the DOME project (see Chapters 1 and 3), is active in the European Travel and Tourism Action Group (ETAG), and enjoys Consultative Status with ECOSOC, the United Nations Economic and Social Council.

Regular EFCT publications include an annual member Directory and a newsletter, 'Destination Europe'. EFCT holds a General Assembly each year, and an annual Summer School (see Chapter 7).

Further information is available from: European Federation of Conference Towns, BP 182, 1040 Brussels, Belgium (tel.: +32 2–732–6954; fax: +32 2–735–4840; email: secretariat@efct.com; website: www.efct.com).

Incentive Travel & Meetings Association

The Incentive Travel & Meetings Association (ITMA) was founded as the Incentive Travel Association for the United Kingdom in 1985, changing to ITMA in 1991. It is the trade association for companies involved in the organization of corporate events, including meetings, product launches and travel incentives. ITMA's key objectives are:

- to provide a register of the most highly respected companies, all of whom are able to offer their clients financial security;
- to protect members' interests through representation to law-makers, the media and relevant commercial bodies;
- to raise standards of professionalism by pooling members' collective expertise and protecting clients' interests.

It offers two categories of membership, which are available to companies and not to individuals:

1 agency membership – for professional event organizing companies; and
2 partner membership – for suppliers of travel, hospitality and ancillary services (airlines, hotels, representation companies, tourist offices, destination management companies, cruise lines and air charter brokers).

Agency members are required to be bonded through an Air Travel Organiser's Licence (ATOL) if their activities include licensable activities involving the use of air travel. All agency members are required to hold worldwide public liability and professional indemnity insurance. In 2002, ITMA had some 40 Agency members and 190 Partner members.

Membership benefits and services include: joint exhibition opportunities; website listing; information on new legislation and lobbying issues; educational seminars and training workshops; advice on a range of subjects such as taxation, insurance and legal obligations, including a free hotline for legal and accounting queries; documentation and market research; networking with other members and publicity through the ITMA National Awards Programme.

Contact details: Incentive Travel & Meetings Association Ltd, 26–28 Station Road, Redhill, Surrey RH1 1PD, UK (tel.: +44 (0)1737–779928; fax: +44 (0)1737–779749 email: info@itma-online.org; website: www.itma-online.org).

International Association of Convention and Visitor Bureaus

The International Association of Convention and Visitor Bureaus (IACVB), now with over 1200 members in approximately 500 destination management organizations in 30 countries, was founded in 1914 to 'promote sound professional practice in the solicitation and servicing of meetings, conventions and tourism'. As the international association representing destinations around the world, IACVB now has as its mission 'to enhance the professionalism, effectiveness, and image of destination management organizations worldwide'. It provides public relations for the industry, represents convention and visitor bureaux on legislative and regulatory issues, publishes a bimonthly newsletter and two annual directories (one for members and one that sells destinations to meeting professionals and tour operators), offers educational programmes and a professional designation for members (CDME; Certified Destination Management Executive – see Chapter 7), runs the online Convention Industry Network (CINET) with a broad spectrum of data on client meetings (over 19 000 association and corporate meeting profiles, most of which are of North American organizations), and sponsors three 'Destinations Showcase' trade show events where members exhibit their destinations to meeting professionals, in Washington, Chicago and New York.

The IACVB Foundation was established in 1993 to meet the needs of the destination management community and its clients by facilitating research, scholarship and philanthropy, and by providing recognition and visibility for the destination management profession.

Further information is available from: International Association of Convention and Visitor Bureaus, 2025 M Street, NW, Suite 500, Washington, DC, USA 20036 (tel.: +1 (202) 296–7888; fax: +1 (202) 296–7889; email: info@iacvb.org; website: www.iacvb.org).

International Association for Exhibition Management

The International Association for Exhibition Management (IAEM) was born in 1928 as the National Association for Exposition Managers. Today IAEM is the premier international association for individuals with business interests in the exhibition industry, representing over 3500 individual members who organize and support exhibitions around the world.

The mission of IAEM is 'to promote the expansion of the exhibition industry by providing its members with education, and unique and essential services and resources through an international networking community'.

It oversees the 'Certified in Exhibition Management' (CEM) programme and awards the designation of CEM to those who complete the programme successfully. The CEM was created to raise professional standards and provide a vehicle for certification in the exhibition industry.

Further information from: International Association for Exhibition Management, 8111 LBJ Freeway, Suite 750, Dallas, Texas 75251–1313, USA (mailing address: PO Box 802425, Dallas, Texas 75380–2425, USA). Tel.: +1 (972) 458–8002; fax: +1 (972) 458–8119; email: iaem@iaem.org; website: www.iaem.org.

International Association of Professional Congress Organizers

The International Association of Professional Congress Organizers (IAPCO) is a professional association exclusively for organizers of international meetings and special events, and has

70 members in 29 countries around the world. Prospective members are required to provide evidence of their experience and competence. IAPCO aims to:

- further recognition of congress (conference) organizing as a profession;
- further and maintain a high professional standard in the organization of meetings;
- study theoretical and practical aspects of international congresses, research problems that confront professional organizers and promote solutions;
- offer a forum for PCOs and provide members with opportunities to exchange ideas and experiences;
- maintain effective relations with other organizations concerned with international meetings;
- assist PCOs in obtaining the skills and expertise required to organize congresses;
- encourage meetings' convenors (organizers) to seek the assistance of reputable PCOs.

IAPCO is well known for its congress management courses, particularly the annual 'Wolfsberg' Seminar in Switzerland (see Chapter 7 for further details). It also publishes a range of useful conference guidelines for PCOs, planners and suppliers, such as: *How to Choose the Right PCO*; *Pre-requisites for a Conference Hotel*; *Guidelines for Co-operation between the International Association, the National Organizing Committee and the PCO*; *Guidelines for the International Scientific Programme Committee*; *First Steps for the Chairman of an International Meeting*; *Sponsorship Prospectus*; and *Housing Guidelines*. Its newsletter is published twice a year. IAPCO is one of the members of the Joint Meetings Industry Council.

Contact details: International Association of Professional Congress Organizers, 42 Canham Road, London W3 7SR, UK (tel.: +44 (0)20 8749–6171; fax: +44 (0)20–8740–0241; email: info@iapco.org; website: www.iapco.org).

International Congress and Convention Association

The International Congress and Convention Association (ICCA) was founded in 1963 and is the only international association that represents the interests of all the various professional meetings suppliers. Its membership (numbering over 600 in almost 80 countries) is organized in nine chapters (by regions of the world) for networking, and structured into seven categories: (1) congress travel agents; (2) airlines; (3) professional congress and/or exhibition organizers; (4) tourist and convention bureaux; (5) meetings information and technical specialists; (6) hotels; (7) congress, convention and exhibition centres.

ICCA exists to help all types of suppliers to the meetings industry to develop their skills and understanding of the industry, to facilitate the exchange of information between members, to maximize business opportunities for members, to raise and encourage professional standards in line with client expectations, and to provide quality networking opportunities. ICCA is a member of the Joint Meetings Industry Council.

ICCA membership benefits and services include:

- ICCA pavilions for members to exhibit at international trade shows;
- business workshops, where members can discuss business with potential clients;
- *International Meetings News* – a quarterly magazine distributed to 6500 international associations and corporate meeting planners;
- worldwide distribution of the annual Membership Directory, which includes detailed information on every member and their services;
- access to privileged information via ICCA data (a selection of ICCA statistics is reproduced in Chapter 1);
- monthly published factsheets containing detailed information on international meetings;
- access to the ICCA database for tailor-made listings;
- international networking, and education and training programmes.

Contact details: International Congress and Convention Association, Entrada 121, NL – 1096 EB Amsterdam, The Netherlands (tel.: +31 20–398–1919; fax: +31 20–699–0781; email: icca@icca.nl; website: www.iccaworld.com).

ICCA also maintains regional offices in Malaysia and Uruguay.

International Pharmaceutical Congress Advisory Association

The International Pharmaceutical Congress Advisory Association (IPCAA) is a group of senior managers from the global pharmaceutical industry who have responsibility for medical congresses and exhibitions. IPCAA's main objective is to promote the highest standards at international medical meetings. These standards most importantly refer to scientific content, but they also include appropriate location, facilities and security.

Contact details: International Pharmaceutical Congress Advisory Association, PO Box 182, CH-4013 Basel, Switzerland (tel.: +44 (0)1625–890035; fax: +44 (0)1625–890112; email: secre tariat@ipcaa.org; website: www.IPCAA.org).

Joint Meetings Industry Council

The Joint Meetings Industry Council (JMIC) was founded in 1978 as a forum for the exchange of conference-related news and views, and to explore ways of cooperating in conference education, publications and research. It meets twice a year and now includes 13 associations as members: Asian Association of Convention and Visitor Bureaus, Association Internationale des Interprètes de Conférence, Association Internationale des Palais de Congrès, Confederación de Entidades Organizadoras de Congresos y Afines de América Latina, European Federation of Conference Towns, International Association of Convention and Visitor Bureaus, International Association of Municipal Sports and Multi-purpose Centers, International Association of French-speaking Towns, International Association of Professional Congress Organisers, International Congress and Convention Association, Meeting Professionals International, Society of Incentive and Travel Executives, and Union of International Associations.

JMIC was the coordinating body behind a 'Millennium Leaders' Summit' held in Malaysia in 2000, at which the decision was taken to give priority to the following areas of activity: recognition, technology, globalization, standardization and training.

Contact details are those for whichever member body is currently acting as JMIC President. In October 2002, this was Jean Delobel of the Association Internationale de Villes Francophones de Congrès (tel.: +33 1–302–11582: email: Delobel. Jean@wanadoo.fr).

Meeting Professionals International

Meeting Professionals International (MPI) was founded in 1972 and is now the world's largest association of meeting industry professionals with more than 19 000 members in 64 countries. Membership belongs to an individual, not to a company/ organization. Membership categories include planners, suppliers and students. Planners and suppliers are represented in equal proportions. MPI's 75 staff members work at its International Headquarters in Dallas (USA) as well as at its regional offices in Canada and Luxembourg. Members are organized in National Chapters (and Chapters-in-Formation). Membership benefits and services include the following.

- Education: three major conferences – the World Education Congress (WEC); the Professional Education Conference, North America (PEC-NA); and Europe (PEC-E); Institutes in Meeting Management; the Certificate in Meeting Management programme (see Chapter 7); regular network evenings; and other educational programmes.

- Publications: a monthly magazine, MPI Global Membership Directory plus a European Membership Directory, 'Meeting Europe' (European newsletter), Chapter newsletters.
- Information: MPI Foundation (research and development arm), Resource Centre (library), MPINet (global on-line communications network).
- Professional recognition: Meeting Professional Awards.

Further information is available from:

- Meeting Professionals International, 4455 LBJ Freeway, Suite 1200, Dallas, Texas 75244, USA(tel.: +1 (972) 702–3000; fax: +1 (972) 702–3070; email: information@mpiweb.org; website: www.mpinet.org).
- MPI European Office, 22 Route de Grundhof, L-6315 Beaufort, Grand Duchy of Luxembourg (tel.: +352 2687–6141; fax: +352 2687–6343; email: dscaillet@mpiweb.org).

Professional Convention Management Association

Founded in 1957, the mission of the Professional Convention Management Association (PCMA) is to deliver breakthrough education and promote the value of professional convention management. Membership in PCMA was initially restricted to meeting managers in the medical and healthcare fields. In 1990, the Association opened its membership to chief executives and meeting professionals from not-for-profit associations in all sectors. And, in 1998, PCMA further opened its membership by removing the requirement that meeting professionals be employed by 501 (c) 3 (i.e. not-for-profit) organizations. PCMA has 16 chapters located across North America. In addition to large conventions and exhibitions, PCMA members plan an estimated 250 000 smaller meetings each year.

In 1985, PCMA created an Education Foundation, designed to support college and self-study courses, professional training and book publishing. The Foundation recently published the fourth edition of *Professional Meeting Management*, widely recognized in North America as the 'bible' of the industry. PCMA publishes its own magazine, *Convene*, one of the leading industry magazines. In 1994, PCMA initiated the 'Space Verification Program', designed to help meeting managers and hotels validate meeting room specifications.

Contact details: Professional Convention Management Association, 2301 South Lake Shore Drive, Suite 1001, Chicago, Illinois 60616, USA (tel.: +1 (312) 423–7262; fax: +1 (312) 423–7222; website: www.pcma.org).

Society of Incentive and Travel Executives

Founded in 1973, the Society of Incentive and Travel Executives (SITE) is a worldwide organization of business professionals dedicated to the recognition and development of motivational and performance improvement strategies of which travel is a key component.

Membership, which numbers just under 2000 in 81 countries, is open to qualified individuals who 'subscribe to the highest standards of professionalism and ethical behaviour'. Members are drawn from airlines, cruise lines, corporate users, destination management companies, ground transportation companies, hotels and resorts, incentive houses, official tourist organizations, travel agencies and supporting organizations, such as restaurants and visitor attractions. As representatives of every discipline in the incentive travel industry, SITE members design, develop, promote, sell, administer and operate motivational programmes as an incentive to increase productivity in business.

SITE has almost 30 national and regional Chapters around the world. Among the membership benefits and services offered are:

- an annual conference that brings together experts from around the world to examine business trends and the application of business products that apply to them;
- SITE certifies members who meet stringent requirements as 'Certified Incentive Travel Executives' – proof that they have achieved the highest level of expertise in the industry;
- members subscribe to a 'Code of Ethics' that is recognized by both users and suppliers of incentive travel as a guarantee of trustworthy service;
- SITE provides opportunities worldwide – seminars, networking and social functions – for members to increase their level of professionalism. Such opportunities include three annual Universities of Incentive Travel: in Europe, in the Americas and in Asia;
- SITE funds research into the nature and effectiveness of motivational methods through its SITE Foundation, established in 1987;
- the publication of a Resource Manual and a Directory of Members.

Contact details: Society of Incentive and Travel Executives, 401 North Michigan Avenue, Chicago, Illinois 60611, USA (tel.: +1 (312) 644–6610; fax: +1 (312) 527–6783; email: hq@site-intl.org; website: www.site-intl.org).

Union of International Associations

The Union of International Associations (UIA) was formed in 1907 as the Central Office of International Associations, becoming the UIA in 1910. It was created in an an endeavour to coordinate international organization initiatives, with emphasis on documentation, including a very extensive library and museum function. Gradually, the focus has shifted to promoting internationality, as well as to a role in representing the collective views of international bodies, where possible, especially on technical issues.

The UIA is an independent, non-governmental, not-for-profit body that undertakes and promotes study and research into international organizations. Of particular importance to the conference industry is the UIA's production of statistics on international congresses and conventions, statistics that have been collected annually since 1949. The meetings taken into consideration are those organized or sponsored by international organizations appearing in the UIA publications *Yearbook of International Organizations* and *International Congress Calendar*. Some of the UIA's conference statistics are reproduced in Chapter 1.

The UIA is represented on a number of international conference industry forums, including the Joint Meetings Industry Council.

Contact details: Union of International Associations, Congress Department, Rue Washington 40, B-1050 Brussels, Belgium (tel.: +32 2–640–4109; fax: +32 2–643–6199; email: gdc@uia.be; web site: www.uia.org).

The roles of selected national trade associations

In addition to the international industry associations described above, there is a much larger number of trade bodies operating at a national level. This section provides brief profiles of a small selection of these as examples of the types of organizations to be found within individual countries.

Association of Australian Convention Bureaux Inc.

The Association of Australian Convention Bureaux Inc. (AACB) consists of 13 city and regional bureaux dedicated to marketing their specific region as a premier Business Events destination. The mission of the Association is 'to participate in and foster the development of Australia's Business Events industry'.

AACB has several key focus areas, which include the following.

- Information and research. The AACB Bureaux Comparison Survey provides members with statistical reports for effective lobbying, planning and performance review. The AACB also furnishes the Australian Tourist Commission (ATC) with annual updates for compilation of the ATC Conventions, Trade

Shows and Exhibitions Calendar. A more recent innovation is the National Business Events Survey (NBES) in partnership with ATC and Cooperative Research Centre for Sustainable Tourism (CRC). It measures the size, scope and value of the segment. The Survey began in November 2002 and is intended to be ongoing (and is the first survey of its kind since 1996).

- Education – an annual staff conference is held for members to develop sound professional practices, educate members and provide networking opportunities. In addition, a Staff Scholarship and Staff Prize (for newcomers to bureaux) are offered annually to encourage excellence, in partnership with ATC and Qantas.
- Publicity and promotion, significantly offshore development through the Team Australia Alliance with the Australian Tourist Commission (see Chapter 4). The AACB investigates opportunities where the role and function of convention bureaux can be promoted to meeting planners on an international basis through vehicles such as trade shows and road shows. As an incentive for individual bureaux to promote their city/area internationally, the AACB holds approved body status for eligible bureaux to receive a rebate on international marketing expenditure through the Export Development Grant Scheme.
- Lobbying and Government liaison. The AACB communicates a coordinated industry view and voice to the Governments of Australia and to the public, strengthening industry influence on policy formulation. It also seeks to further industry liaison through its involvement with two organizations: the National Tourism Alliance and the Business Events Council of Australia.

Contact details: Association of Australian Convention Bureaux Inc., Level 13 / 80 William Street, East Sydney, New South Wales 2011, Australia (tel.: +61 (0)2–9326–9133; fax: +61 (0)2–9326–9676; email: mcannon@aacb.org.au; website: www.aacb.org.au).

Association of British Professional Conference Organizers

Formed in 1981, ABPCO is the only association in the British Isles whose membership comprises exclusively professional conference organizers (PCOs). Membership is selective and is limited to individuals who have a proven record of achievement nationally and (in many cases) internationally. Membership is on an individual not a company basis, is open not only to conference and event organizers from independent conference organizing businesses, but also to in-house organizers working within associations, educational/official bodies and corporate organizations. Members are required to uphold an agreed Code of Practice.

ABPCO's main aims are to:

- position ABPCO as the leading body representing the interests of professional conference organizers and increase its profile and recognition;
- constantly develop and enhance the benefits it provides to ABPCO members by creating opportunities for networking and by encouraging its members to achieve the highest possible standards of excellence;
- raise standards of professionalism across the meetings industry through the provision of education, training and personal development opportunities;
- increase the volume and value of business being won by ABPCO members through a range of marketing activities.

The benefits of ABPCO membership include:

- *recognition* – as a leading professional conference organizer – membership requires a high level of experience and proven competence;
- *networking* – sharing ideas and problems with a peer group of event organizers at regular meetings, residential 'think tank' weekends, and through an Internet chat room;
- *business leads* – access to business leads and enquiries;
- *promotion* – promotion through the ABPCO website www. abpco.org , an annual Directory, and other publications;
- *training and education* – professional development opportunities at the regular ABPCO meetings, as well as teaching opportunities at ABPCO's HNC in Business (Conference and Event Management) course at the City of Westminster College in London (see Chapter 7).

Contact details: Association of British Professional Conference Organisers, 6th Floor, Charles House, 148–149 Great Charles Street, Birmingham B3 3HT, UK (tel.: +44 (0)121 212 1400; fax: +44 (0)121 212 3131; email: information@abpco.org; website: www.abpco.org).

British Association of Conference Destinations

The British Association of Conference Destinations (BACD) was founded in 1969 and represents some 80 destinations throughout the British Isles, from the north of Scotland to the Channel Islands. Its members are conference offices (of local authorities), convention bureaux and area tourist boards, through which it represents around 3000 conference venues. BACD also has formal links with the British Tourist Authority and the three National Tourist Boards, which have seats on its Management Board. BACD activities include:

- an enquiry fulfilment service ('Venue Location Service'), providing a destination response to clients via BACD members;
- participation in a number of key industry trade shows, and organization of the annual 'Confer' workshop;
- publication of annual directories (*British Conference Destinations Directory* and *Get Organised*);
- maintenance of several industry databases (buyers, venues, destinations, universities and colleges, trade press, trade associations);
- maintenance of a website (www.bacd.org.uk);
- organization of an annual educational conference;
- supporting conference industry research programmes, and providing information and consultancy services;
- contributing to various collaborative initiatives with government agencies and other professional associations to increase recognition of, and support for, conference and business tourism as a major benefactor to the national economy. BACD is a founder member of the Business Tourism Partnership.

Contact details: British Association of Conference Destinations, 6th Floor, Charles House, 148–149 Great Charles Street, Birmingham B3 3HT, UK (tel.: 44 (0)121–212–1400; fax: 44 (0)121–212–3131; email: info@bacd.org.uk; website: www.bacd.org.uk).

Hellenic Association of Professional Congress Organizers

The Hellenic Association of Professional Congress Organizers (HAPCO) was established in 1996, when five far-sighted Greek PCOs decided to bring together their working knowledge and experience with the aim of promoting Greece as a competitive business travel destination.

Today, HAPCO has more than 60 members from all over the country. Apart from PCOs, membership also includes conference centres, hotels, audiovisual companies, interpretation services, airlines, cruise and publishing companies, all of which cooperate closely with one another.

HAPCO's main activities consist of:

- promoting the destination through participation in national and international exhibitions and conferences, publications, press releases, IT, etc.;
- creating opportunities for networking, educational programmes and seminars for its members;
- cooperating with the Greek National Tourist Office, and other national and international associations serving the conference industry;

- providing full and updated information to its members on the conference industry and carrying out relevant studies.

HAPCO is the sole body that exists in the country legally representing the whole of the Greek conference industry.

Contact details: Hellenic Association of Professional Congress Organizers, 2–4 Alkmeonidon Street, 16121 Athens, Greece (tel.: +30 10 72 58 486; fax: +30 10 72 58 487; email: hapco@hapco.gr; website: www.hapco.gr).

Meetings Industry Association

The Meetings Industry Association (MIA) was established in 1990. It now has over 700 organizations in membership, drawn from the supply side of the conference industry in the UK and Ireland. The MIA aims to improve the quality of service and facilities offered by its members, encouraging the highest possible standards. It seeks to strengthen the position of its members' businesses in an increasingly competitive market place and raise the profile of the United Kingdom as an international conference destination. Specific member services and benefits include:

- marketing opportunities via publications, exhibition representation, and media relations;
- sales opportunities;
- networking at MIA national and regional events (an Annual General Meeting, Autumn Convention, Annual Golf Classic and regional events);
- training courses, including a five-module programme entitled the 'MIA Certificate in Management Development' launched in October 2002;
- research and information;
- consultancy and arbitration services;
- management of the quality assurance scheme 'Hospitality Assured Meetings';
- the unique MIAtracker System for measuring Customer Satisfaction with Expectation, providing a benchmarking tool for industry suppliers.

Contact details: Meetings Industry Association, 34 High Street, Broadway, Worcestershire WR12 7DT, UK (tel.: +44 (0)1386–858572; fax: +44 (0)1386–858986; email: mia@meetings. org; website: www.meetings.org).

Meetings Industry Association of Australia

The Meetings Industry Association of Australia (MIAA) is the largest meetings and events industry association in Australia with over 1700 members (both individual and corporate, plus a category for international subscribers) from all sectors of the industry. The Association is an independent not-for-profit body dedicated to fostering professionalism and excellence in all aspects of meetings management. In addition to promoting the value and effectiveness of meetings as a communications medium, MIAA also promotes meetings as a high-yield sector of business travel and tourism.

Education and accreditation are key services offered by MIAA. Two accreditation programmes exist: a general industry system (AMIAA) and a specialist accreditation for meetings managers (AMM). The Association offers training, including an annual five-day residential course in meetings management, which draws participants from Australia, New Zealand and Asia.

Other member services include: newsletters, special interest forums and site visits, social activities, representation to government and the wider industry, and an awards programme. MIAA also maintains a comprehensive website (www.miaa.com.au) where information and contact details for local meetings managers, venues and conference suppliers can be obtained.

Contact details: Meetings Industry Association of Australia, PO Box 1477, Neutral Bay, New South Wales 2089, Australia (tel.: +61 2–9904–9922; fax: +61 2–9904–9933; email: miaa@miaanet.com. au; website: www.miaanet.com.au).

Southern African Association for the Conference Industry

The Southern African Association for the Conference Industry (SAACI) was established in 1987, and is dedicated to maintaining and improving the standards of efficiency and professionalism of the conference industry in Southern Africa. The need for an organization of this kind was originally recognized by SATOUR (now known as South African Tourism, the Government tourism body). SAACI is managed by a Coordinating Council elected every two years and members are representative of the broad spectrum of the conference industry. All members are obliged to accept the SAACI Code of Conduct. The organization is divided into geographically based branches, which organize a number of functions for their members. Categories of membership are now being introduced – the first of which is an 'Accredited Conference Organizer' category. SAACI holds an annual conference, which rotates around the country.

Membership benefits and services include:

- the official SAACI journal, the definitive 'Southern Africa Conference, Exhibition & Events Guide', which is produced on a monthly basis as well as a Yearbook, in which members have an entry;
- a membership database;

- distribution of the SAACI catalogue at trade shows;
- generation of business enquiries;
- international exposure via the SAACI website;
- attendance at the annual SAACI conference and regional events.

Contact details: Southern African Association for the Conference Industry, National Secretariat, PO Box 414, Kloof 3640, South Africa (tel.: +27 31–764–6977; fax: +27 31–764–6974; email: admin@contactpub.co.za; website: www.saaci.co.za).

The exhibitions sector has its own trade associations. Among the key British associations are:

- *Association of Exhibition Organisers* (AEO), 113 High Street, Berkhamsted, Hertfordshire HP4 2DJ, UK (tel.: +44 (0)1442–873331; fax: +44 (0)1442–875551; email: info@aeo.org.uk ; website: www.aeo.org.uk).
- *British Exhibition Contractors Association* (BECA), 36 The Broadway, Wimbledon, London SW19 1RQ, UK (tel.: +44 (0)20–8543–3888; fax: +44 (0)20–8543–4036; email: info@ beca.org.uk; website: www.beca.org.uk).
- *Exhibition Venues Association* (EVA), 15 Keeble Court, Fairmeadows, North Seaton, Northumberland NE63 9SF, UK (tel.: +44 (0)1670–818801/523568; fax: +44 (0)1670–854445; email: info@exhibitionvenues.com; website: www.exhibition venues.com).

An assessment of the conference industry's fragmentation

It cannot be denied that the tourism industry as a whole is fragmented. It is composed of thousands of mainly small operators and businesses, providing accommodation, restaurants, attractions, coach and taxi services, and so forth. The conference sector shares this same infrastructure, but also encompasses conference venues and other suppliers specific to the industry. With the exception of chain hotels, conference venues are, for the most part, run as discrete business units, independent of any centralized management or structure.

The sense of fragmentation is reinforced by the apparent proliferation of trade associations and similar bodies representing segments of the conference industry. In comparison with many other professions and industries, architecture or the automotive industry, for example, the conference industry can be said to lack a single, cohesive voice.

At another level, however, the industry enjoys a very real sense of unity across the world. It is characterized by an openness and sharing, by friendships and networking between colleagues, which are immensely attractive and create almost a sense of family. Martin Lewis pays eloquent testimony to this aspect of the industry in his career profile in Chapter 7, quoting another colleague who described the industry as a 'global village hall'.

There is undoubtedly scope to bring some greater harmonization to the industry, and there would also be benefits arising from a rationalization of the industry's representative bodies, but it is to be hoped that these can be achieved without damaging the international friendship and collaboration that is such an important, and winsome, feature of the conference sector today.

Summary

There are many trade associations and similar bodies operating within the conference sector, both at national and international levels. Some have clearly defined roles and a niche membership, which is not being served by other associations. Some, however, appear to duplicate the activities of other associations, suggesting that rationalizations and mergers may become necessary both to ensure their own survival and for the wider health of the industry.

Review and discussion questions

1 To what extent is the description of the conference sector as 'fragmented' justified? Is there a greater degree of fragmentation within the conference and business tourism sector than in the leisure tourism sector?

2 Read through the descriptions of the various international and national trade bodies described in this chapter. Identify those characteristics that are common to a number of the bodies and comment on why these seem to be important. Then make a list of some of the key unique features that differentiate one from another. What features and services would you expect to be crucial to the future survival and prosperity of these associations?

3 'There should just be one conference industry association per country'. Discuss the pros and cons of such a development.

CHAPTER 9

The future of the conference industry

Introduction

Tourism is on the verge of becoming the world's largest industry. As a subsector of tourism, conference and business tourism showed sustained growth during the 1990s. This chapter looks at whether this growth is likely to continue into the 21st century by examining current trends and the impact of new communications technology. It also discusses a number of other key factors and issues affecting the industry as it matures and develops. Finally, it concludes with an optimistic prediction for conferencing in the 21st century. The specific chapter sections are as follows:

- Market trends
  - the conference market
  - conference and meeting trends
  - trend towards disintermediation
  - use of the Internet
- Issues and developments
  - what role for government and government agencies?
  - the design of conference facilities
  - the needs of disabled delegates
  - environmental issues and sustainable conference tourism
- In conclusion
  - an optimistic forecast

Market trends

The conference market

The World Tourism Organization has been predicting for some time (see Chapter 3) that tourism is set to become the world's largest industry and, indeed, may already have become such. But what of conference and business tourism? Is there likely to be the same exponential growth in this sector of the industry? Or is the pessimistic forecast of Munro (1994), who predicts the demise of the conference industry within 50 years, nearer to reality?

Munro's scathing attack on the value of conferences includes the following reasons why delegates like to attend conferences (the author's comments are shown in italics).

- International 'first-class' air travel. *In reality, only a small proportion of delegates travel first class.*
- Luxury hotel rooms 'with a chocolate on the pillow'. *This ignores the fact that many large conferences require a wide range of accommodation, from guest house provision to five-star facilities. Luxury is an overused word. While it may be true to say that accommodation standards have risen significantly over recent years, and are expected to continue to rise, only a very small percentage of hotel rooms could be described as luxurious.*
- Events being scheduled to coincide with the 'Olympics' or 'British Open Golf Championship'. *This is completely to misunderstand the scheduling of international conventions and the bidding processes which determine their actual locations. International sporting and cultural events can themselves generate new meetings and conferences. But few, if any, organizers of association conventions would deliberately try to arrange their conventions to coincide with such events, not least because hotel accommodation would simply not be available.*
- 'Delegates spend a lot of time putting together their itinerary to take in as many events as possible in a round-the-world trip'. *No organization could possibly afford to employ a 'professional conference-goer' when ever-higher levels of employee productivity and performance are expected. The phrase 'cash rich but time poor' is now quite prevalent in the societies of many developed countries, and it is certainly very true of conference organizers and delegates that they face increasing pressure to achieve more from their working day, a major contributory factor to the reduction in conference and meeting duration.*

Munro outlines a typical conference day as starting at 9.30 am and finishing by 4 pm – explain that to the corporate executive who is still in session at 10 pm and is then given work to prepare in time for an 8.30 am start the following morning! Munro suggests that organizations will no longer be willing to waste time and money on sending their employees off to attend conferences where only a small part of the whole conference will be relevant and beneficial. Video conferencing is put forward as the panacea for company communications, and as the great destroyer of the conference centre building boom of the late 20th century. 'With a little imagination, the whole conference interaction can be handled without leaving home,' concludes Munro.

There is no doubt that video conferencing has, and will continue to have, a significant role to play in the evolution of the conference industry into the 21st century. Almost certainly, other developments in technology, many as yet quite unforeseen, will affect the style and quality of interaction in the conference of 2020 and beyond. But will they decimate the conference industry in the way that Munro suggests? Eight years on from when Munro was writing, let us look at what is happening, and what seems likely to happen during the early years of the 21st century.

The confidence and buoyancy of the conference and meetings industry does seem set to continue. Downturns in national and global economies will, of course, have repercussions for the industry, but history has shown how resilient the conference sector can be. It may be that conference activity has reached some kind of plateau overall but, with variations from segment to segment, it is not easy to gain a clear comprehensive view. There are indications that the number of corporate meetings may be reducing (see Chapter 2), but whether this is just a temporary phenonemon is not yet certain. International association conventions still show consistent growth: the UIA research summarized in Chapter 1 covered 9259 international meetings held in 2001; in 1983, fewer than half this number of events (a total of 4864) was held. A growth of 268 such events was recorded in the five-year period from 1996 to 2001. In a presentation to the IACVB Global Executive Forum held in Dublin in May 2002, Lode Beckers predicted that the enlargement of the European Union and the establishment of European Monetary Union would trigger major increases in meetings/conventions/incentives, both within the for-profit and not-for-profit sectors.

Conference and meeting trends

Conferences in the 21st century are now much more active and participatory in style than was the case just a few years ago. The emphasis is on dialogue rather than declamation, networking and sharing rather than on passive listening, getting hands-on experience and forming workgroups so that conference themes can be understood and digested.

This means delegates spend less time in plenary sessions in the main conference auditorium, and much more time in smaller groups and syndicates. There is still a requirement to bring delegates together for keynote presentations, whose aim may be motivational or inspirational, or to provide an opportunity to present new corporate strategy, or to give leadership and direction, but the emphasis is on delegate involvement and participation. Campbell (2000) describes the trend as follows:

> The idea of a hundred or two delegates all happily sitting together to be lectured at for eight hours is woefully out of date. Instead, the key requirement is the syndicate room, and plenty of them! It is no longer unusual to receive requests for a large room for a one-hour introductory address followed by the dispersal of delegates into a dozen or more syndicate groups. More and more venues are, therefore, having to provide up to 20 such rooms for training and interactive discussions, and no, the converted bedroom is no longer good enough. Purpose-designed, air-conditioned, high-tech syndicates are essential. One consequence of this trend towards the learning (as opposed to the listening) conference is the growing success of the single-purpose Conference Centre and, therefore, a real challenge to the dominance of hotels. A further trend is the growing popularity of venues for exclusive use by one organization.

Meetings and conferences also now have a much stronger business focus. They are more intensive events than in the 1980s and early 1990s, using an interactive approach through personal computers and multi-media technology. In the words of Peter Berners-Price, speaking at a BACD conference as long ago as 1994:

> The strength of multi-media, the result of technology that is based on transmitting text and pictures digitally through telephone wires, or rather through microwave technology off satellites and down fibre-optic cables, is that it will revolutionize interactive learning. It will be far more efficient in communicating information than listening to someone speaking from a stage or a teacher in a classroom.
>
> Why? Well, first it will go at the speed at which you want to go. It will ask questions depending on how you have answered the last one. It will appeal to the creative imagination through colourful video, and dramatic animation. It will speak to you. It will play you music. And yes, of course, it will test you! So why is this technology good for the conference industry? Primarily because the technology will bring an amazing dimension of inter-activity right into the conference room itself.

Large association conferences typically involve a combination of plenary and workshop sessions. Many have poster sessions (displays of reports or scientific/academic papers put up by authors, sometimes with a short presentation or question-and-answer session between the author and interested delegates) and a concurrent exhibition, often used by conference organizers as a way of generating income to defray the costs of the business sessions. In an increasingly commercial climate, with convention centre managers now under pressure to achieve operational profits, the requirement is much greater for hall hire charges to be set at market rates, even for not-for-profit organizations. This, in turn, brings pressure on association organizers to keep a much closer eye on the 'bottom line' and to be imaginative and creative in obtaining sponsorship, or finding other ways to generate funds that can help to keep delegate fees at affordable levels.

Forecasting the likely structure and format of conferences in 10 or 15 years' time is a sure way to invite questions as the pace of change continues to accelerate. Buyer research summarized in Table 2.4 (Chapter 2) highlights the growing use and importance of new technology in the administration and marketing of events as well as in the production of events. MPI's *2001 Meeting Outlook Survey* asked meeting planners about what they saw as the most significant changes to affect the industry over the succeeding two years: technology was ranked highest (as it had been in the previous year's survey). The other changes, in ranking order, were predicted as: educational topics and format, pricing structures, duration of time for meetings, sponsorships, and virtual trade shows.

Trend towards disintermediation

The 2002, *EIBTM European Meetings & Incentive Report*, written by Philip Alford and published by Mintel, noted the trend towards disintermediation (i.e. cutting out the middleman) in hotel and venue bookings. It comments that:

> business travel agents are increasingly having to struggle to persuade buyers and suppliers that their role in the market is an essential one, as a growing number of suppliers and buyers are choosing to bypass the 'middlemen'. They prefer to deal directly with each other for the same reason – to make savings on the fees and commissions they pay to intermediaries. This trend is seen most clearly in the hotel conference sector. A growing number of hotel chains are looking to increase their conference revenue by offering, along with direct sales, their own in-house events management services, which circumvent the need for clients to use any intermediaries at all. As well as offering the meetings

facilities themselves, a growing number of hotel chains are providing creative input and expert consultancy on audiovisual support, people management, themed events, catering, delegate management and even crisis management.

This same point is made in Chapter 2 in the description of Destination Management Companies.

The Internet facilitates direct booking between buyer and supplier and seems likely to have a major impact on the role and activities of convention and visitor bureaux, as increasingly sophisticated venue searches can be undertaken through the web and bookings made online. It seems likely that disintermediation will lead CVBs to place a greater focus on the services needed by their customers. There may be a need for them to integrate themselves into the 'value chain' for customers, and be in a position to steer their customers to the 'best in class' facilities and services in their destination, rather than seeking to offer unbiased, impartial information as has traditionally been their role. 'The CVB Futures Project' undertaken on behalf of the IACVB Foundation concluded that the successful CVB of the future 'must engage in best practice strategic planning, share knowledge, engage in alliance partnering, be customer focused, and be part of an established industry-wide branded approach to marketing'.

Use of the Internet

The EIBTM Report suggests that:

> the use of e-mail and the Internet have become useful additional tools for the meetings organizer: use of the Internet for marketing meetings events is one example of an application of this technology to the meetings sector, as organizers can directly target any potential delegates, using their e-mail addresses. It is already common practice for organizers of large events to set up a dedicated website for each event, with details of the venue and the programme, together with links to sources of information on, for example, leisure and recreational facilities at the destination.
>
> Actual registration for many events is also now possible via the Internet, streamlining planners' organization and enabling them to keep delegates up to date with e-mailed messages about the forthcoming meeting. Specifically for this purpose, software designers have created a number of Internet-based registration systems (see Chapter 5) for use by meetings organizers.

Online survey tools can also be set up that can be used, for example, to ask delegates and potential delegates what topics should be covered at the next conference. An increasing number of conventions will provide cyber cafe facilities, enabling delegates to collect their emails while attending the event.

The EIBTM Report says that:

> in a further application of the Internet to meetings planning, a number of websites now offer powerful search engines with extensive venue and other supplier listings, which claim to enable buyers to carry out their research and book venues on-line.
>
> Research suggests that surfing for venues has become established practice among many in the meeting planners' profession. Interestingly, research conducted in the US has linked this method to shrinking lead times. The Menlo Consulting Group notes that: 'The most noticeable trend in the corporate meetings segment is a shift towards meetings with planning lead times of three months or less. Technology is helping to shift the market in this direction. It is now possible for a corporate planner to search for a site (venue), select one, contact the hotel's salesforce and sign a contract in the span of a single day. This trend shows no sign of slowing: 50 per cent of corporate planners expect an increase in short-term meetings in the next 12 months.'
>
> One application of the Internet capable of causing obvious concern to facilities and services providers is virtual conferencing, also known as 'electronic' or 'web-cast' conferences, which are increasingly being offered as an alternative to more traditional forms of meeting. Delegates send and receive information, meet other delegates, interact, even buy and sell in a digital environment fashioned for the purpose. In other words, the actual venue becomes redundant. The potential advantages of such a system, for the initiator of the meeting, include the potential for much wider participation than could be created for a traditional conference.
>
> The same advantage is offered by video conferencing, which enables two-way, remote on-screen discussions to take place. A number of conference centres have also installed satellite-linked video conferencing equipment, most often to enable keynote speakers who are unable to attend in person to address the delegates.

An article entitled 'What the Taleban did for teleconferencing', published in the September 2002 issue of *Association Meetings International* magazine, states that:

analysts Frost & Sullivan say the worldwide web conferencing market generated US$266 million in revenue in 2000 and (this) could grow to as much as US$2 billion by 2008. The visual component of a web conference can include anything from running through a PowerPoint presentation or demonstrating just about any piece of desktop software, to touring websites, conducting virtual polls or even interacting with the audience to run a Question and Answer session as part of the meeting.

In considering whether this technology is being used to replace the traditional form of face-to-face meeting, the EIBTM Report concludes that:

most surveys indicate that video conferencing is increasingly being used *in addition to* meetings, but only in a small minority of cases *instead of* face-to-face meetings. However, there is general agreement that, for reasons of economy and security, video conferencing is likely to reduce the need for face-to-face meetings in the future. Many companies have been experimenting with video conferencing as a way to limit costs and eliminate hotel availability concerns. However, the indications are that companies use video conferencing primarily for short meetings with few participants.

The Report suggests that these technologies will remain 'niche applications' that are not suited to the mainstream conference industry, which uses face-to-face meetings. It says that:

most commentators would appear to support this forecast, basing their arguments on two key observations: the potential of new technology to enhance and complement aspects of 'real meetings' and the essential value of the face-to-face experience. Video conferencing is certainly being used as a resource to improve the quality and efficiency of existing modes of meetings communication, but as far as new technology replacing live meetings goes, there are two factors which should continue to limit this trend:

- Conferences are now much more active and participatory in style, the emphasis is on dialogue, networking and sharing rather than on passive listening
- Delegates enjoy them not only for the opportunities they provide to update knowledge and network with like-minded people, but also due to the fact that they are often located in cities of tourist interest, and offer

other peripheral pleasures such as the social programme and the partners' programme.

Tony Carey, industry writer and trainer, makes the point (in an
article entitled 'The Personal Touch', *Meetings & Incentive Travel*
magazine, July/August 1999) that:

> the Internet and the telephone, the CD-Rom and the
> video recording can give us voices and pictures but they
> can't give us 'presence', that intensely individual aura
> that is both intellectual and chemical. You can't share a
> glass of wine over the Internet or enjoy the same walk in
> the park. You can't see deep into someone's eyes when
> you ask them a question, nor banter in the company of
> friends. So people arrange to meet. It's pretty obvious
> really.

Fisher (writing in 1998) predicts that:

> information alone will not be a good enough reason in
> the future to call a conference, because information will
> be disseminated in a variety of ways. The large-scale
> meeting in future may well primarily be about motivation
> and attitude. Changing beliefs and opinions should be
> the mission of conference organizers of the future, rather
> than imparting information. Perhaps the future role of
> conferences lies in promoting behavioural and attitudinal
> change, creating loyalty, applauding success, and con-
> centrating on targeted messages to individuals rather
> than the grand gesture and the big show. This will be the
> challenge for tomorrow's conference organizer.

Issues and developments

The second half of this chapter examines some of the principal
issues and developments facing the conference industry as it
gears up to the changes and challenges of the new millennium.
Rod Cameron, Vice-President of Criterion Communications Inc
(Vancouver, Canada), writing in the September 2002 issue of
ICCA's *International Meeting News*, suggests that, post '9/11', two
things are needed for the meetings industry.

> The first is for a vision for the industry that addresses
> things such as the realities of new technology, changes
> in travel patterns and economic pressures that could
> impact participation. We continue on the assumption that
> people will always want to meet face to face and, while
> that's probably true, there are mounting pressures that
> will make this both more challenging and expensive at a

time when technological alternatives are becoming increasingly attractive. There is a growing need to ensure that meetings remain relevant and the value of face-to-face meetings is actually promoted, rather than simply leaving people to reach that conclusion themselves. The second need is for a concerted effort to change the way our communities regard the meetings industry and its overall value. Here, the greatest obstacle is the tendency to 'lump' meetings together with tourism, which often has completely different agendas and priorities and as often as not is competing for the same resources. If anything, tourism is a beneficiary of the meetings industry – not the other way round. Congress delegates often become tourists, either through pre and post activities or by returning to a destination they discover through meetings-related travel, but I'm not aware of any cases where a tourist suddenly decided to become a congress delegate. The key point is that, while tourism is basically measured in purely economic terms, meetings and congresses deliver a whole array of additional benefits, such as education, professional development and trade enhancement. But while this means there is a much greater range of promotional opportunities, such attributes are seldom recognized by the communities they benefit because no-one is promoting them.

What role for government and government agencies?

A seminar organized jointly by the World Tourism Organization's Commission for Europe and the European Travel Commission, held in Salzburg in April 1997 (and reported in *WTO News* – May 1997) discussed what should be the role and responsibilities of European governments in the face of increasingly global competition and structural changes in tourism markets. The seminar's main conclusion was that governments should assume the role of catalyst, bringing together all the different public and private sector players involved in tourism. The seminar found that, although governments have traditionally played a key role in the development of their countries as tourism destinations, there have been increasing signs of disengagement over the past decade – at least in Western Europe. To some extent, the trend has been a natural consequence of decentralization, which, in many countries, has resulted in powers of decision-making being shifted to provincial and local authorities. Budget constraints have also been a major contributing factor to governments' increasing withdrawal from tourism development and marketing.

Two speakers at the seminar (Peter Keller, Switzerland, and Egon Smeral, Austria) identified the following as the core tasks of governments *vis-à-vis* the tourism industry:

- definition and elaboration of the fundamental principles of tourism policy;
- creation of a tourism-friendly environment;
- acting as a catalyst for promotion and marketing;
- stimulating innovation and international cooperation;
- creation and protection of 'brand image';
- regular upgrading of tourism infrastructure;
- providing support for the accommodation sector.

In their keynote address to the seminar, they suggested that:

> As destinations now compete worldwide through globalization, we have to ask ourselves with increasing frequency why some destinations succeed in international competition and why others fail. The focus of tourism is no longer on air travel, hotel rooms, and meals, but rather the experiences of fantasy worlds connected with specific destinations. It seems that the old thinking does not work any more and that there is a growing need for a new paradigm in tourism policy to influence the competitive position of a destination under the conditions of global competition.
>
> A market-oriented approach makes it easier to integrate matters relating to tourism policy with economic policy. A consistent market-oriented approach can make it easier to prepare and implement tourism policy measures, because it forces those responsible for tourism policy to concentrate on what is essential and feasible. This in turn makes the task of allocating funds for carrying out tourism policy easier. Even so, the need to fight for the thinly stretched budget available to governments today is certain to make an obstacle course out of anything to do with tourism policy.
>
> When attempting to put market-oriented policies into practice, it is important always to bear in mind the peculiar nature of the tourism sector. Unlike the manufacture of watches, in which state participation is nil, in tourism the state is co-producer, an active partner in the creation of tourism products. Is it not the state which ensures the availability of such basic necessities as education, the essential infrastructure of airports, railways, roads, supply and disposal networks, and such all-important 'soft' factors as peace, order and security? Tourism is the marketing of a location. It, therefore, relies on the ability of the state to provide a full complement of modern services.

While the presentation by Keller and Smeral concerned itself with tourism in the broadest sense, with perhaps a bias towards leisure tourism, the principles which they outline, as the role for government, apply equally to business and conference tourism.

There does need to be a greater recognition by governments of the contribution that conventions and business tourism plays in the economic prosperity of communities, at national and local levels. Central governments have a role to play in bringing together in true partnership – with shared investment, risk and benefits – the industry's major players, public and private sectors, venues and hotels, trade associations and airlines, buyers as well as suppliers, to formulate policies and marketing strategies, to create a strong brand for their country, which will make an impact in domestic and international markets.

The design of conference facilities

Projecting the design requirements of conference centres and facilities to be constructed in the 21st century is not easy, especially as the pace of technological and social change continues to gather momentum. Flexibility is likely to remain a key consideration, enabling maximum use of venue rooms and space in order to maximize occupancy, through increased demand, by allowing different types of events to take place and, indeed, a number of mutually exclusive events to take place simultaneously. While few of the major, purpose-built conference centres have been run at a profit hitherto, there is now increasing pressure on centre managements to achieve operational profits, as confirmed by the European Federation of Conference Towns in *A Report on Europe in 1996*, their annual survey of the European conference scene, published in April 1997.

The principles of good design that applied to conference facilities in the 1990s seem likely also to apply through the early years of this new millennium, at the very least. The exposition of these principles in the following paragraphs is based on the experiences and expertise of venue design consultancy, The Right Solution Limited.

The designer of conference facilities, whether a major convention centre or a new conference room for a hotel, needs to consider the same basic principles.

First and most importantly, who will be using the facilities and for what purpose? The target markets and the likely occupancy of the facilities are crucial to their viability and must be considered carefully at every stage of the design. In other words, form should follow function, not the other way round, which is so often the case.

The basic shape of conference rooms determines their ease of use, their flexibility, and the degree to which they can accommodate different seating layouts. Plenary sessions, for example, usually require a large room, often with raked seating. However, the plenary frequently lasts only a short time, with the rest of the event being split into breakout sessions. Normally, fixed-seating auditoriums are inflexible. In the case of the Edinburgh International Conference Centre (EICC), one of the newest purpose-built centres in the United Kingdom which opened in 1995, two sections of the main auditorium revolve to transform a 1200-seat theatre into three rooms, of 600, 300 and 300 seats.

The most flexible shape is the 'shoebox' – a rectangular space with adequate ceiling height. The key to this type of space is access. Access is one of the most important criteria – it needs to be easy for delegates, equipment and staff. The larger the space, the more important this becomes. Direct vehicle access into a conference room or hall is frequently required. A loading bay, under cover and large enough to accommodate several articulated lorries at a time, is a useful feature, especially with a lift to enable goods to be moved easily and quickly to the stage of the auditorium.

Getting equipment in and out quickly reduces set-up and breakdown times and leaves more time for the events themselves, which for venues means maximizing the opportunities to sell food and beverages. For the client, venues that enhance flexibility of event production are popular because there are no technical constraints. If the technicians can install and remove a production in half the time it would take in a poorly-designed venue, this will save enormously on labour, equipment and room hire costs.

Delegate access is also a prime consideration. It has to be remembered that delegates do not necessarily know the layout of a venue, so simplicity of circulation is important. A main entrance giving direct access to a spacious foyer, for delegate registration and access to stairs, escalators and lifts, will facilitate delegate movement around the building while, at the same time, enabling the organizer and venue staff to monitor and control the flow, for security and safety's sake.

The configuration of facilities can greatly influence the easy running of the conference schedule. Particular issues are the proximity to the main auditorium of breakout rooms and catering areas. It also helps event organizers to site an exhibition area where people will naturally walk through without having to make a huge detour. This will encourage the sale of stands (often a pre-requisite of financing major conferences). Office facilities and other essential services should also be easily accessible. If a speaker arrives five minutes before he is due to start presenting and needs his notes photocopying several hundred times before he has finished speaking, it does help if the organizer does not have to walk half a mile to the office.

Ensuring a plentiful supply of toilets close to the function room, enough telephones, large enough cloak-rooms and plenty of space in the reception area, are points not often appreciated if they are well thought through. However, they will cause a barrage of complaints if they are inadequate.

The meeting rooms should have a good ceiling height so that screens, sets and presenters are above the audience and clearly in view of everyone. This also helps the lighting to point downwards, rather than at the presenter, which both dazzles and causes shadows. To enhance the staging possibilities, it is worth building load-bearing points into the ceiling to hang lighting, sound and video equipment.

If a room is used for special dinners and occasions requiring either an intimate or a grand ambience, as well as more functional meeting uses, then good lighting systems will help create the necessary flexibility. It is possible to install chandeliers with electric motors so that they can be raised into roof recesses, and to add variations into the lighting to suit all types of event. In the EICC's Cromdale Hall, a grid of hanging bars ensures that lighting can be hung anywhere in the room. This means that each table in a banquet can have a pin spot illuminating it, reflecting the shining cutlery and glass-ware – a spectacular effect. It also has a practical application. Standard table layouts are quickly achieved by simply putting the spotlights on and aligning each table under the pool of light on the floor. In this way, room set-up can be completed speedily and accurately.

The general decor of facilities also affects their adaptability. It is possible, with due thought and consideration, to design interiors so that they are attractive enough for gala dinners and practical enough for conferences. The most common errors are lining the walls with mirrors, which causes a lot of reflection and is not good for acoustics; windows which cannot be blacked out for audio-visual presentations although they are of obvious benefit for social occasions, if there are attractive grounds or views; and colours that could potentially clash with set designs and company logos. With neutral decor, a room can be decorated to suit any event.

Chairs always need to provide adequate comfort for delegates who are seated for long periods of time. They may also need to be sufficiently attractive to suit the setting for wedding receptions. Adequacy of comfort is defined, in conference terms, as 8-hour sittings. Standard banqueting chairs found in most venues are usually comfortable for a couple of hours. Then that well-known medical condition appears: NBS (for the less medically informed, 'Numb Bum Syndrome'). This can only lead to dissatisfaction and is clearly a pain in the . . . neck!

On a more technical note, an efficient and well-designed cabling infrastructure, to include water and compressed air services as well as the provision of electrical power and cabling for multi-media communications, will assist a venue to respond efficiently to the many-faceted demands of today's event organizers. It will also prevent the need for the all-too-common yet dangerous and unsightly practice of having cables running all over the floors which can trip people up, cross fire exits and mean that doors have to be propped open – adding to the concerns of the fire officer. The use of tie-lines – built-in cabling to link sound, video and lighting in various parts of a room – can easily prevent these problems. The provision of large power will always stand a venue in good stead. Communications technology today means that telephone, data and broadband video can all be sent down one set of cabling – if it has been installed in the first place.

The present conference climate demands high levels of both tele- and data communications facilities. This demand will increase, as more and more bandwidth, at ever-increasing speeds, is required to relay information required within conferences. Presentations are now regularly sent 'down the line' from anywhere, direct into a video projector, to support a presenter on stage. Presenters can image 35mm slides digitally, or manipulate digital photographs, and instantly transform the presentation into a flexible, adjustable format. This is only possible if the communications medium – the way of getting from point A to point B – is available.

Peter Berners-Price also emphasizes the importance of wiring and cabling for conference venues:

Any new investment in conference facilities, whether building anew or adapting what already exists, must take into account the wiring needs. There may still be differences between the compatability of computer hardware, and the intelligence of computer software, although problems of incompatibility are now far less than they were. But information signals will be fed to and from the facility via a dish on the roof, or by an ISDN (Integrated Services Digital Network) or ADSL (Asymmetric Digital Subscriber Line) telecommunications socket, which can carry signals throughout the country and throughout the world. New exhibition halls have made allowances, but conference rooms, whether they be in hotels or so-called purpose-built centres, are still remarkably unfriendly when it comes to wiring up equipment within the room itself. Flexibility is the watchword, and wiring is the key. Wiring for sound, wiring for lighting, and wiring for the new technology that will drive multi-media.

The Right Solution suggest that:

> Despite having a good cabling infrastructure, there will be times when clients will not want to use the in-house cabling – outside broadcast being a prime example. In this instance, integral temporary cable routes can mean a fast and safe installation. Where routes pass through walls, fire-protected cable pass-throughs can ensure that fire exit doors are not propped open by errant cables.
>
> Sound systems are also one of those areas that are taken for granted if they work well but cause much dissatisfaction among delegates or guests if they cannot hear, or if sound is broken or disrupted. This is particularly the case if poor partitions and inadequate sound-proofing mean that they can hear what is happening in the next room, or can hear plates being cleared in the kitchen.
>
> The design of conference facilities should be driven by users and operators, rather than by designers. All the decisions taken during the design stage of venue planning can impact its revenue-earning potential and, in many cases, that of its home city. Large numbers of happy delegates will tend to spend more in hotels, restaurants and shops. Ultimately, this is the reason any city builds a convention centre. Extra care and consideration taken at the concept stage and followed through in the development of the design will, undoubtedly, be paid for many times over by higher occupancy, increased revenue and maximum profitability.

The needs of disabled delegates

In the UK, the Disability Discrimination Act (DDA) gives disabled people rights of access to buildings, transport, work, services, decision-making and all the cultural, commercial and social activities of a modern and civilized society. It provides the legislative backbone to a growing movement that seeks to ensure that disabled people can play the fullest possible part in society, including participation in meetings and conferences. The full force of the DDA takes effect from October 2004, and it is important that all delegates are well provided for and that all venues and facilities are 'reasonably accessible'. The principles of the DDA, and their recommended practical outworking as detailed below, should be applied equally in all countries around the world.

For conference venues it means that access and facilities should be designed in a way that takes full account of the needs of people with disabilities. These include wheelchair users, those with hearing and visual impairments, but also many others, such as people with cerebral palsy or facial disfigurements, and those with learning difficulties. All will be delegates at some time, all with differing losses but also with differing gifts, and all at different stages of coming to terms with their particular disabilities.

Venues are gradually adapting their facilities to meet the needs of their disabled guests, but much work remains to be done, not only in the design and equipping of buildings, but also in the education of their staff. The following incident, relayed at the BACD annual conference in 1996 by Dr Scott Hutchison, a disabled person for 49 years, epitomizes the challenge faced by the industry:

> Some time ago, I was told by a fairly reliable source that a certain Glasgow hotel was ideal for the disabled. However, as always, I first phoned up. 'Is your hotel accessible for wheelchair users?' 'Yes, sir, we have a portable ramp at the front and all is on the level inside.' Just to make sure about things, I asked: 'Now about the portable ramp. Being portable it's not likely to be in position when I arrive?' 'No problem, sir, just come into Reception and we will get a porter right away to put it down for you.'

The UK Holiday Care Service charity provides consultancy to venues on the needs of disabled people. Their advice to conference venues and destinations includes the following.

- In general terms, extend the same positive approach to disabled clients as you would to others. In other words, do not treat disabled clients differently.
- Have a copy of destination information available in large print, braille or even on audio tape. Or, if you use a promotional video, ensure that it has commentary and text description. It

should also describe facilities that have been designed to be accessible.

- If you book accommodation for wheelchair users, ensure that it has been inspected under the 'National Accessible Scheme', and that it has an access category and facilities appropriate to your clients' needs.
- Where an induction loop/inductive coupler system has been fitted for hard of hearing delegates, the appropriate symbols should be prominently on display – for example, at the reception desk, in the conference room and beside the public telephones. A public telephone should be placed at desk height 700–800 mm.
- Venues should try to place posters/display/merchandise that specifically express a welcome to people who use a wheelchair at a height of 900 mm, for example, at registration points. At this height it also remains accessible for delegates who can stand up. Print styles should be large and clear for delegate packs and signage.
- Where practical, venues should allow 800 mm minimum aisle width for people using wheelchairs, with a turning circle at the end of the aisle of 1500 mm minimum. Is there a ramp available up to the stage?
- Venues should avoid placing items where they may be a danger to, or become easily dislodged by, delegates who are blind or partially sighted.
- Try to put yourself in a disabled person's position. How 'user friendly' would your destination or venue appear if you were seated at a height of 400–500 mm, or if you had your eyes closed?

The Holiday Care Service may be contacted at 7th Floor, Sunley House, 4 Bedford Park, Croydon, CR0 2AP, UK (tel.: +44 (0)845–1249974; fax: 44 (0)845–1249972; email: holiday.care@ virgin.net; website: www.holidaycare.org.uk).

Catering professionally and in a caring way for the needs of disabled delegates is not only good from an ethical standpoint. It also makes sound business sense. There is a huge potential market for venues that can provide the correct combination of well-designed facilities and well-trained staff. Training in disability awareness is a sensible investment for destination managers and venue operators. The Holiday Care Service is able to supply details of suitable training providers.

Environmental issues and sustainable conference tourism

Reference has been made in Chapter 1 to the fact that conference and business tourism has fewer negative impacts on the natural environment than mass leisure tourism. Nonetheless, there is still enormous scope within the conference sector to minimize waste and introduce policies that are genuinely 'green'. The World Travel and Tourism Council's 'Green Globe' programme and the International Hotels Environment Initiative (IHEI) are just two examples of ventures that aim to encourage those working in the tourism and hospitality industries to adopt environmentally-friendly practices and thus create sustainable tourism. The IHEI promotes continuous improvement in the environmental performance of hotels throughout the world. It represents 11 multinational hotel groups representing 68 brands and hotels on five continents (www.ihei.org).

The March/April 2002 newsletter of the IMEX (Frankfurt) trade show gives details of a new Internet-based environmental benchmarking tool (www.benchmarkhotel.com), which has been launched to help hotels around the world to make substantial cost savings, while improving environmental performance. Hotels can use the facility to monitor energy management, fresh water consumption, waste management, waste water quality, purchasing programmes, community relations and biodiversity improvements. Hotel managements can compare their environmental performance with that of hotels with similar facilities in three major climate zones and design a programme to reduce their costs and environmental impact. All individual hotel data remain confidential. IHEI member hotel groups (including Six Continents Hotels, Hilton International, and Marriott International) were involved in developing the tool by testing and data provision to ensure that it is useful for small, medium and large independent hotels as well as major brands.

Another website to assist meetings professionals is to be found at www.bluegreenmeetings.org. It has been set up by the Oceans Blue Foundation and aims to help meeting planners, suppliers, and host hotels and destinations to make meetings and events environmentally responsible. The website provides resources and tips on choosing environmentally friendly cities, selecting accommodation and facilities, communications and general office procedures, transportation, food and beverages. It features a planning guide, sample environmental policies, case studies, a Green Meeting quiz, and questionnaires to send to destination cities and hotels about how they reduce impacts from meetings. Checklists are available to send to suppliers to detail their environmental performance so that planners can give preference to those that score well.

Companies now exist that work out the carbon dioxide (CO_2) emissions of conferences and events, and provide compensation for this through reafforestation programmes. One such company is Clevel based in Brighton, England (email: info@clevel.co.uk).

Whether at the macro level of a broad strategy for a destination or international hotel chain, or at the micro level of, for example, avoiding overproduction of brochures to promote a new meeting venue and thus reducing the wastage element, green issues will be increasingly important in the years ahead. The limited research so far undertaken suggests that suppliers are taking environmental concerns more seriously than buyers. But this is clearly another area where a positive espousal of green practices makes good business sense, both in eliminating waste (and so reducing costs) and in being seen to support policies which protect the earth's fragile ecology (and thus enhancing the public image of the company or organization).

In conclusion

An optimistic forecast

The author makes no claim to have covered all of the topical issues facing the conference industry in this chapter or even in this book. Reference has been made to a number of important issues elsewhere in this book – the need to continue improving the industry's statistical base, the desirability of rationalizing the number of trade associations, the importance of enhancing education and training programmes, the need to attract and retain staff with the right personal qualities and skills, for example – but space has precluded adequate coverage of other key issues.

Readers must, and will, draw their own conclusions on whether this great conference industry faces future expansion or contraction. In the author's view, and in the opinion of many leading figures in the industry, the importance of face-to-face contact and personal networking will continue to sustain the conference and meetings industry. People are social, gregarious creatures by nature, and conferences and conventions are a wonderful way of bringing people together in beneficial inter-action, and for communicating and sharing experiences through inspirational presentations, educational workshops and memor-able social programmes.

To those working in this dynamic industry, buyers and suppliers, it offers variety, stimulation, scope for creativity and imagination, travel, fulfilment, excitement, enjoyment, constant challenges, the chance to build friendships around the world, and so much more. Few other industries can offer as much. Surely, none can offer more. Industry journalist Rob Spalding, writing in *Association Meetings International* magazine (September 2002), sums it up well when he writes about the 'sense of warmth, the heart, and the personality of the meetings phenomenon'. He refers to the 'skill and devotion, the generosity of sharing and the loyalty of service of those who make meetings that makes the profession so unique. Oh yes, and that meetings have saved the world from self-destruction once or twice'.

The Congress of Vienna marked the beginning of a long period of peace and stability for Europe in the 19th century. Conferences have the potential for ensuring a permanent peace for the world throughout the 21st century and beyond, as they provide the framework for discussion rather than conflict, for uniting rather than dividing communities and nations, and for encouraging the sharing of ideas and information for the benefit of all mankind. Whether 'conference' will still be the most appropriate word to describe what the industry will become in this millennium is another matter, and perhaps a keynote topic for a 21st-century congress!

Summary

- The conference market is resilient and still remains generally buoyant, despite the impacts of economic downturns, political instability and new technology.
- The format of conferences and meetings has undergone a significant change of emphasis in recent years, with much greater active participation on the part of delegates. The application of new multimedia technologies is revolutionizing communication systems and learning methods, but not reducing significantly the need for delegates to confer on a face-to-face basis.
- The role of governments *vis-à-vis* the tourism industry has been changing. They can play an important catalytic role, both in giving impetus to public and private sector partnerships and in helping the industry set strategic objectives for its long-term development.
- The design of conference facilities should be based on the requirements of conference organizers and venue operators rather than on the whims of architects and designers. Effective practical design and appropriate fitting out of conference venues can only arise from close collaboration between all parties.
- In responding positively and promptly to other contemporary issues, such as the needs of disabled delegates or the concerns for environmental conservation, the industry can demonstrate its growing maturity and sense of social responsibility. It should also see that there are good business reasons for adopting an ethical approach to these issues.
- The conference industry faces an exciting future at the beginning of the 21st century. The potential is huge, the competition is immense, the rewards in terms of enjoyment and job satisfaction are incalculable.

Review and discussion questions

1 Television, computers and the Internet have had a dramatic effect on society and on the lives of individual people. Television, in particular, has been accused of creating a

generation of 'couch potatoes'. Is the home, therefore, likely to become the conference venue of the future as we all become 'virtual' delegates? Or are people's social and gregarious instincts strong enough to ensure that face-to-face communication remains the pre-eminent form of human interaction? Outline the arguments for and against both scenarios, with specific reference to the conference industry.

2 Should governments disengage from tourism development and marketing, as the speakers at the WTO seminar suggested has been happening in Western Europe over the past ten years? Or is a greater 'hands-on' approach by governments to be preferred? Support your conclusions by analysing two different countries, with particular reference to the conference and business tourism sector.

3 Arrange to visit two conference venues and assess the degree to which they meet the principles of good design described in this chapter. To what extent could their design be said to be customer- and operator-driven, rather than architect-driven?

Notes and references

2001 Meeting Outlook Survey. Meeting Professionals International (2002).

A Report on Europe. European Federation of Conference Towns (April 1997).

Alford, Philip. *EIBTM European Meetings & Incentive Report 2002.* Mintel International Group Ltd (www.mintel.com)(2002).

Berners-Price, Peter. *Looking Ahead. . . . The Conference Industry in the 21st Century.* Presentation at the BACD annual conference (1994).

Campbell, David. Market-driven venues adapt to meetings needs. *Catering* (December 2000), Croner CCH Group Ltd.

Fisher, John G. *How to Run a Successful Conference.* Kogan Page (1998).

Munro, D. Conference centres in the 21st century. In Seaton, A.V., editor. *Tourism: The State of the Art.* John Wiley & Sons (1994).

Spalding, Rob. Packaged at last! (editorial article). *Association Meetings International* (September 2002 issue), CAT Publications.

The CVB Futures Project. A study carried out for the IACVB Foundation by Arthur Andersen and D.K. Shifflet & Associates (2000).

WTO News (May 1997) World Tourism Organization.

Case studies

Manchester

Manchester is England's third largest city with a population of approximately 400 000 at the heart of a conurbation of 2.5 million people. Located in the northwest of the country, it is an exciting and energetic city in the centre of a vibrant and diverse region. The city's wealth was established in the 19th century through the development of its textile industry. Nowadays, Manchester's economy is based on very varied manufacturing and service industries. Sporting and leisure-based industries feature prominently among the latter, with Manchester United Football Club enjoying international renown. In 2002, the city also staged a very successful Commonwealth Games, the largest multisporting event ever held in the UK.

For visitors there is a mix of culture, heritage and sport. There are hotels, shops and restaurants to meet every need, and a nightlife that extends right through until dawn. From Wigan's pier to Stockport's historic market, the conurbation's two cities (Salford being the other) and eight boroughs offer an extremely varied choice of attractions and experiences.

For those staying longer, Manchester has four universities, world-famous medical facilities, and one of the most vigorous and comprehensive business communities in the UK.

Beyond convention: Manchester as an international conference destination

As a conference destination, Manchester has developed rapidly over the past few years. The impact of the new Manchester International Convention Centre (MICC), opened in May 2001 and seating up to 800 people, has been immense (MICC handled 25 major meetings in its first year of operation) and has enabled Marketing Manchester (see below), the agency charged with promoting Greater Manchester, to target new business opportunities. The MICC was built alongside the existing G-Mex Exhibition Centre, which, with adjacent hotels, has created Manchester's innovative 'Conference Quarter'. This development, together with simultaneous construction of wide-ranging new accommodation, visitor attractions and improvements to the city's already impressive transport systems, has given Manchester its place as one of the UK's top convention cities.

Manchester's world-class airport has undoubtedly been a key player in this growth. Winning an award for the second year running as Best UK Airport, it provides access for over 19 million passengers a year from over 175 destinations. A unique 'Fly in/Fly out' promotion has also been launched by the airport hotels, offering special rates for meetings and conferences that encourage delegates to fly in for a meeting and then fly back out!

In addition to the Commonwealth Games, 2002 saw the launch of a number of unique visitor attractions. Urbis is a new kind of museum challenging visitors to see their world differently. It is set not only to become one of the most innovative attractions, but also an impressive and imaginative corporate events venue. The impressive structure of the Imperial War Museum North, built by acclaimed architect Daniel Libeskind, is based on the concept of a world shattered by conflict, a fragmented globe reassembled in three interlocking shards of clad aluminium. The main exhibition gallery provides a dramatic setting for events and corporate hospitality and can seat 350 for dinner.

Manchester offers a selection of over 35 000 hotel bedrooms and this is ever-expanding. The £30m Lowry Hotel is currently Greater Manchester's only five-star hotel, and has already become a well-established haunt for the many stars of stage and screen that visit Manchester. Its corporate clientele plays an important role at this venue, where a whole floor is dedicated to meeting facilities providing cutting edge audiovisual technology.

A range of hotels offering budget accommodation have also recently arrived, including the 164-bedroom Novotel in central Manchester and the 121-bedroom Tulip Inn positioned near the Trafford Centre.

What is Marketing Manchester?

Marketing Manchester was established in 1996 when it was recognized that Manchester needed to change its image, or more importantly, change the external perceptions of the Greater

Manchester region. Marketing Manchester is an agency charged with promoting Greater Manchester on a national and international stage, and was set up with a clear brief:

- To develop a strategic framework for the national and international promotion of Manchester.
- To create partnerships to make the difference in securing projects, events and investment.

Around 50 per cent of Marketing Manchester's funding comes from Manchester Airport plc, the ten Greater Manchester local authorities and the Greater Manchester Passenger Transport Executive. The remainder comes through initiatives with the private sector.

An organization chart for Marketing Manchester is shown at Figure 1.1.

Marketing Manchester and the private sector

Marketing Manchester has been working with the private sector on specific initiatives and events since its inception. Much work has been done with businesses in the tourism industry, and this has proved very successful in bringing in tourists on short breaks through campaigns, such as the Irish Campaign and the Shopping Campaign. Marketing Manchester has also enticed key national and international conferences to the region, such as the Confederation of British Industry conference, held in November 2002. Other initiatives involve the property and construction sector, where close links have been established over recent years, and the public/private sector partnership has worked together to promote both the region and the individual companies involved. One of the promotional events is described below.

London Sales Mission

In 2000, Marketing Manchester staged, with some of its member organizations and regional partners, an inaugural London Roadshow. Over 350 invited guests attended an awareness evening targeting the tourism/conference/incentive market at London's Vinopolis attraction, intended to update 'buyers' on recent Manchester developments and secure bookings for local hotels, venues and attractions. It was so successful that it was decided to run the event again the following year (and subsequently in 2002), with some additional features, such as the Property Event. This allowed the property and construction companies in Manchester to showcase their key developments and themselves to key audiences in southeast England. In both 2001 and 2002, the venue became Manchester Square in central London, which was occupied for a full week.

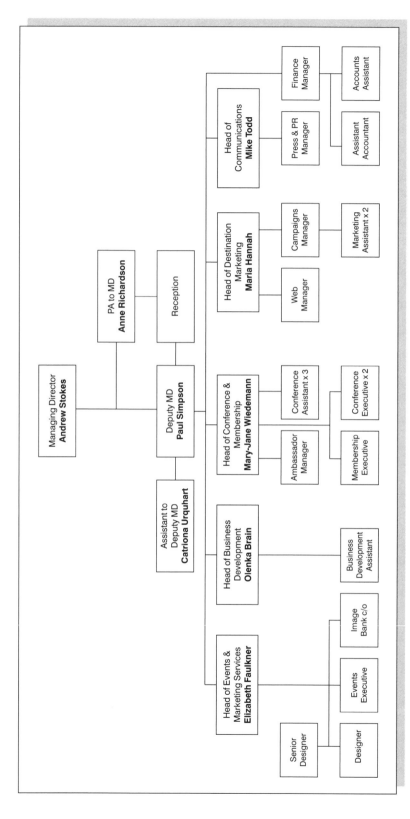

Figure 1.1 Organization chart for Marketing Manchester.

The Corporate Sponsorship Scheme

The Commonwealth Games achieved great things for the region and provided a platform on which to capitalize on this success. The Corporate Sponsorship Scheme provides a vehicle through which the expertise and knowledge of local private sector businesses can be harnessed in tandem with the public sector. Such businesses become members of Marketing Manchester's Corporate Sponsorship Scheme, and so influence the future promotion of the city and region.

The benefits of the scheme are not always easy to define but include:

- the ability to work closely with the public sector and to influence the way in which the region is promoted;
- the opportunity to network with the people that run Greater Manchester;
- the chance to influence the promotion of their own industries;
- the ability to be involved in initiatives being run by Marketing Manchester.

There are also some tangible benefits for businesses:

- branding their logos on the Marketing Manchester website and in the Annual Report;
- meetings – invitations to quarterly meetings to be updated on Marketing Manchester's activities and to discuss future promotional initiatives;
- newsletter – receipt of Marketing Manchester's newsletter;
- images – access to Marketing Manchester's Image Bank with a 50 per cent discount.

The cost of becoming a member of Marketing Manchester's Corporate Sponsorship Scheme is £15 000 per year, and the membership runs for a period of three years.

Conference Ambassador Programme

Marketing Manchester's Conference Ambassador Programme is aimed at helping to support academics or professionals who are interested in raising the profile not only of their organization but also their home city by bidding and winning major national or international conferences. The programme is administered and developed by an Ambassador Team, comprising Marketing Manchester, the Manchester International Convention Centre, and three of Manchester's universities. Since its inception in 1999, the Ambassador Programme has attracted national and international conventions, generating over 23 000 booked delegate nights, resulting in an estimated £12 million revenue for Manchester.

Further information

Websites: www.destinationmanchester.com and www.manchesterconferences.com.

Case study 1.2

Pattaya Exhibition and Convention Hall (PEACH), Pattaya, Thailand

Pattaya Exhibition and Convention Hall, or PEACH as it is better known, has its origins in the development of the Royal Cliff Beach Resort – the resort property which is home to PEACH.

The Royal Cliff Beach Resort

From modest beginnings with the 88-room Royal Cliff Terrace in 1973, the Royal Cliff Beach Resort demonstrated tremendous growth in the years following. In 1974, the Royal Cliff Beach Hotel (527 rooms) came into existence. Apart from the many rooms available, the Royal Cliff Beach Hotel also signalled the beginnings of the resort as an attractive place for meetings, with its large (divisible) ballroom as well as a number of separate meeting rooms and lounge areas. Over the next 12 years, the two hotels established a worldwide reputation as one of *the* places to stay in Asia.

The next major change occurred in 1986 when the Royal Wing & Spa (85 suites), an all-suites hotel with an accent on the highest standards of service and hospitality, opened its doors to guests. The last of the four hotels that make up the Royal Cliff Beach Resort, the Royal Cliff Grand (372 rooms) was completed in 1992. Today, the four hotels combined offer a total of 1072 rooms and suites, all conforming to five-star standards.

The resort currently occupies a total area of 64 acres and offers a total of ten restaurants, four bars, five swimming pools, two health spas, a Thai cooking school, a state-of-the-art fitness complex alongside six floodlit tennis courts, and a private catamaran available for excursions to nearby tropical islands.

The Royal Cliff Grand is an important venue in its own right for meetings and other group business. Having two large ballrooms as well as ten meeting rooms, the Royal Cliff Grand was to be the Royal Cliff Beach Resort's first serious step into the fledgling MICE arena in Thailand.

PEACH (Pattaya Exhibition and Convention Hall)

The development of the Royal Cliff Beach Resort as shown above was never completely by design. In most cases, the investments and new additions were in response to a perceived business opportunity. And such was the case with PEACH.

Figure 1.2 PEACH (Pattaya Exhibition and Convention Hall).

The MICE industry in Thailand was only *just* gaining a foothold within the travel sector in the early 1990s. By the late 1990s, having seen the steady growth of foreign conventions and congresses taking place in Thailand as well as the growth of the worldwide MICE market in general, the ownership of the Royal Cliff Beach Resort felt that there was sufficient demand to warrant expanding further to cater to this particular segment.

A number of factors, which are listed below, were instrumental in making this decision.

Globalization of MICE industry

The nature of the industry has changed dramatically over the past 10–15 years, particularly in the Asia–Pacific region. The region's share of international meetings business has escalated for numerous reasons, including the considerable growth of the region's economies, new state-of-the-art infrastructure, and effective well-targeted marketing, both by individual destinations and collectively through such bodies as ICCA (International Congress and Convention Association) and the Asian Association of Convention and Visitor Bureaux (AACVB).

In addition, many trade and professional associations, with their headquarters historically based in Europe, have seen a large increase in membership from Asia, thus creating both awareness and the need to give new destinations the opportunity to host meetings and events.

With modern communication and transportation links it is now much easier to explore new destinations, facilities and cultures. Asia has been one of the front-runners in taking advantage of this interest from the traditional markets, such as Europe and North America. Thailand, in particular, has been no exception.

Thailand: An emerging MICE market with significant growth potential

Thailand has a number of strengths as a tourism destination:

- an abundance of both natural as well as cultural attractions;
- a safe and hospitable environment;
- very good value for money;
- good accessibility.

These and other factors have been instrumental in making Thailand one of the most sought-after destinations as far as leisure travel is concerned. With a number of additional improvements that have taken place in recent years, such as an expanded and improved internal infrastructure, Thailand has grown in importance as a MICE destination.

And at this time (July 2002), the potential for growth remains strong. The go-ahead has been given for the formation of a dedicated convention bureau in Thailand, which should be in place before the end of 2002. Estimates project that, with the establishment of the bureau, by 2005 the proportion of MICE travellers to leisure tourists will increase from 2.77 to 5 per cent and generate 38 billion baht (or almost US$1 billion) in revenues.

But, with much of this revenue accruing to the capital city of Bangkok, why build a centre that is a two-hour drive away from Bangkok, in Pattaya? The answer put forward by those behind PEACH is 'comparative advantage'.

Pattaya: the alternative to metropolitan Bangkok

Prior to the opening of PEACH, there were no stand-alone purpose-built convention and exhibition centres outside Bangkok. With the opening of PEACH, organizers were given an alternative to Bangkok, a fully fledged convention centre that was uniquely Thai but at the same time not situated within a metropolitan area.

Pattaya is a seaside resort destination, seeking to offer a more relaxed setting. The hustle-and-bustle and traffic problems of the capital are not experienced in Pattaya. Secondly, unlike other beautiful seaside destinations around Thailand, Pattaya is relatively easy to get to from Bangkok, located just a two-hour drive by motorway. Finally, Pattaya has numerous attractions that can be used for off-site functions, partner programmes or incentives.

The Royal Cliff Beach Resort factor

The other major factor in deciding to build PEACH was the Royal Cliff Beach Resort. In particular, the readily available resources, including staff and support facilities, the experience that has been gained from over 27 years in operation, and the reputation for hosting successful events were all considered as major advantages when the decision to build PEACH was taken.

The only significant addition that needed to be made to the resort post-PEACH was the recruitment of experienced sales and marketing personnel with direct knowledge of the convention industry. As far as operational personnel were concerned, most were already in place handling pre-PEACH group activities, so it was simply a matter of building up the numbers.

The PEACH development has been judged to be complementary to the Royal Cliff Beach Resort, with both centre and resort deriving mutual benefits. With four hotels offering almost 1100 rooms, it is found that large groups utilizing PEACH almost always prefer to use the accommodation on its doorstep as well. And PEACH has confirmed initial research that a greater proportion of international meetings take place during the summer months between May to September. With the leisure business at the Royal Cliff Beach Resort primarily centred around the winter months of December, January and February, both markets can be catered for to the full extent.

PEACH the venue

PEACH is a four-storey building adjacent to the Royal Cliff Beach Resort's four hotels, opened in 1999. The pillarless convention and exhibition hall, located on the first floor, occupies an area of 4851 square metres, and can accommodate up to 5800 persons in theatre-style seating or 2100 for banquets. The hall is highly flexible and can be divided into three large sections and further subdivided into a total of seven sections, all soundproofed. There are also nine meeting rooms located within PEACH with capacities ranging from 50 to 140 persons.

The investment required to build and equip PEACH was approximately US$38 million, which includes the land, interior decoration and operational equipment.

PEACH target markets

There are four primary markets (zones), with designated sales and marketing personnel allocated to each. The first is local business from around Thailand, primarily companies based in Bangkok. The local market provides maximum flexibility to attract both short-term and long-term business, and a wide range of events. Past events originating from this market have ranged from conventions to exhibitions to wedding banquets.

The second primary market is that from around the Asian region, or short-haul international events. The last two markets are both long-haul – Europe and Australia/New Zealand. PEACH currently has representatives in the UK and in Australia responsible for the venue's sales and marketing activities.

PEACH is a genuinely multipurpose facility that can accommodate a wide variety of events. In the long term, association meetings, and in the short term, corporate meetings, will be the focus of sales and marketing activity, as well as larger incentive gatherings (smaller meetings generally choose the meeting facilities situated within the four hotels themselves). PEACH is also capable of hosting exhibitions; however, the destination of Pattaya does not perform as well in this area as it does in others (primarily due to the limited number of local visitors that such events can attract).

PEACH in the context of the Thailand MICE market

PEACH is Thailand's newest convention and exhibition centre and is positioned as an attractive venue option for MICE business coming into Thailand, given its ease of accessibility from Bangkok, stunning location and strong conference infrastructure.

PEACH aligns itself very closely with its industry partners, such as the Tourism Authority of Thailand (TAT), Thailand Incentive and Convention Association (TICA) and Thai Airways International (TG), as their endorsement and support play an integral part in bidding for MICE business.

The MICE industry is still in its development stage in Thailand. However, Thailand is already one of the top five countries for MICE business in Asia attracting an estimated 100 000 delegates and 25 billion baht in revenue per annum. The newly established Thailand Convention and Exhibition Bureau is expected to contribute to further growth for PEACH and the Royal Cliff Resort complex.

Further information

Websites: www.peachthailand.com and www.royalcliff.co.th.

Case study 1.3

Dubai

History and infrastructure

Dubai is one of the seven emirates of the United Arab Emirates (UAE), a federation formed in 1971, following British withdrawal from the Persian Gulf, for 'mutual defence, security, prosperity and law and order'. The other six emirates are Abu Dhabi, Sharjah, Ajman, Ras Al Khaimah, Umm al Quwain and Fujairah.

As recently as the middle of the 20th century, Dubai was little more than a small pearling settlement. In 1958, Sheikh Rashid became Ruler of Dubai (which, at the time, was a British colony), and he proved to be a visionary figure instrumental in the establishment of Dubai's industries. The discovery of oil in 1966 led to the development of Dubai's oil industry, providing the resources that have enabled Dubai to build its commercial and communications infrastructure.

As such, the city and emirate is young and developments in the tourism industry are also relatively recent. Dubai International Airport opened in 1971, and the first international five-star hotels, the Dubai Intercontinental and the Sheraton Deira, opened in 1975, followed by six more major new hotels by the end of 1978. In 1979, the principal port, Jebel Ali, was completed and the same year saw the opening of the Dubai World Trade Centre, a landmark development, which now plays host to a great number of international conferences and exhibitions.

1985	Launch of Emirates airline
1989	Dubai Desert Classic golf tournament initiated, the first golf tournament to be held in Dubai as part of the PGA European Tour
1989	Dubai Commerce & Tourism Promotion Board was established, with a remit to market the emirate's tourism and commercial potential
1992	Jebel Ali Free Zone inaugurated. There are currently some 2000 international companies in residence
1996	Dubai World Cup, the richest horse race in the world, was held for the first time
1996	Dubai Shopping Festival launched, attracting 1.6 million visitors
1997	The Jumeirah Beach Hotel opened
1999	The Burj Al Arab, the world's tallest hotel, opened
2000	The new Sheikh Rashid Terminal was opened at Dubai International Airport
2001	The Dubai Cruise Terminal was officially opened at Port Rashid

Table 1.9
Dubai: other major tourism-related developments since 1980

Investments in the general tourism infrastructure have continued apace over the succeeding 25 years. By 2001, the number of hotels had reached 268, providing a capacity of 22 194 rooms (88 of these hotels were of three-star, four-star or five-star standard). Continuing investments will see at least a further ten more hotels opening by 2004. Other major tourism-related developments since 1980 include those listed in Table 1.9.

Other major development projects due to open within the next few years are shown in Table 1.10.

Completion date not yet confirmed	**Hatta Heritage Village Resort:** this resort, an exclusive multi-million dollar Arabian-style resort, will be located in the midst of the spectacular Hajjar Mountains. It will cater mainly for small incentive groups, meetings and conventions. The development will combine a state-of-the-art convention centre, an open-air amphitheatre, a village plaza, traditional souk, handicraft plaza and workshops as well as food and beverage outlets.
2004	**The Palm Project:** two of the world's largest man-made islands shaped like palm trees will be created off Dubai's coast. Each island will house up to 40 hotels offering 4000 rooms per island. There will also be luxury villas, marinas, a water theme park, shopping, leisure and boutique facilities.
2006	**Dubai Festival City:** a multi-phase project expected to transform the 4 kilometre site along the creek waterfront in Al Garhoud into a world-class one-stop destination for dining, shopping, family entertainment and conventions, at an estimated cost of Dh 6 billion.
2008	**Dubai Marina:** this project will create a 'city within a city', able to house 150,000 people. The Marina will have a sea frontage stretching for up to 3 kilometres. 42 per cent of the total area will be for construction of low, medium and high-rise buildings. The remainder will comprise open space, water surface, roads and public facilities.

Table 1.10
Dubai: Other major development projects due to open within the next few years

The historical links between the UAE and the UK have contributed to the strong presence of British companies in Dubai. Factors such as Dubai's general efficiency, high-quality infrastructure, openness, flexibility and the creation of a cosmopolitan environment have stimulated the inward investment by British companies.

In 2000, Dubai received 3 420 209 overseas visitors, compared with just 1 791 994 in 1997. The UK has also evolved as the main European source market for business and recreational travel. In 2001, over 355 000 visitors to Dubai originated from the UK and Ireland (348 477 from the UK, 7065 from Ireland), representing a 15.6 per cent growth over 2000.

Dubai as a conference and exhibition destination

Strategically located at the crossroads of three continents – Europe, Asia and Africa – Dubai can claim to be a natural meeting place: London is seven hours away, Hong Kong eight and Nairobi four. A major aviation hub, Dubai International Airport has direct flights to more than 136 destinations worldwide.

Dubai is now being increasingly recognized as a premier conference and meetings destination, offering facilities and services of a very high standard, with venues ranging from purpose-built to hotel-based. About half of the conference and exhibition space in Dubai is provided by four-star and five-star hotels and golf clubs. The other half, approximately 60 000 square metres, comprises the Dubai World Trade Centre and the Dubai Airport Exhibition Centre.

Scheduled for completion in March 2003, the Dubai International Convention Centre (DICC) will have the capacity to accommodate events for up to 11 000 delegates in 11 500 square metres of space, including a 6000-seat Auditorium and 44 break-out rooms that can hold from 60 to 600 delegates. The facility will be complemented by more than 1000 on-site bedrooms (including apartments and two hotels). The first key event to be staged in the Convention Centre will be the 58th Annual General Meetings for the International Monetary Fund and the World Bank, in September 2003. The International Convention Centre will be managed by the Dubai World Trade Centre team, an organization that has been at the forefront of the region's exhibition industry for more than two decades. The DICC will be located adjacent to the Dubai International Exhibition Centre, which offers more than 37 000 square metres of exhibition space.

The Dubai International Convention Centre's main auditorium will be divisible by 'operable walls', offering capacities to range from 600 to 6000. When set for its maximum 6000 capacity, it will accommodate 2500 delegates in retractable tiered seating and 3500 delegates in seating 'on the flat'. There will also be a link to Hall 8 of the Dubai International Exhibition Centre, expanding the Centre's capacity significantly to provide a single venue with up to 11 500 square metres of gross floorspace all on one level.

Technology features of the DICC will include:

- a high-tech security system;
- an electronic voting system infrastructure;
- simultaneous interpretation facilities;
- individualized signage capacity using plasma screens and poster light boxes;
- a video conferencing system;
- video projection systems;

- satellite linkage services;
- quality sound systems.

Other significant additions to Dubai's conference infrastructure include the new Grand Hyatt Hotel, opening at the end of 2002 and, in 2004, the Madinat Jumeirah Hotel, catering for conferences with a purpose-built conference venue and 900 bedrooms.

Marketing Dubai as a conference destination

In 2002–2003, the Dubai Department of Tourism & Commerce Marketing (DTCM) launched a dedicated Dubai Convention Bureau. Seven of the DTCM's network of 15 overseas offices will provide international marketing representation for the Bureau. The DTCM has set a target of attaining 600 000 additional visitor bed-nights from the international meetings market by 2008, which, if achieved, will generate cumulative revenues for Dubai's hotels in excess of 137 million pounds sterling.

The Bureau will carry out promotional activities for Dubai as a meetings and convention destination, including awareness campaigns and the organization of familiarization visits to enable conference buyers to experience the Dubai product at first hand. It will also work with all the hotels, venues and airlines in Dubai, supporting them extensively in marketing their facilities locally and overseas.

Further information

Government of Dubai, Department of Tourism and Commerce Marketing, PO Box 594, Dubai, United Arab Emirates. Tel: +97 14 2230000; Fax: +97 14 2230022; Email: info@dubaitourism.co.ae; website: www.dubaitourism.co.ae.

Case study 1.4

Creta Maris Hotel and Conference Centre, Hersonissos, Crete, Greece

The Creta Maris Hotel is one of the Maris Hotels, a group of mainly five-star hotels situated on the Greek island of Crete. The Creta Maris Hotel is located some 25 kilometres east of the island capital, Heraklion, in the resort of Hersonissos on the northern coast of Crete overlooking the Cretan Sea.

When it first opened in 1975, the Creta Maris marked the starting point of tourism development in Hersonissos, which was then just a fishing village. It also acted as one of the catalysts for the tourism industry in Crete as a whole.

Now, through a programme of ongoing investment and expansion, the hotel has 547 rooms (including bungalows and suites), combining Aegean architecture with luxury facilities. There are also special facilities both in the bedrooms and communal areas for guests with special needs. In 2000, a complete refurbishment of all bedrooms and communal areas was undertaken. Other facilities include a comprehensive health and fitness centre, tennis centre, taverna and open-air theatre.

In May 2002, further expansion of the hotel was completed with the opening of a new wing directly connected to the Conference Centre (see below). The new wing provides an extra 145 bedrooms as well as a range of other amenities including: lounges, bars and restaurants, medical services, Internet services, an open-air theatre/cinema, swimming pools and sporting facilities, shops, Thalasso Centre and a beauty salon. The new wing can function independently of the main hotel and be available for 12 months of the year, whereas the hotel itself closes during the winter months (December–February).

Conference centre

While the Creta Maris Hotel has had some extensive and high-quality meeting rooms since its inception, including the Apollo Conference Hall with a capacity of 500 theatre-style, the hotel's standing as a conference venue was taken to an altogether higher plane in June 2000 with the opening of a new purpose-designed Conference Centre.

The very impressive Conference Centre is a two-storey, stand-alone building with a capacity of 1800 theatre-style in its main ('Zeus') room on the upper floor. In total, the Centre covers a surface area of 3500 square metres for conference and exhibition use, plus an additional 1500 square metres of subsidiary exhibition space. Through the use of soundproof partitions, the Centre has up to a maximum of 16 rooms, of various dimensions, depending upon the requirements of each event.

The Conference Centre is equipped with the latest audiovisual technology and systems to international standards: built-in fibreoptic cabling for the operation of computer networks and Internet access, ISDN lines, three screens on which parallel three-dimensional projections can be made, video conferencing and projection equipment, as well as special seating approved by the British Standards Institute and suitable for nine-hour use. Such amenities are complemented by interpretation facilities, an area for the press/media, two secretariat offices (each of 137 square metres), six external access points, including two entrances for vehicles, and five heavy-duty lifts/elevators. The Centre also has internal connections with the hotel's new wing, which itself offers an additional 49 small and medium-sized meeting rooms.

Scale of investment and return

The total cost of the construction of the Conference Centre and the new wing of the hotel was six billion drachmas (over 17 million euros, approximately 12 million pounds sterling). The Greek Government provided a 35 per cent subsidy of loan interest on 70 per cent of the loan granted for the construction work (see also below).

During 2001, 35 conferences and incentives took place at the Creta Maris, generating 24 270 overnight stays. These in turn were worth over 2.3 million euros (approximately 1.6 million pounds sterling), equating to 17 per cent of the total hotel turnover. In the first six months of 2002 (January–June), 20 conferences and incentives were held generating 12 860 bed-nights.

Target markets

Maris Hotels have made this huge investment in conference facilities at the Creta Maris Hotel both to win a larger share of the lucrative conference and incentive market, and also to increase occupancy levels during the months (i.e. March, April, May, September, October, and the winter season) when leisure tourist business booked via tour operators is limited.

While the hotel believes that it can cater well for all market sectors, markets of specific interest include:

- medical association conferences;
- conferences organized by pharmaceutical companies;
- product launches/presentations;
- exhibitions;
- company incentives.

The challenge for the hotel (and similarly for conference hotels and venues situated on other Greek islands, such as Rhodes and Kos) is to enhance communications to the island, primarily scheduled air services from key markets such as Germany, the UK and other European destinations. Clearly, this is not something within the control of any hotel group or conference venue – it is up to airlines to action with encouragement and possibly risk funding from the Greek Government.

Quality systems

Maris Hotels were the first hotel group in the Mediterranean region to be accredited (in 1995) under the ISO 9000 quality system for the hotel industry. In June 1995, the Creta Maris was awarded the International Quality Certificate ISO 9001 by the Greek Organization for Standardization EΛOT, a member of the International

Quality Network (IQNET). Since 1997, Maris Hotels have been applying the HACCP system (Hazard Analysis Critical Control Point) in each hotel's food and beverage department. The HACCP system defines the general food-hygiene regulations kept during the production, preparation, storage, transport, delivery and final disposal of products by staff working in these areas.

In 2000, Maris Hotels were the first hotel chain in Greece, the third in the Mediterranean and among the top 100 on a world scale to have been certified with the ISO 14001 Standard, covering their System of Environmental Management.

Social programme activities

Apart from the myriad facilities offered by the hotel itself for leisure time activities, the area surrounding the Creta Maris also provides a variety of options for social programmes and pre- and post-conference tours. These include visits to the Palace of Knossos (centre of the Minoan civilization), exploration of the natural beauty of the island in locations such as the Samaria Gorge and Agios Nikolaos, and many opportunities for water sports, as well as for off-road pursuits in the Cretan mountains. The resort of Hersonissos itself is now a modern cosmopolitan resort with many restaurants, shops and attractions, due in significant measure to the investments in the area pioneered by the Maris Hotels chain.

Greek Government financial and fiscal incentives

The financial support provided by the Greek Government for the construction of the Creta Maris Conference Centre is one of several support measures directly aimed at the conference industry in Greece. The Ministry of Development offers financial and fiscal incentives for investments in developing purpose-built conference centres. Financial incentives typically entail subsidies of up to 40 per cent of costs or interest or lease payments, while fiscal incentives include tax exemption of up to 100 per cent.

Further information

Website: www.maris.gr.

Case study 2.2
International Federation of Library Associations and Institutions

This case study describes the annual conference of the International Federation of Library Associations and Institutions (IFLA), an international association that was founded in Edinburgh in

1927 and now has its headquarters in The Hague, Netherlands. The IFLA is a membership organization with 1750 members in 150 countries. Members comprise national library associations, national libraries, large university and public libraries, and other kinds of libraries as well as 'personal affiliates'.

The IFLA annual conference:

- attracts 2000–5000 participants (4765 attended in 2002) from up to 150 countries;
- attracts up to 175 exhibitors;
- lasts for up to nine days;
- has some 220 conference sessions.

Recent and future IFLA conferences have been/will be held in:

- 1998 – Amsterdam
- 1999 – Bangkok
- 2000 – Jerusalem
- 2001 – Boston
- 2002 – Glasgow
- 2003 – Berlin
- 2004 – Buenos Aires
- 2005 – Oslo
- 2006 – Seoul
- 2007 – Durban.

The selection process entails the following:

- Invitations to tender are issued six years ahead of the event.
- Expressions of interest from national members are received. Such members must be of good standing within the Association (i.e. have paid their membership fees for the current fiscal year and be deemed to be 'supportive' of the organization). (N.B. Proposals from other organizations, such as convention centres, convention and visitor bureaux, or PCOs, cannot be accepted.)
- Two to three national members are invited to prepare a 'bid book'.
- Two sites are visited.
- A special committee considers the merits of the two sites visited.
- The IFLA Governing Board makes the final decision.

IFLA selection criteria are as follows:

- Geographic spread, ensuring that the conference takes place in different parts of the world for member accessibility. IFLA wishes to hold meetings regularly outside Europe and North America, and to include a range of geography over any five-year period.

- The venue must be capable of accommodating plenary sessions of up to 3000 people and have good registration areas.
- The venue must also have the rooms to handle 8–12 simultaneous sessions. Such sessions include workshops, open meetings and business meetings.
- It should be wired for Internet applications and be able to provide good audiovisual services. The Internet wiring is now essential for the cyber cafe and exhibition areas, but not yet for the professional sessions.
- It must also be able to provide interpretation facilities for conference sessions in five languages.
- There needs to be an exhibition/exposition hall nearby with 3000 square metres of space.
- The destination must offer a wide range of hotels, ideally with email facilities in the hotels. There should be sufficient supply of hotel rooms in each category. Alternatives to hotels (home-stays, dormitories, hostels, etc.) are also considered.
- There should be an efficient transport system. Transportation is assessed against its speed, cost, frequency, hours of service and safety.
- Details of meals and food services are assessed against both quality and variety-of-price criteria. Availability of different kinds of food to suit a range of cultures/religions is important.
- Support from national government/local city administration/ sponsors. The national members must be able to provide evidence of financial support to fund the conference and extra activities. Typical evidence will include: letters, money already raised/promised, or a reasonable strategy for raising money. There should also be an assurance that participants from all over the world will be able to enter the country.
- The quality and availability of local professional support. This relates particularly to there being active, long-time IFLA members who have attended previous conferences and have some experience in organizing conferences.
- The availability of local libraries for study visits, and interesting professional activities going on in the region/area. Support for the IFLA conference from local libraries is also assessed.

Other desirable facilities ('desiderata') are:

- a cyber cafe open all hours;
- all facilities are within easy walking distance;
- a bank and post office;
- plenty of places for delegates/attendees to meet and sit down;
- newsagents selling foreign newspapers;
- a souvenir shop;
- air conditioning within the conference venue that is not too fierce;

- pleasant weather;
- cheap and enjoyable post-conference tours;
- social events that capture culture; and, finally,
- a safe and welcoming environment.

Proposal document

National members interested in hosting the 2007 IFLA conference were required to submit their proposal by the deadline of 1st November 2001. Those short-listed were then invited to make a brief presentation to the Governing Board during the IFLA conference in Glasgow in August 2002. The written proposal was required to answer the following points/questions.

1 Provide short details of your Association (including membership details, structure, governance and financial situation).
2 Has your organization had experience of organizing conferences of this kind, including international conferences? Please give details.
3 First indications of expected support, either in-kind or monetary, from government (city/province/region, national) and from sponsors.
4 Indications of support from the local profession.
5 What is the anticipated impact of the IFLA meeting in your country and what would the advantages be to IFLA? If there is a special significance in meeting in your country/city in the year 2007, please indicate.
6 Does the city/conference venue have a main lecture theatre that can accommodate 2000–3000 delegates?
7 Give a short overview of the accessibility of your city for both national and international visitors, and transportation available within the city between hotels and the conference venue.
8 Provide an overview of the hotel situation in your city. Please focus on the number of beds in the various categories and the proximity to the main conference venue, as well as the price range that would be available to IFLA participants.
9 Please respond to the following requirements for the conference venue.
   - The congress complex must be large enough to accommodate the various professional sessions and meetings that are to be held during the meeting week.
   - It must be possible to have at least eight concurrent sessions. Facilities for interpretation in five languages need to be available in designated parts of the conference complex (at least the main lecture theatre and two meeting halls).
   - A large hall (indication 3000 square metres) needs to be available near the main halls to accommodate the stands of the exhibitors and other stands. Describe security and medical provisions in the centre.

- What innovations would you propose in holding the conference?

Durban was chosen as the host destination for 2007. IFLA has now appointed a core PCO to work on five conferences beginning with Oslo in 2005.

Further information on IFLA can be accessed via their website: www.ifla.org.

Case study 3.1
Cape Town International Convention Centre (CTICC), South Africa

Reference has been made (see Chapter 1) to South Africa's pre-eminent position among meetings destinations on the African continent. Within South Africa itself, there is keen competition among several cities to be the number one convention destination, with Durban and Cape Town regularly vying for top spot. The International Congress and Convention Association (ICCA) figures put Durban first in 2001, with 14 meetings fitting its criteria for inclusion compared with ten for Cape Town. The Union of International Associations (UIA), on the other hand, ranked Cape Town ahead of Durban with 29 international meetings, against 23 for Durban.

In 1997, Durban opened its International Convention Centre, a venue with three large halls, the largest seating 3000 delegates. In July 2003, Cape Town is due to open its own International Convention Centre, further strengthening its position in South Africa and enabling it to compete aggressively for the larger international conventions for the first time. This case study outlines the CTICC project and the economic impact it is expected to have both on the city of Cape Town and the wider Western Cape Province.

CTICC specification

The Convention Centre is located on Cape Town's northern foreshore, beneath Table Mountain. It is designed to provide flexible convention and exhibition space, and contains under one roof:

- one raked seating auditorium for 1500 people;
- one raked seating auditorium for 620 people;
- one roof terrace meeting room seating 400 people, with an independent foyer and spectacular views of Table Mountain;
- 33 more breakout rooms varying in size from 25 to 320 people each;
- 10 000 square metres of state-of-the-art exhibition and trade show space;

- banqueting and function rooms including a ballroom (2000 square metres);
- three restaurants (one *à la carte* and two day restaurants), one of which will be open 365 days per year.

There is also a 483-room five-star Arabella–Sheraton Grand Hotel integrated with the Centre, and 1400 secure parking bays under and adjacent to the Centre, and good transport links.

The CTICC is a 20-minute drive from Cape Town's International Airport. Within walking distance of the Centre are Cape Town's leading recreational amenities (including major hotels providing 3000 rooms of three-star quality and above), shopping areas and cultural attractions, among which is the internationally acclaimed Victoria and Alfred Waterfront. On the doorstep is Table Mountain and within an hour's travel are some of South Africa's leading tourist attractions: The Kirstenbosh Botanical Gardens, Robben Island, the Winelands and Cape Point.

Specialist convention support services comprise the Cape Town Convention Bureau, experienced destination management companies (DMCs) and professional conference organizers (PCOs).

The Centre will be operated and managed by the Dutch company RAI Communications Group, which manages the RAI exhibition and conference centre in Amsterdam. RAI have been able to apply their 100 years of convention and exhibition experience to the CTICC development process.

Economic impact

Convention centres are big business for any city. Tourism, for some cities, is also big business. Tying convention centres and tourism together by using convention centres to promote a city's tourist attractions is even bigger business. This is what the CTICC sets out to do.

Construction of the CTICC is estimated to cost 582 million rand (approximately 36 million pounds sterling, based on September 2002 exchange rate). During the construction phase (April 2001–July 2003), an estimated R400 million will be added to the Gross Geographic Product (GGP) of Western Cape Province, generating 4000 direct new jobs in the city as well as 14 000 indirect employment opportunities.

Assessments of the economic impact of the Centre, once construction is completed, confirm that it will have a huge impact on both the provincial and national economies. A study undertaken by the Graduate School at the University of Cape Town, in partnership with Peninsula Technikon, has forecast that the CTICC will provide a cumulative contribution to Gross Domestic Product (GDP) of R25 billion over ten years, and create 47 000 new direct and indirect jobs within the same period. Projections

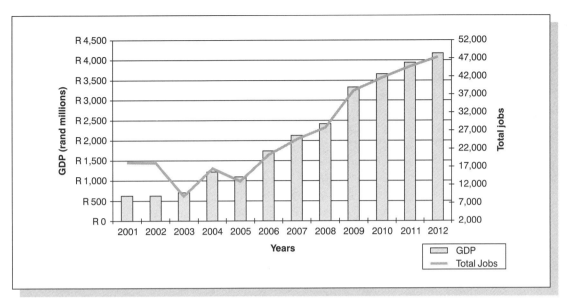

Figure 3.3 CTICC contribution to gross domestic product and job creation.

are for the Centre to make a direct and indirect contribution to GDP of R709 million in its first year, increasing to R4.175 billion in 2012, the tenth year after opening.

The Centre is expected to generate over 1.8 million new overseas visitor bed-nights by 2012, with the capacity to stimulate significant increases in foreign exchange. Estimates are for annual foreign exchange earnings of R1.5 billion by 2012, worth a cumulative total of R7.4 billion.

Figure 3.3 illustrates the anticipated contribution by the CTICC to GDP and job creation.

Other economic benefits

While the most obvious immediate beneficiary of the CTICC project will be the tourism industry, other established and developing local industries are expected to benefit, such as businesses that operate in, and provide support to, the predominantly high-technology and knowledge-based economic sectors. The Study suggests that the Convention Centre can be used to 'showcase the Western Cape and its industrial base which, if handled sensitively, will have the potential to grow these industries at a faster rate'. Such industries include film-making, financial services, business services, phyto-medicinal products and boat building.

The CTICC will also transform the physical area from a dirty, dusty and unsafe environment to a place that is clean, friendly and attractive.

Confirmed events

A selection of national and international conferences taking place at the CTICC during the first three years of operation, and which were booked over a year before the scheduled opening date, include the following:

- Heavy Minerals Conference in 2003 for 300 delegates;
- World Wind Energy Congress in 2003 for 1000 delegates;
- The Society of American Travel Writers in 2003 for 500 delegates;
- South African Production & Inventory Control Society (SAPIC) in 2004 for 1000 delegates;
- The World Blind Union General Assembly in 2004 for 850 delegates;
- 7th Annual International Conference of Principals (ICP) in 2005 for 1500 delegates;
- International Congress on Radiology in 2006 for 4000 delegates.

Further information

The CTICC website: www.capetownconvention.com.

Case study 4.1

The Aberdeen and Grampian Convention Bureau

The Aberdeen and Grampian Convention Bureau (AGCB) represents a destination in northeast Scotland comprising the City of Aberdeen, Scotland's third largest city, and the rural hinterland of the Grampian Mountains. Aberdeen, known as the 'granite city' because of the use of local granite in the construction of many of its buildings, is now the administrative headquarters for the UK's offshore oil and gas industries. The Grampian Mountains are home to many whisky distilleries of international repute, to castles (including the British Royal Family's summer retreat at Balmoral), and to outdoor pursuits centres, such as Braemar, location of the world-famous Highland Games.

The destination's conference product includes a purpose-built conference and exhibition centre, Aberdeen Exhibition and Conference Centre (which completed an £18 million re-development in 2003, adding significant new convention and meetings space), good-quality city hotels, some excellent country house hotels, and unique rural facilities and attractions, world-renowned universities and research institutes, and an airport with frequent flights to most parts of the UK and with gateways to Europe.

	1997–1998	1998–1999	1999–2000	Total
Estimated net additional value from confirmed events (£000s)	114	162	914	1190
Estimated indirect effect through sales activities (£000s)	247	954	1083	2590
Total estimated net impact (£000s)	**361**	**1116**	**1997**	**3780**
Local enterprise company funding	30	60	70	160
Cost/expenditure ratio	1:12	1:19	1:29	1:24

Table 4.4
Estimated net value generated by AGCB in the period 1997–2000

The AGCB was established in the mid-1990s. It is the Business Tourism division of the Aberdeen and Grampian Tourist Board. Business tourism is a rapidly growing sector within the Scottish tourism industry, worth more than £450 million a year to Scotland.

AGCB struggled to establish itself in its first few years of operation, mainly because of a lack of consistent and reliable funding from the public sector. The turning point came in 2001 when the sole public-sector funding partner announced that it was in the process of implementing an exit strategy for the Bureau because of inadequate financial resources. The Bureau drafted a report, which incorporated past achievements and future operational plans in the hope of generating funding from local government to ensure the Bureau's survival in the short term, and to enable activities to be planned and incoming events to be supported in the longer term. Agreement was reached with key funding partners to commit resources, which underpinned the work of the Bureau, and allowed a strategy and a four-year business plan to be developed. In part, this agreement resulted from research into the role of AGCB carried out by external consultants, which demonstrated a return on investment of 1:24 (£24 of economic benefit for every £1 invested in marketing the destination), supporting 113 jobs per year and representing 'reasonable value for money in comparison with other tourism marketing activities and improving year on year'. The key research findings are set out in Table 4.4.

The research also revealed high levels of client satisfaction with support and services provided by the Bureau, another important factor in securing longer-term funding. A total of 47 per cent of clients rated AGCB support as 'better than average', and a further 13 per cent rated it as 'one of the best'.

Area tourism strategy 2002–2005

The AGTB Strategy for 2002–2005 states that:

> the business tourism target segments lead to premium tourism opportunities, such as establishing Aberdeen as a world class conference centre on environmental, oil and gas, health, food sciences and sustainability issues. This is why the Strategy sees town, gown and corporate sector working together to create a 'must do' package to encourage conferences to Aberdeen and delegates to make the most of their stay by extending bed nights and activities in the area, and to bring their partners.

Business tourism is seen as one of the ways to diversify the local economy, which has had a high level of dependence on the offshore oil and gas industries for the past 20–30 years, generating weekday occupancy levels of up to 85 per cent in Aberdeen's hotels.

Key market segments are identified in the Strategy as:

- international associations
- UK associations

with subsegments as listed in the preceding paragraph. Such segments are attractive because they:

- generate high economic impact
- create a high destination profile
- incorporate social programmes
- provide an opportunity to 'sell on' extended stays
- allow the destination the opportunity to focus on broadening business links
- provide the greatest return on destination investment and resources.

The Strategy also envisages an extensive conference care training programme for venues, accommodation providers and support services; underlines the need for increased air links, particularly within Europe, and for improved transport infrastructure development; and makes the case for the setting up of a subvention fund and an Ambassadors Scheme.

Specific aims for business tourism from the business plan 2002–2006

- To increase awareness of Aberdeen City for major conferences and the region as a whole for business tourism.
- To increase the volume and additionality value of discretionary business tourism for the region.

- To focus activities on key business tourism segments identified in the Area Tourism Strategy.
- To maximize the economic impact of business tourism.
- To develop the Conference Ambassador Programme to its full potential.
- To use effectively information communications technology (ICT), particularly the Internet and customer relationship marketing techniques.
- To maintain private and core public sector funding support.
- To create sales and marketing platforms for the local business tourism trade.

Specific actions highlighted for 2002–2003 included the following.

- Recruitment of Ambassadors.
- Expansion of the Ambassador database to include profiled information. A dedicated part-time member of staff (Ambassador Executive) to play a key role in the development of the Ambassador Programme.
- Creation of awareness of the Ambassador Programme through the website and promotional literature.
- Accelerated development of the Ambassador Programme through Ambassador newsletter, presentations, a reception attended by local dignitaries and possible launch of an 'Ambassador Awards Scheme'.
- Creation of awareness of Aberdeen and Grampian as a business tourism destination through participation at relevant trade exhibitions, being featured in national directories, through hosting familiarization visits and by attending industry meetings.
- Joint promotional activity to target conference sectors with the Aberdeen Exhibition and Conference Centre and with national and international bodies.
- Monitoring of individual Bureau membership packages, and delivery of benefits to members in full and on time.
- Maximization of the economic impact of conferences through promotion of extended breaks for delegates plus 'welcome desks' during events.
- Bureau involvement/representation on relevant committees pertaining to Aberdeen's infrastructure (e.g. transport and air links, hotel planning).

AGCB Budget 2002–2003

AGCB is typical of most British convention bureaux in terms of staffing, with 2.5 full-time equivalent staff. In 2002–2003, income was derived from both public and private sectors, as outlined below:

Public sector income

Local enterprise company	£30 000
Local enterprise company (specifically for Ambassador Programme)	£20 000
Local government	£50 000
European Union	£28 808
Total	£128 808

Private sector income

Membership	£22 500
Advertising income	£2 000
Other (e.g. commissions)	£12 000
Total	£36 500
Total operational income	£165 308
Less salaries/costs	£68 308 (£10 000 for Ambassador Programme)
Total marketing budget	£97 000 (£30 000 for Ambassador Programme)

For further information, see the website: www.agcb.org.

Case study 4.2

Tourism Vancouver

The city of Vancouver is located on Canada's Pacific seaboard, close to the Canada/USA border. It enjoys a stunning setting around the islands of its natural harbour and against the backdrop of the Pacific Ocean. The population of Greater Vancouver was just under two million in 2001, with more than 80 per cent of the working population engaged in the service sector. The most important manufacturing industries are related to food and drink, and to wood products.

Vancouver's strategic location and breathtaking natural beauty have made it a magnet for leisure tourists for generations, but it was not until 1989 that Tourism Vancouver, the marketing body for the city and for the Greater Vancouver area, began to promote to the conventions and meetings market. This resulted directly from the institution of a hotel tax by the City of Vancouver, which generated revenues that could be ploughed back into the marketing of the city and enabled Tourism Vancouver to recruit convention sales staff. By the year 2000, conventions business accounted for 15 per cent of all hotel room-night occupancy, with corporate meetings representing a further 14 per cent. In 2001, conventions business was estimated to have had an economic impact of $142 378 193 on the Greater Vancouver area.

This case study examines the strategies adopted to win more convention and meetings business, the resources and structures available, and some of the issues facing the city and Tourism Vancouver.

Tourism Vancouver

Tourism Vancouver focuses on generating demand from travel influencers (e.g. meeting planners and tour operators) and end users (e.g. independent visitors, convention delegates, cruise passengers). Efforts are targeted towards *generating demand* for Greater Vancouver hotel rooms, attraction visits, retail sales, sightseeing tours, airline seats, restaurant meals, event tickets and more besides. As an organization, Tourism Vancouver represents over 1000 member businesses in tourism and related fields. Its job is to 'build the business of its members through results-driven Greater Vancouver sales and market development programmes aimed at increasing leisure travel and meetings and events business, as well as by encouraging visitors to stay longer and visit more often'.

Vision and mission

Tourism Vancouver's *vision* is as follows:

> Tourism Vancouver is committed to being the best destination sales, marketing and visitor servicing organization in the world.

Its *mission* is:

> Tourism Vancouver's focus is on building exceptional customer relationships with meeting planners, travel influencers, travel media and independent tourists. Its efforts generate demand for the destination, thereby creating value for members and stakeholders. Innovation, partnership, research and accountability guide our approach. It utilizes person-to-person and technology-based sales, marketing and visitor servicing activities to achieve results. Through positive positioning of both the organization and the destination, its leadership benefits the society, culture, environment and economy of Greater Vancouver.

Strategies for generating demand

Tourism Vancouver has a five-year 'Business & Market Development Plan' (1999–2003). The following extracts are based on

Year Three (i.e. 2001) of the Plan, under the heading of 'Generating Demand'. Tourism Vancouver instituted a six-part approach to generating demand with its range of sales and market development initiatives as follows.

1 *Branding Vancouver* – by positioning the destination brand as 'Vancouver. Spectacular by Nature' to targeted markets world-wide. The brand message is designed to convey the notion of Greater Vancouver as an exciting, cosmopolitan city with the beautiful outdoors at its doorstep. It aims to have a distinct, clear image for Greater Vancouver that matters to its customers and truly differentiates it from the competition.

2 *Establishing trust* – the destination brand is supported by Vancouver's Service Edge promise. Tourism Vancouver repre-sents a 'knowledgeable, reliable and integrated membership that provides its customers with "best ever" experiences'. While the brand grabs the attention of its customers, its quality of service aims to ensure they keep coming back by establishing trust with them and 'consistently delivering products and services that meet or exceed expectations'.

3 *Market priorities* – as Greater Vancouver is a popular inter-national destination, Tourism Vancouver must be engaged in multiple markets at various levels of maturity: emerging, growth and maintenance. Its margins will come from building business in markets where Tourism Vancouver can make a difference to its members, while ensuring a positive return on investment. It is 'less inclined to be in markets where its members are already very active (e.g. British Columbia) or where the market is better served through the broader sell of the Canadian Tourism Commission (e.g. Italy)'.

4 *Strategic partnerships* – Tourism Vancouver has built and continues to develop important industry partnerships with organizations, such as Vancouver Convention and Exhibition Centre, the Canadian Tourism Commission, Tourism Whistler and Tourism Victoria to 'achieve efficiencies by levering marketing dollars and support in key markets throughout the world'. It is also:

augmenting marketing reach through formal multi-year partnership agreements established through the Vancouver Signature Program. Corporate partnerships exist with VISA and AT&T, and community partnerships with Metropolitan Fine Printers, EasyPark, and The Vancouver Sun and Province. This marketing alliance not only allows Tourism Vancouver to extend its market-ing reach and generate demand for Greater Vancouver, it also brings customers and members together to build business.

Its global alliance with BestCities.net has enabled it to collaborate on the world stage with other cities in the network, seeking to provide meeting planner customers with exceptional service standards across the network.

5 *Broad appeal* – Greater Vancouver is known for its 'appeal to both the meeting planner and tour operator, consistently delivering a 15–20 per cent increase in delegate attendance over the previous meeting destination'. Tourism Vancouver recognizes the strength of the destination across market segments by allocating a similar amount of resources to meetings and events, and leisure travel.

6 *Customer relationships* – although a membership organization, Tourism Vancouver's customers come first, based on the philosophy that, 'if its customers are satisfied, its members will be as well'. It utilizes one-to-one relationship techniques in a variety of ways, and listens to its customers by holding regular Customer Advisory Board meetings. It aims to build long-term relationships and work closely with its key customers to develop sales and market development initiatives that deliver value and business to the city.

Strategic priorities

The Plan identified three strategic sales and market development priorities:

1 Meetings & Events;
2 Leisure Travel;
3 Visitor Servicing.

Its priority for 'Meetings & Events' placed the emphasis on generating long-term, citywide impact and short-term (2001–2003) smaller meetings. The Meetings & Events team of Tourism Vancouver sells and markets Greater Vancouver to targeted markets worldwide (typically trading as 'Greater Vancouver Convention and Visitors Bureau' rather than as 'Tourism Vancouver' because of the affinity such wording has for meeting planners, especially those in the US market). Its primary market segments are international congresses, associations, corporate and incentive meetings, sports and recreation, and trade shows ranging in size from 10 to 10 000 visitors. Building citywide business (minimum of 1000 rooms on the peak night of the meeting) for the long term and non-citywide business for the short term have become 'the pillars of its sales and market development efforts'. With an increase in the total number of rooms available in Greater Vancouver, the ability to secure meetings, conventions and corporate business over the next three years was 'paramount to the success of the entire tourism community'.

In 2001, 14 citywide conventions were secured for the period 2001–2007, an increase from six the previous year. Total Meetings & Events room nights were up 8 per cent, while the number of definite bookings and leads generated were the highest ever recorded.

Goals set for the Meetings & Events team for 2001 were:

- to secure 18 citywide conventions annually over the next three years, to build business for the city;
- to increase overall meetings and events leads by 5 per cent for a greater opportunity to close definite business;
- to maintain a 40 per cent conversion ratio from leads to definite bookings for meetings and events, to earn a solid return on investment;
- to increase the number of non-citywide group bookings less than three years out by 10 per cent, to provide business value and fill need periods;
- to realize an industry total of 5 million room-nights (2001–2003) from group conventions and corporate meetings segments to help fill hotel rooms.

Key issues

Some of the issues identified in the Plan that could impact on Tourism Vancouver's ability to generate demand for the destination were as follows:

- Revenues from the city's voluntary hotel tax were seen as vulnerable to City and Provincial Government interference, thus threatening revenue flow and impacting on Tourism Vancouver's ability to make longer term commitments in order to remain competitive in the international marketplace. Tourism Vancouver receives 2 per cent of the 10 per cent tax paid to the City of Vancouver.
- Airline restructuring and subsequent issues related to air capacity, airfare and service standards was affecting the number of visitor arrivals to Greater Vancouver.
- Extraordinary hotel room growth had exceeded the rate of growth in the number of visitors to the city, impacting hotel occupancy levels even though room demand was increasing. In 2001, Greater Vancouver was in the midst of a forecast 35.8 per cent increase in the number of hotel rooms (i.e. 2003 over 1997).
- Convention Centre expansion was needed for Greater Vancouver to remain competitive and meet the needs of meeting planner customers who generate citywide economic impact. Expansion of the Centre would bring 7500 new jobs and $1.5 billion in economic benefits. Tourism Vancouver's

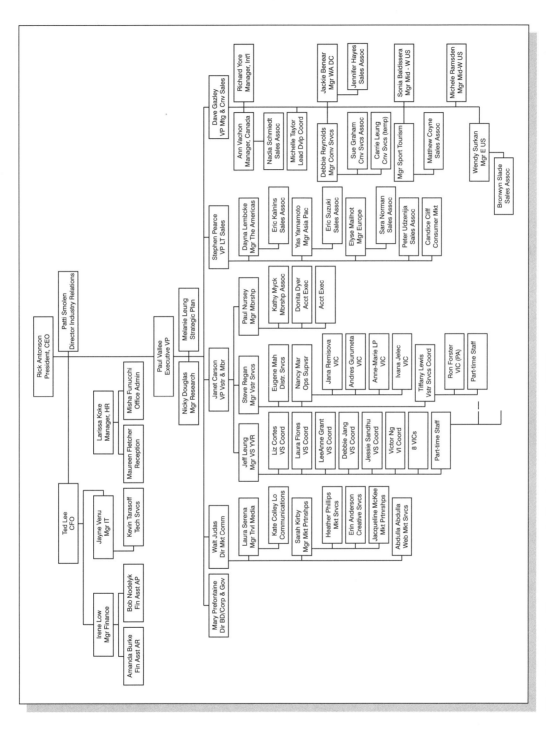

Figure 4.3 Tourism Vancouver: organizational chart (at 13th March 2002).

31-member Board of Directors voted unanimously to commit $33 million over 30 years towards the $90 million industry contribution to the funding of the expansion of Vancouver's Convention Centre.

Budgets and resources

In 2001, Tourism Vancouver operated on a budgeted expenditure of $11 985 000, of which 30 per cent was allocated to 'Meetings & Events'. Budgeted income was the same amount, with 74 per cent of such income expected to accrue from the 'voluntary 2 per cent hotel tax'.

An organization chart showing the staffing structure for Tourism Vancouver is shown in Figure 4.3.

Further information

Tourism Vancouver – The Greater Vancouver Convention and Visitors Bureau, Suite 210–200 Burrard Street, Vancouver, British Columbia, Canada V6C 3L6. Website: www.tourismvancou ver-.com. Other useful background information can be found at www.gvrd.bc.ca.

Case study 4.3

Vienna Convention Bureau

In recent years, Vienna has been one of the most successful convention destinations in the world. Statistics released by the International Congress and Convention Association ranked Vienna in second place for staging association meetings in 2001, and the Union of International Associations placed Vienna fourth in the same year. Reference has already been made to Vienna's place in the history of the conference industry through its hosting of the Congress of Vienna in 1815, but even so, for one of the smaller and less populous of European countries, Vienna's achievements and current status among convention cities are impressive indeed. While there are a number of contributory factors to this success, including the roles played by the Austrian National Tourist Office, the Austrian Convention Bureau, together with venues and suppliers, there is little doubt that the real driving force has been the Vienna Convention Bureau. This case study will examine the structure, resources, activities and services of the Vienna Convention Bureau, and will summarize its economic impact on Austria's capital city.

Structure

Vienna Convention Bureau is one of four departments within the Vienna Tourist Board, the others being: Visitor Services, Staff & Finance; Strategy & Communication; and Market & Media Management. The Tourist Board is established as an independent legal institution, and is guaranteed a voice on any issues affecting tourism within the city. It is managed by a board of directors, whose composition reflects the current political situation in the City Parliament. Representatives nominated by the political parties to serve on the Board, which meets four times a year, are required to have a link to tourism in their business lives.

Resources

The Vienna Tourist Board had a budget of 16.7 million euros (approximately 10.5 million pounds sterling) in 2002. Sources of budget income were the city tax (2 per cent bed tax levied on hotel guests) (46 per cent), direct funding from the city administration (32 per cent), the Chamber of Commerce (3 per cent) and commercial activities (e.g. advertising, hotel booking service, sponsorship) (19 per cent). The 2 per cent bed tax is ring-fenced for use by the Tourist Board – money cannot be diverted for expenditure on other 'deserving causes' as happens in certain other cities, especially in North America, which also generate revenues from taxing visitor stays.

Vienna Tourist Board expenditure in 2002 was allocated as follows: marketing, 59.3 per cent; staff costs, 29 per cent; operating expenses, 6.5 per cent; other expenditure, 5.2 per cent.

The *Vienna Convention Bureau* was founded in 1969, the same year that the city's first international class hotel was opened. The City Administration and the Chamber of Commerce provide marketing funding on an equal 50:50 basis, while the Vienna Tourist Board provides office space and supporting infrastructure. The Convention Bureau has its own board of directors (reporting to the board of directors of Vienna Tourist Board), with a 50:50 representation between the City and the Chamber.

In 2002, the Convention Bureau had a budget of 1.5 million euros (approximately one million pounds sterling), made up of contributions of 39 per cent from the City of Vienna, 39 per cent from Vienna Chamber of Commerce, 10 per cent from industry collaborative activity, 7 per cent from industry sponsors, and 5 per cent interest and reserves. Expenditure was 30 per cent on staff costs, 70 per cent on marketing (advertising, exhibitions, work-shops, study groups, site inspections, printed materials, website, etc.). The Bureau is allowed to operate as a company, and any moneys unspent at the end of a year can be placed into a Convention Bureau reserve fund, a fund that, at the end of 2001, held an amount of 780 000 euros (almost 500 000 pounds sterling). Since 1969, the annual budget has increased by approximately 5 per cent each year.

Vienna Convention Bureau staffing and structure

The Convention Bureau began life in 1969 as a part of the Sales Promotion Department of the Tourist Board. In 1990, it became a department in its own right and was relaunched with new staff, a new strategy, corporate identity, statistics and new working standards.

Undoubtedly one of the key ingredients of Vienna Convention Bureau's success in the conference market has been the quality of staff recruited, and the investments made to develop and retain staff. Minimum criteria to be met by new staff joining the Bureau include having experience of working in the MICE private sector, being bilingual and having 'personality'. Rewards for staff are based on a philosophy that believes in paying higher salaries (with an average remuneration of 61 000 euros a year) (approximately 38 000 pounds sterling) and payment for overtime worked. The practical outcomes of such a philosophy include stability and continuity of staff and the ability to build client confidence.

Staff training is taken very seriously, and staff are encouraged to familiarize themselves with new developments in the Vienna infrastructure and make regular site inspection visits. They are also expected to participate fully in the international convention industry through attendance at events such as the Summer School of the European Federation of Conference Towns, ICCA researchers' meetings, the MPI conference and the ICCA congress. The Director of the Convention Bureau, Christian Mutschlechner, personifies this international approach as a regular speaker at industry events around the world.

The staffing structure is shown in Figure 4.4.

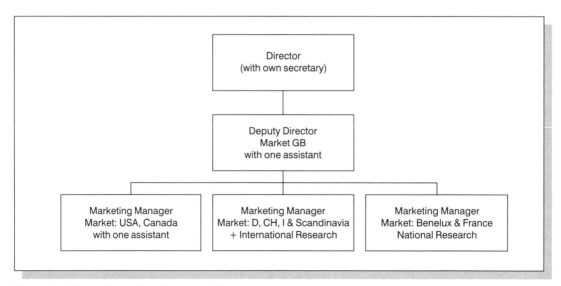

Figure 4.4 Vienna Convention Bureau: staffing structure.

Convention Bureau strategy

The strategy can be summarized in the phrase 'being proactive'. Being proactive in its relationships with clients (both international and domestic), in its attitude towards the MICE industry, and in its involvement with international industry associations. Such pro-activity gives Vienna Convention Bureau a leadership role within the sector and is one of the keys to its success.

The Bureau places great emphasis on the importance of industry research and intelligence. Monthly data are collected from the city's hotels, which now fully recognize the benefits of pooling information (a situation of which many other destinations would be envious!), and other suppliers provide data on a quarterly basis. There is a law in Austria requiring meeting planners to supply data to Vienna Convention Bureau – failure to do so can lead to a fine. While this law is not actually enforced, it does have its uses! The Vienna University of Economy is also actively involved in collecting and collating research data on behalf of the Bureau. One of the outcomes of all this data collection is the publication of an annual report on MICE business for Vienna, which underlines the importance of the sector for the city's economy. The research also helps in lobbying for product investment and for greater marketing budgets, and stimulates cooperation among suppliers.

The other cornerstones of the strategy are:

- an approach that says every client is important;
- all business is of value, regardless of its size;
- a staff focus on 'acquisition' (i.e. sales);
- regular networking with the international head offices of organizations;
- promotional material in foreign languages ('Meeting Planners' Guide in English and French, as well as German, and website in German and English);
- financial assistance for international conferences taking place between November and March, and during the months of July and August.

The outworking of the strategy is underpinned by adherence to key working standards, which include:

- a maximum 24-hour response time to enquiries from clients, anywhere in the world;
- staff competence – knowing the value and nature of the business they are handling;
- quality and professionalism;
- a desire to be better than the rest of the industry.

Hotels, venues and other suppliers in Vienna are treated as 'partners'. The Bureau does not have a membership scheme.

Results and economic impact

In 2001, MICE business in Vienna made a contribution of 174.1 million euros (approximately 110 million pounds sterling) to Austria's gross domestic product (GDP), with delegates contributing an average of 353 euros to GDP per overnight stay. A bed tax revenue of 5.7 million euros (3.6 million pounds sterling) was generated for Vienna. A total of 4282 jobs were secured as a result of MICE sector revenues into the economy.

The volume of conference business in 2001 is shown in Table 4.5.

	Events	Persons	Overnights
Association congresses	339	114 213	495 527
National	74	17 702	38 102
International	265	96 511	457 424
Corporate events	1 064	70 940	186 414
Total	**1 403**	**185 153**	**681 941**

Table 4.5
Volume of conference business in 2001

While the number of international conferences held in 2001 rose by 26 per cent, the total of overnight stays was at a similar level to 2000. However, revenue generated fell by 11 per cent to 233 million euros, owing mainly to the staging of fewer 1000+ delegate conventions (86 per cent of events attracted less than 500 delegates). Congresses, conferences and incentives now account for 9.3 per cent of all overnight stays in Vienna, an increase from 6.6 per cent in 1991.

For further information, see the website: www.vienna.convention.at.

Case study 5.1

A PCO philosophy

This case study has been written by PCOs Peter Mainprice and Rebecca Lawrence Bristol of Index Communications Meeting Services Ltd, Hampshire, England (email: icms@dial.pipex.com), and describes the ways in which PCOs help their clients and bring added value to clients' events.

Of the millions of conferences and meetings that take place every year, a large number of them are supported by a professional conference organizer (PCO). Since research has proved that many people believe that they have the necessary skills to organize a conference, the inevitable question is asked: what does a PCO contribute to a conference and what extra is achieved for a client who contracts a PCO?

Take a look at a job advert for a PCO and the essential skills are outlined: methodical administration, attention to detail, impeccable customer care, commercially orientated approach, etc. – all very predictable attributes for anyone providing any kind of administrative service interfacing with clients. However, for conferencing, this is just the pencil sketch of a picture on to which the rich hues of organizing an excellent conference are added. These skills represent the basic starting points of someone taking on a conference and while this outline could still, in the end, constitute an effective result, a real masterpiece requires a different level of operation, organization and determination.

While an amateur conferencer has a vision in mind, a PCO has knowledge and experience balanced with a healthy cynicism, paranoia and 'worst ways' mentality, contributing a realistic idea of how a conference is really going to turn out. They have 'been there, done that' in most cases and can steer (overtly or otherwise!) the client and the conference away from danger – be it the inappropriate (e.g. location), the vulnerable (e.g. budget) or the practical (e.g. a programme that goes on too long). PCOs act as consultants, advisers and sometimes decision-makers, and the reliance upon them is often overlooked and underestimated by the more confident clients at the outset of the project, only to change later in the life of a conference.

Some advantages of having a PCO involved are well documented and often flouted within the marketing associated with PCOs. Lists of promises, generated to reassure potential clients of impeccable service while pointing out the possible 'Bermuda Triangles' within non-PCO conferences, are common. But, however over the top these claims and warnings seem, they flow from both the positive and negative experiences of a PCO, and with conferences there is always the need to be careful, to pay close attention to all the details and to use all potential problem analysis skills available. Only through meticulous attention to these will an excellent event be staged.

PCOs frequently promise to relieve the stress involved with conference organization. The slogan of ABPCO (The Association of British Professional Conference Organizers) – 'sleep easy with a PCO' – typifies this. Most clients who set out to organize a conference are specialists at something else. This does not mean that their competence to organize a conference is in question, but it is very obvious that, if the administrative planning, logistical management and routine processing aspects are taken away from them, they will have more time and more brain space to concentrate on their vision of the meeting. Some clients find conferencing stressful simply contemplating how they will be judged by their peers and superiors after the conference is over. ABPCO's view is that to cash in on a PCO's experience and ready-made systems means to have fewer sleepless nights. The views of ABPCO members' clients would seem very much to support this.

Leading on from relieving stress, PCOs are also able to make up for a client's skill deficit in terms of some professional skills and tricks, which can be crucial to a conference's welfare (e.g. budget generation and control). Even a small conference of 100 people can represent very significant expenditure by a client organization or very large liability carried by an underwriter. *Realistic* budget models should be produced early on to flag up some very major key elements. For example, can sufficient sponsorship be obtained? What is the target number of registrants? Can the venue really be afforded or does the programme need to change to work in line with the budget? (Budgets are addressed in more detail elsewhere is this book.) Budgets can often be a *bête noire* to an amateur organizer. The responsibility can weigh heavily because of the potential consequences of a failure and this is often the area where the client obtains the most comfort from the involvement of a PCO.

The fact that conferences are commercial entities is also frequently overlooked by the client. While to the client the event is educational, an auditing accountant sees a conference as a very long list of transactions with the need to keep all costs tight, negotiate wherever possible and keep a constant eye (not just a periodical glance) on the accounts as also being key to its success. Where a client may lack the confidence to negotiate, it quickly becomes part of everyday life, even for a junior PCO within a conference management company.

Because conferences can regularly make a profit, many organizations ambitiously set about launching a conference or even a series of conferences in order to contribute financially to the organization, hand in hand with the provision of education. This seems a logical step, but this plan can often be blighted by over-optimism, lack of business planning and minimal commercial strategy. Many PCOs are involved with a series of meetings by the same client, run over a period of many years. The result of this involvement is that they are able to see conferencing in the context of real growth and development year on year. This knowledge can be invaluable to a client about to embark on a set of meetings and helps in setting appropriate objectives.

A PCO can also enlighten a client as to the market value of his product. A good PCO can create sponsorship opportunities and marketing outlets for any event. Often wearing a more commercial hat than the client, the PCO takes an objective view of the mutual benefits to client and sponsor. A PCO new to a project will frequently identify and locate new streams of financial support simply by using objectivity, relevant contacts and previous conferencing experience.

Logistically, having a PCO involved in the running of the conference is an option second to none. While many venues provide exemplary support to conferences, many do not, and, in the final lead-in particularly, a conferencing expert on hand to spot potential problems and iron out ambiguities can be invaluable. Most PCOs have used hundreds of venues and they come to the table of each conference organizing team with one objective in mind: to ensure an excellent event. This remains their focus, whatever effort (within reason) it takes, adding creativity where there are philosophies such as 'we always do it like that' and cross-fertilizing good ideas from previous experience of other conferences and other venues to best effect. PCOs have experience of people flow, queue management, efficient conference registration practice, and speaker liaison and management, and these skills clock in at each event. To envisage several hundred people collecting together and moving effectively and safely around a building without utilizing some professional knowledge and careful planning is to turn down an opportunity for improving the experience of all participants at a meeting. You could say that PCOs enjoy the bits that other people, frequently the clients, do not want to be bogged down with, or even do not consider.

Q: So, if a PCO can achieve all this – enable a host to sleep better, ensure that participants have the optimal experience at the conference, etc etc. – what is the astronomical cost associated with their service?

A: The good news is that a good PCO can help to construct a conference budget, which means that their fees are included without additional expenditure by the client, because the cost is covered by the income to the project, e.g. via registrations or sponsorship. PCOs construct their fees in different ways depending upon the size of the conference. Sometimes there is a fixed management fee covering all aspects – including management of the venue, speakers, delegates, sponsors, marketing, print, etc., and sometimes the fixed fee is lower, being subsidized by a per unit fee for processing delegate registrations. It should be said that because of the nature of conferencing and the potential for repeat business, PCOs often fix their rates to reflect their interest in a long-term relationship, working to establish themselves and illustrate their value over the medium to long term, unlike other kinds of agencies who charge 'for the moment'.

Table 5.3 Specimen planning budget. Reproduced with permission of Index Communications Meeting Services, the PCO company involved with the event)

Assumptions

	Early	Late		
No. of delegates			Exhibition stands sold	15
Sponsorship sold				
Registration fee (incl. VAT)	*Early*	*Late*	Catering per head	£17.00
Member	293.75	323.125		
Non-member	0.00	0		
Allied member	223.25	258.5		
Allied non-member	0.00	0		
Day delegates	176.25	188	Conference duration	2

	£ ex VAT	VAT @ 17.5%	Total £
1. Venue rental	£1 889.00	£330.58	£2 219.58
2. Audiovisual	£720.00	£126.00	£846.00
3. Furniture	£410.00	£71.75	£481.75
4. Poster boards	£–	£–	£–
5. Staff	£–	£–	£–
6. Administration	£10 000.00	£1 750.00	£11 750.00
7. Print	£7 695.00	£786.63	£8 481.63
8. Marketing (e.g. mailings/postage)	£4 825.00	£323.75	£5 271.25
9. Social events	£1 028.00	£144.90	£1 172.90
10. Committee expenses	£1 500.00	£262.50	£2 262.50
11. Speakers expenses	£9 500.00	£–	£9 500.00
12. Press/pPR	£–	£–	£–
13. Abstract handling	£–	£–	£–
Total of fixed costs	£37 573.12	£3 797.17	£41 992.79
Contingency @ 5%	£1 878.66	£328.76	£2 207.42
Total fixed costs	£40 451.78	£4 175.94	£45 250.21
Insurance	£670.00	£–	£670.00
GRAND TOTAL OF FIXED COSTS	**£41 121.78**	£4 175.94	£45 920.21

Cost of exhibition					
		£4 822.00		**£843.85**	
No of delegates	214	150	200	250	300
Costs	£16 162.35	£11 328.75	£15 105.00	£18 881.25	£22 657.50
VAT	£2 704.64	£1 895.78	£2 527.70	£3 159.63	£3 791.55
TOTAL PER CAPITA EXPENSES	£18 866.99	£13 224.53	£17 632.70	£22 040.88	£26 449.05
Total costs	£69 865.55	£64 223.09	£68 631.26	£73 039.44	£77 447.61
Income					
Sponsorship	£0.00	£0.00	£0.00	£0.00	£0.00
Exhibition income	£20 000.00	£20 000.00	£20 000.00	£20 000.00	£20 000.00
Grants	£0.00	£0.00	£0.00	£0.00	£0.00
Total	£20 000.00	£20 000.00	£20 000.00	£20 000.00	£20 000.00
Registration	214.00	150.00	200.00	250.00	300.00
Net	£47 545.00	£33 652.50	£44 870.00	£56 087.50	£67 305.00
VAT					
Total	£47 545.00	£33 652.50	£44 870.00	£56 087.50	£67 305.00
GRAND TOTAL OF INCOME	£67 545.00	£53 652.50	£64 870.00	£76 087.50	£87 305.00
PROFIT	-£2 320.55	-£10 570.59	-£3 761.26	£3 048.06	£9 857.39
Contingency values	£3 502.19	£2 874.41	£3 039.66	£3 204.91	£3 370.16
Undercharge delegate fee	-£10.84	-£70.47	-£18.81	£12.19	£32.86

Conclusion

Conferences are like paintings. They can be very similar, but never exactly the same. There can be variances within the basic design of the picture or the way in which the paint has been applied. Sometimes the originator has the whole idea complete before beginning and sometimes the picture takes shape over a period of time. Some artists are able to paint without first mapping out the plan, while others are more laborious and careful.

To refer back to the basic skills required of a PCO, these are really just the start of what is behind an impressive conference – like a sketch behind a painting. Building on these basics, the colours of the meeting get added, and the design of the end product evolves and is influenced by all of those behind the project, shaped by their vision and previous experience of what works and what does not. It is almost impossible to ascertain at the beginning of a project exactly what the role of all of those involved will end up being and the extent of their involvement, but in the end a PCO can act as a more experienced artist working with the other painters, used for reference and expertise where they seek advice, comfort and experience.

A good PCO is there to advise, manage, juggle, pre-empt, negotiate, steer, process, buffer and liaise. To balance these things – to make a conference a client's pride, a delegate's pleasure, a sponsor's benefit and an organization's financial success, while managing the personal stress of responsibility and protecting the profit-margin of your conference management company – is the art of being a PCO. For any client to turn down this potentially pivotal and crucial addition to a conference organizing team would be for an amateur artist to ignore Monet.

Case study 5.2

Conference planning budget

This case study shows an actual planning budget (Table 5.3) developed by a professional conference organizer (PCO) for a client event. The event is a typical clinical (i.e. medical) association conference attracting approximately 230 international delegates over a two-day period, with some 20 speakers. It is taken from a real conference but the name of the organization is disguised for confidentiality purposes. The event has a history of more than 12 years, and registration fees are kept to a minimum, with the aim of achieving break-even financially.

Other features of the conference were:

• it had a social event, and a small concurrent exhibition with 15 exhibiting companies;

- proceedings were distributed to delegates and the abstracts published on the conference website;
- as well as the involvement of a PCO, the conference had a voluntary committee steering the programme.

This planning budget is the initial stage in preparing an overall budget, which includes detailed breakdowns for all income and expenditure items, including the accompanying exhibition. It is designed to illustrate the varying degrees of financial risk attaching to the event, enabling the PCO and client to make appropriate management decisions on the viability and profitability of the event. The break-even point on this budget assumes that the contingency will not be used.

The spreadsheet 'tool' allows for the input of various income and cost scenarios such as varying the registration fee or enhancing the quality of the programme. It gives immediate feedback by showing the effects of such changes.

Appendix A

List of conference industry trade magazines

The list below provides details of some of the international conference industry's leading trade magazines.

Title	Contact details
Association Meetings International	CAT Publications Ltd, Ashdown Court, Lewes Road, Forest Row, East Sussex RH18 5EZ, England (www.meetpie.com)
Association Meetings	The Meetings Group/Primedia Business, 132 Great Road, Suite 200, Stow, MA 01775, USA(www.assocmeetings.com)
Conference & Exhibition Fact Finder	Batiste Publications Ltd, Pembroke House, Campsbourne Road, Hornsey, London N8 7PE, England
Conference & Incentive Management	CIM Verlag GmbH & Co KG, Postfach 10 07 51, D-64207 Darmstadt, Germany (www.cim-publications.de)
Conference & Incentive Travel	Haymarket Marketing Publications Ltd, 174 Hammersmith Road, London W6 7JP, England
Congresos, Convenciones e Incentivos	Meetings & Incentive SL, Plaza de España 18, 28008 Madrid, Spain (www.cci@cciweb.info)

Title	Contact details
Convegni	Via Ezio Biondi 1, 20154 Milano, Italy (www.convegni.it)
Convene	Professional Convention Management Association, 2301 South Lake Shore Drive, Suite 1001, Chicago, IL60616–1419, USA (www.pcma.org)
Conventions & Incentives Marketing	Rank Publishing Co Pty Ltd, Box 189 St Leonards PO, NSW 1590, Australia (www.cimmagazine.com)
Incentive Travel & Corporate Meetings	Market House, 19–21 Market Place, Wokingham, Berkshire RG40 1AP, England
L'Evenementiel	84 rue de Villiers, 92683 Levallois-Perret, France (www.evenementiel.fr)
Meeting & Congressi	Ediman srl, Corso San Gottardo, 39, 20136 Milano, Italy (www.mconline.it)
Meeting News	VNU Publications, 770 Broadway, New York NY1003, USA (www.meetingnews.com)
Meeting Planner	VIP Centre, Ghyll Road, Heathfield, East Sussex, TN21 8AW, England (www.meeting-planner.com)
Meetings & Conventions	Northstar Travel Media, 500 Plaza Drive, Secaucus, NJ 07094–3626, USA (www.meetings-conventions.com)
Meetings & Incentive Media	Mechelseplein 23, B-2000 Antwerp, Belgium
Meetings & Incentive Travel	Canada (www.meetingscanada.com)
Meetings & Incentive Travel	CAT Publications Ltd, Ashdown Court, Lewes Road, Forest Row, East Sussex RH18 5EZ, England (www.meetpie.com)
Quality in Meetings	Postbus 341, 1700 AH Heerhugowaard, The Netherlands
Quality Travel	Promos Edizioni SRL, via Giacomo Watt 32, 20143 Milan, Italy (www.qualitytravel.it)
Successful Meetings	VNU Publications, 770 Broadway, New York NY10003, USA (www.successmtgs.com)
The European Conference Monitor	Victor Braeckmanlaan 107, B9040 Ghent, Belgium
TW Tagungs Wirtschaft	Mainzer Landstrasse 251, D-60326, Frankfurt-am-Main, Germany (www.tw-media.com)

The author wishes to acknowledge the assistance given by the British Tourist Authority and CMP Information (organizers of the 'International Confex' exhibition) in the compilation of this list.

Index

Aberdeen & Grampian
    Convention Bureau, 292–6
Academic venues, 47–8
Accor Hotels, 135
Adelaide Convention and
    Exhibition Centre, 5
Alice Springs Convention Centre,
    5
Ambassador programmes, 112,
    124–5, 273
American Society of Association
    Executives (ASAE), 228
APEX (Accepted Practices
    Exchange), 18
Argentina, 12
Asia Pacific Incentives and
    Meetings Exhibition (AIME),
    77–8, 156
Asian Association of Convention
    and Visitor Bureaus
    (AACVB), 4, 59, 228–9
Association Internationale des
    Palais de Congrès (AIPC), 4,
    59, 229
Association Internationale des
    Villes Francophones de
    Congrès (AIVFC), 229–30

Association of Australian
    Convention Bureaux Inc
    (AACB), 239–40
Association of British
    Professional Conference
    Organisers (ABPCO), 4, 51,
    146, 204–5, 240–1
Association of Exhibition
    Organisers (AEO), 57
Australia, 12
  Association of Australian
    Convention Bureaux. Inc
    (AACB), 239–40
  Destination survey, 78–80
  Meetings Make Their Mark, 19,
    70, 79–80
  Team Australia, 113–15

Belfast Waterfront Hall, 6
Best Western Hotels, 134
BestCities.net, 108, 299
Bid proposals, 35
Birmingham, 90–1
  International Convention
    Centre, 6, 47, 174, 188–90
  National Indoor Arena, 5

Bournemouth, 91–2
Branding, 106–8, 135–7
Brisbane Convention and
    Exhibition Centre, 5
British Association of Conference
    Destinations (BACD), 4,
    44–6, 49, 128, 167–8, 241–2
British Conference Market Trends
    Survey, 19, 65, 70, 88–9
British Exhibition Contractors
    Association, 58
British Tourist Authority, 65,
    128–30
Budgeting, 149–53, 310–13
Business tourism, 20–3
Business travel agency, 57

Cairns Convention and
    Exhibition Centre, 5
Canada, 12
    Canadian Tourism
        Commission, 115–17
    trends in the MC&IT market,
        80–5, 93–4
    Vancouver/Tourism Vancouver,
        296–302
Canberra:
    Canberra Convention Bureau,
        99–100
    Canberra National Convention
        Centre, 5
Cape Town International
    Conference Centre, 289–92
Cardiff International Arena, 6
Career profiles, 211–25
Careers, 208–9
Catering, 91–2
Certificate in Meetings
    Management (CMM),
    199–201
Certified Association Executive
    (CAE), 203
Certified Destination
    Management Executive
    (CDME) programme, 201–2
China, 12, 65
City of Westminster College, 204
Civic venues, 48
Clyde Auditorium, 6
Confederation of Latin American
    Congress Organizing Entities
    and Related Activities, 230

Conference Centres of Excellence,
    134–5
Conference office, 35, 49, 112–13
Conference production company,
    52, 156–7
Conference venue definition, 20
Consortia, 133–5
Consultants, 60–1
Convention and visitor bureau,
    49, 108–12, 252
    bid proposals, 35
    national convention bureau, 60
    origins, 3–4
Convention Industry Council
    (CIC), 16, 92–3, 230–1
Corporate conference industry
    sectors, 28, 31
Corporate events company, 56
Corporate meeting types, 30
Cranfield Management
    Development Centre, 191
Crete, Creta Maris Hotel, 22–3,
    282–5 (case study)
Cuba, 12
Cumberland Hotel, 173
Customer relationship
    management, 30, 104–5

Denmark (Danish Tourist Board),
    117–18
Design of conference venues,
    173–5, 258–62
Destination branding, 106–8
Destination management
    company (DMC), 50, 55–6,
    156–7
Destination marketing
    organization (DMO), 49,
    108–33
Detroit, 3
Disabled delegates, 262–4
Displacement effects, 72
DOME Project, 15, 77–8
Dubai case study, 279–82

Economic impact, 70–6, 256
Edinburgh International
    Conference Centre, 6, 259–60
Education and training, 198–206

EIBTM, 7–8, 155
    EIBTM European Meetings &
        Incentive Report 2002,
        251–5
Entrepreneurial buyer, 43
Environmental issues, 24–5, 76,
    264–6
European Federation of
    Conference Towns (EFCT), 4,
    59, 202, 231
Event evaluation, 167–9
Events Sector Industry Training
    Organisation (ESITO), 207–8
Exhibition (exposition) organizer,
    57–8
Exhibition Venues Association
    (EVA), 58

Fife College, 205
Finland Convention Bureau,
    118–19
Fragmentation, 69, 245–6
France, 31, 54, 65
    France Congrès, 75–6
    Maison de la France, 119–20

Germany, 31, 47, 48, 54
    German Convention Bureau,
        120–1
    German Meetings and
        Convention Market
        1999–2000, 85–6
Glasgow, 288
    SECC/Clyde Auditorium, 6, 91
Greece, Creta Maris Hotel and
    Conference Centre, Crete,
    282–5
Green tourism, 24, 76

Hellenic Association of
    Professional Congress
    Organizers (HAPCO), 242–3
Hilton Hotels, 135
Historic Conference Centres of
    Europe, 135
Hobart – Federation Concert Hall
    and Convention Centre, 5
Holiday Inn Hotels, 135

Hong Kong:
    Convention and Exhibition
        Centre, 47
    Hong Kong Tourism Board,
        121–2
Hyatt Hotels, 173–4

IMEX, 155
Incentive travel:
    incentive travel house, 52–4
Incentive Travel & Conventions,
    Meetings Asia (IT&CMA), 156
Incentive Travel & Meetings
    Association (ITMA), 59,
    231–2
Incentive Travel & Meeting
    Executives Show (IT&ME),
    155
International Association for
    Exhibition Management
    (IAEM), 4, 58, 233
International Association of
    Convention and Visitor
    Bureaus (IACVB), 4, 59, 70,
    201–2, 232–3, 252
International Association of
    Professional Congress
    Organizers (IAPCO), 4, 59,
    146, 162, 199, 233–4
International Confex, 156
International Congress and
    Convention Association
    (ICCA), 4, 59, 70, 110–11,
    234–5
    ICCA rankings, 8–10
International Federation of
    Library Associations and
    Institutions, 285–9
International Passenger Survey,
    23, 89
International Pharmaceutical
    Congress Advisory
    Association (IPCAA), 235
Internet, use of, 252–5
Inward investment, 24
Ireland, 86–7
    Convention Bureau of Ireland,
        124–5
    Northern Ireland Conference
        Bureau, 123–4
    Tourism Ireland, 122–3
Italy, 31, 65

Japan, 12, 125–6
Job titles, 29
Joint Meetings Industry Council, 236

Le Méridien Hotels, 173
Leading Hotels of the World, 135
Lebanon, 12
Leeds Metropolitan University, 204
Leisure extenders, 22
Leisure tourism, 20, 22
Leonardo Programme, 208
Llandudno – North Wales Conference Centre, 6
London:
    City of Westminster College, 204–5
    Convention multipliers, 73–4
    Cumberland Hotel, 173
    Millennium Conference Centre, 6
    University of Westminster, 204–5

Majestic Hotel (The), 183–6
Malaysia, 12
Manchester:
    Bridgewater Hall, 5
    case study, 269–74
    Manchester International Conference Centre, 6
    Nynex Arena, 5
    UMIST, 48
Market intelligence, 13–15
Marketing (definition), 97
    destination marketing, 106, 257
    event marketing, 164–5
    marketing mix, 101–3
    marketing plan, 98–103
    overseas marketing, 137–8
    relationship marketing, 104–5
Marriott Hotels, 135, 173
Meeting Professionals International (MPI), 4, 37, 59, 70, 206–7, 236–7
    MPI Meetings Outlook Survey 2001, 251
Meetings Industry Association (MIA), 4, 243

Meetings Industry Association of Australia (MIAA), 4, 243–4
Melbourne, 77
    Melbourne Exhibition and Convention Centre, 5, 47
MICE acronym, 15
Moat House Hotels' Seal of Assurance, 135–6
Morocco, 11
Multi-management firm, 50
Multi-media, 250
Multipliers, 72–5

National convention bureau, 60
Negotiating, 158–62, 181–2
New College (Nottingham), 206
New Zealand, 12, 87–8
    New Zealand Convention Association, 126–7
Newcastle upon Tyne Arena, 5

Opportunity costs, 72
Occupational standards, 206–8

Pattaya Exhibition and Convention Hall (PEACH), 274–8
Per diem, 43
Perth Convention and Exhibition Centre, 5
Plymouth Pavilions, 6
Poster sessions, 251
Professional conference/congress organiser (PCO), 50–1, 145–6, 156–7, 306–12
Professional Convention Management Association (PCMA), 4, 59, 202–3, 237
Purpose-built centres, 47

Qualifications (vocational), 207

Rates (conference delegate), 101–2, 179
Relationship management, 104–5
Relationship marketing, 104–5
Return on investment (ROI), 30, 32

Revpar, 180–1
Risk assessment, 148–9

Salary levels, 210–11
Scotland, 130–1
    Aberdeen & Grampian
        Convention Bureau, 292–6
    Edinburgh International
        Conference Centre, 6,
        259–60
    Westin Turnberry Resort (The),
        186–9
Sheffield Arena, 5
Sheffield Hallam University, 205
Singapore, 12
SMERF acronym, 33
Society of Incentive & Travel
    Executives (SITE), 33, 52, 53,
    55, 59, 238
South Africa, 11, 54
    Cape Town International
        Conference Centre, 289–92
    Durban International
        Convention Centre, 47, 289
South African Association for the
    Conference Industry
    (SAACI), 244–5
South Korea, 12
Spain, 31, 54, 65
    Spain Convention Bureau,
        127–8
Sydney:
    bids for international
        congresses, 41
    Convention and Exhibition
        Centre, 5
    Convention Centre South, 5
    Convention Delegate Study
        2001, 80, 81

Teleconferencing, 253–5
Terminology, 15–18

Thailand, 12
    Pattaya Exhibition and
        Convention Hall (PEACH),
        274–8
Thames Valley University, 206
Trade press/media, 60, 156,
    314–15

UK Conference Market Survey
    2002, 29, 31, 32, 34, 37–9, 67
Union of International
    Associations (UIA) statistics,
    11–13, 14, 70, 238–9
United Arab Emirates, 54
University of Westminster, 204–5
USA, 3–4, 12, 36, 40, 43, 47, 54,
    65, 66–7, 92–4, 133, 198

Vancouver/Tourism Vancouver,
    296–302
Venue finding agency, 51–2,
    156–7
Venue inspection, 157–9, 176–7
Venue selection, 153–8, 253
Venuemasters, 135
Video conferencing, 249, 253–5
Vienna, Congress of, 2–3, 17, 266
Vienna Convention Bureau,
    302–6
Vietnam, 12

Wales, 131–2
Webcasting, 67–8, 253–5
Westin Turnberry Resort (The),
    186–9
World Tourism Organization, 65,
    256–8

Yield management, 177–81